Britain's 1961 application was the first time that the European Community was obliged to consider a membership request from one of its neighbours. This book, based on newly released material from the archives, challenges traditional views of the British application and casts new light on the way in which the EEC responded to the challenge of enlargement. The author explains the initial inability of de Gaulle to oppose British membership, and draws attention to the hesitant and conditional nature of Britain's application. In combination these two factors ensured that the sixteen months of negotiations, and the balance the Six struck between their conflicting desires to widen and to deepen the Community, became crucial to the outcome of the UK membership bid. This book provides a detailed analysis of a vital chapter in postwar European history, and offers important insights into differing conceptions of the European Community.

CAMBRIDGE STUDIES IN INTERNATIONAL RELATIONS

Series list continues after index

Dealing with Britain
The Six and the First UK Application to the EEC

N. Piers Ludlow

Balliol College, Oxford

CAMBRIDGE
UNIVERSITY PRESS

PUBLISHED BY THE PRESS SYNDICATE OF THE UNIVERSITY OF CAMBRIDGE
The Pitt Building, Trumpington Street, Cambridge CB2 1RP, United Kingdom

CAMBRIDGE UNIVERSITY PRESS
The Edinburgh Building, Cambridge CB2 2RU, United Kingdom
40 West 20th Street, New York, NY 10011–4211, USA
10 Stamford Road, Oakleigh, Melbourne 3166, Australia

First published 1997

Printed in the United Kingdom at the University Press, Cambridge

Typeset in Palatino 10/12½ pt   CE

A catalogue record for this book is available from the British Library

Library of Congress cataloguing in publication data
Ludlow, N. Piers, 1968–
Dealing with Britain: the Six and the first UK application to the
EEC / N. Piers Ludlow.
      p.   cm. – (Cambridge studies in international relations: 56)
Includes bibliographical references and index.
ISBN 0 521 59242 9 (hb). – ISBN 0 521 59536 3 (pb)
1. European Economic Community – Great Britain – History.
I. Title.   II. Series.
KJE4443.41972.A3L83   1997
341.242′2′0941–dc21   97–7614   CIP

ISBN 0 521 59242 9 hardback
ISBN 0 521 59536 3 paperback

To my parents

Contents

Acknowledgements

The search for funding has been a prominent and sometimes discouraging feature of the five years spent working on this book. But four sources of money were found for which I am very grateful. First, I owe thanks to my parents who allowed the whole project to get off the ground by replacing for a full year the ESRC studentship which I had contrived to lose. Second, I am indebted to the British Academy who paid my college and university fees for two years, agreed to cover the St Antony's College extended fees in my fourth year, and, once I had finished my doctorate, awarded me a post-doctoral fellowship which has allowed me to revise the work for publication. Third, I would like to thank the Wiener-Anspach foundation, whose very generous one-year fellowship made possible the Brussels-based research so central to this book. Fourth, I am grateful to the German Academic Exchange Service, whose funding allowed me to visit Bonn and Koblenz. I must also thank all three of my colleges for their support. Trinity convinced me that I wanted to continue both in Oxford and in history, St Antony's proved an ideally cosmopolitan base for a research project which has attempted to span seven countries, while Balliol has provided a welcoming environment for the start of my academic career.

Equally important were those who helped me in my search through various libraries and archives. Dr Hoffman of the Commission's archives in Brussels and M. Paleyret of the Florence-based Commission archives were both extremely helpful, as were Mr Stols in the archives of the EEC Council of Ministers, Dr von Boeselager in the German Foreign Ministry archives and M. Fournier and Madame Richefort in the Quai d'Orsay. All deserve many thanks.

A third category without whom my research would not have been possible are those who have provided academic guidance. My first doctoral supervisor David Hine very kindly agreed to take me on as a research student at extremely short notice thereby enabling me to start work on the doctorate. Dr Anne Deighton of St Antony's, who took over from David Hine at the start of my third year, has been even more helpful. Her attention to the type of details I was inclined to overlook was invaluable and her constant questioning forced me to tighten up my argument. She was extremely supportive in the final stages of my doctorate and has continued to be a source of encouragement and advice long after my leaving St Antony's. Also helpful during the last five years have been John Young, John Dunbabin, William Wallace, Jean-Victor Louis, Richard Griffiths, Andrew Wyatt Walter, Georges-Henri Soutou, Gérard Bossuat, Maurice Vaïsse, Françoise de La Serre, Barbara Emerson and Hugo Young. I have also benefited greatly from numerous conversations with other young historians working on related topics. Oliver Bange, Bernard Bouwman, Renata Dwan, James Ellison, Wolfram Kaiser, Liz Kane, Sabine Lee, Martin Schaad, Anne de Smedt, Janne Taalas, Stuart Ward and George Wilkes have all helped me place my own research more clearly in its context. Dr Lee has in addition read through the revised manuscript and Dr Dwan the introduction and conclusion, and both have made some very useful comments. Over the last year I have also become very grateful to John Haslam, my editor, and all the other staff at CUP who have guided a total novice through the process of producing an academic monograph.

Finally, I must thank five other people. First, my mother and father who have been enormously supportive throughout and always ready with encouragement, advice and a great deal of unofficial supervision. To them this book is dedicated. Second, my parents-in-law who have always been very welcoming when I have escaped from Oxford to Cheltenham, despite my tendency to clutter up their sitting room with print-outs, computer disks and obscure articles on de Gaulle, Adenauer and the like. And third I must thank Morwenna who, as my girl-friend, then fiancée and now wife, has helped me through every stage of this project, has proof-read page after page of my prose and has acted as sounding-board for many of my ideas. Few other theologians would have been as willing as she was to read about the history of the European Community.

Abbreviations

AAA	Auswärtiges Amt archives, Bonn
AOT	Associated Overseas Territory
BAK	Bundesarchiv, Koblenz
BDI	Bundesverband der Deutschen Industrie
BDT	Bande de Transmission
BKA	Bundeskanzleramt, Bonn
CAB	Cabinet Files
CAP	Common Agricultural Policy
CDU	Christlich-Demokratische Union
CET	Common External Tariff
CMA	Archives of the EEC Council of Ministers, Brussels
COREPER	Committee of Permanent Representatives
CPA	Conservative Party Archive, Bodleian, Oxford
CSU	Christlich-Soziale Union
DE–CE	Service de Coopération Economique, Quai d'Orsay, Paris
ECHA	European Commission Historical Archives, Brussels
ECSC	European Coal and Steel Community
EDC	European Defence Community
EEC	European Economic Community
EFTA	European Free Trade Association
EUI	European University Institute, Florence
FDP	Freie Demokratische Partei
FO	Foreign Office
MAE	Ministère des Affaires Etrangères, Paris
MFN	Most Favoured Nation
MRP	Mouvement Républicain Populaire
MSI	Movimento Sociale Italiano
NATO	North Atlantic Treaty Organisation

NFU	National Farmers' Union
OECD	Organisation for Economic Cooperation and Development
OEEC	Organisation for European Economic Cooperation
PREM	Prime Minister's Files
PRO	Public Record Office, Kew, London
SPD	Sozialdemokratische Partei Deutschlands
UNR	Union pour la Nouvelle République
WEU	Western European Union

Introduction

In 1961, much earlier than had been expected, the six founder members of the European Economic Community (EEC) were confronted by the issue of enlargement. Harold Macmillan's announcement in July 1961 that his government wished to open membership negotiations triggered similar requests from Denmark, Ireland and Norway, and prompted Sweden, Finland, Austria, Switzerland and Spain to seek association agreements with the Community. By mid-1962, the Six were faced with the possibility of becoming the Ten, and of establishing close economic relationships with virtually all the countries of Western Europe. The widespread assumption that the challenge of enlarging Community membership need be overcome only once the Treaty of Rome had been fully implemented among the original member states had been shown to be totally unfounded.

The decision by so many of the states of Western Europe to reassess their relationship with the EEC and to strengthen their ties with the Six was profoundly flattering for the founder members of the Community. Only two months before the British Prime Minister announced to the House of Commons that his government intended to submit a membership application to the EEC, a senior British minister had still felt able to tell a Belgian newspaper that the European Free Trade Association (EFTA) – the looser grouping of seven countries centred on Britain which had been formed in 1960 – was a viable alternative to the integration process underway among the Six, and that, in due course, the Seven might accomplish as much as the EEC.[1] The British application, by contrast, especially when followed by membership and association requests from all but one of its EFTA

---

[1] Reginald Maudling in an interview with *Le Soir* 7.5.1961.

partners, constituted a dramatic acknowledgement that the path chosen by the Six was more attractive than that selected by the Seven. As Sicco Mansholt, the European Commissioner responsible for agriculture, put it in a speech to the European Parliamentary Assembly, 'we can view the British, Danish and Irish membership applications as proof of the success of our Community'.[2] Similarly, the editorial of *Le Monde* two days after Macmillan's statement described the British volte-face as a vindication of the founding fathers of the EEC, while Raymond Aron, writing in *Le Figaro*, commented bluntly that the British decision demonstrated that the creation of EFTA 'was a pointless act'.[3] The division of Europe into two competing economic organisations appeared likely to end on terms dictated by the Six.

Continental satisfaction at the British change of policy, moreover, went beyond mere triumphalism. There were major economic and political gains to be expected from Community enlargement, ranging from the prospect of freer commercial access to the valuable British and Scandinavian markets, to the possibility that British membership might facilitate progress towards the planned political union being discussed among the Six. For the majority of Europe's political elite, the replacement of 'Little Europe' – the somewhat derogatory term for the Six commonly used in Whitehall – by a larger unit including Britain and much of EFTA would add to the attractions of far-reaching European cooperation and bring closer the moment at which, it was hoped, a genuinely united Europe would be able to work together with the United States on the world stage. The potential influence of a Community encompassing all the major states of Western Europe was immense.

Enlargement would also pose the Community a variety of challenges, however. The addition of up to four new members to the EEC was likely to test severely Community institutions which had only been created in 1958 and were thus barely accustomed to work within a six-member grouping, would disrupt patterns of cooperation which had grown up during the EEC's successful first few years of operation, and would alter the balance of opinion within the Community on

---

[2] 'Nous pouvons considérer les demandes d'adhésions de la Grande-Bretagne, du Danemark et de l'Irlande comme une preuve du succès de notre Communauté.' My translation. *Débats de l'Assemblée Parlementaire Européenne 1961–2*, vol. II, p. 78; much the same view was expressed by Emile Noël, the former Secretary-General of the Commission, in an interview with the author, 16.12.1995.

[3] 'Fut un coup pour rien.' My translation. *Le Monde* 2.8.1961; *Le Figaro* 18–19.11.1961.

questions as varied as wheat imports, lead and zinc tariff levels or European relations with former French colonies in Africa. The fact that one of the applicants, the United Kingdom, had a vast array of special requirements and needs which would have to be accommodated before it could join further complicated the issue. Enlargement to include Britain would oblige the Community to reconsider its commercial ties with Australia, Canada and New Zealand, its whole attitude to world agricultural trade, its method of protecting European farmers, and its relationship with large portions of the developing world including the Indian sub-continent and an ever-growing number of newly independent African nations. The internal Community debate about its own institutional evolution, and in particular the question of whether future developments should extend the existing form of integration into fields not referred to in the Treaty of Rome or should instead conform to the intergovernmental pattern favoured by General de Gaulle, was also likely to be profoundly affected by the arrival of new, and in Britain's case opinionated, member states. The widespread desire amongst the Six to press ahead unchecked in their drive for greater integration would thus be difficult to reconcile with the policy reassessments and adaptations that enlargement was likely to bring. Eight years before the Hague Council, when President Georges Pompidou was to speak of the EEC's need to reconcile 'deepening' with 'widening', the dilemma was already acute.

The aim of this study is to examine the way in which the Community responded to these challenges between 1961 and 1963. To ensure that the subject remains manageable, it will restrict its focus in three ways. First, this book concentrates almost exclusively on the impact of the British membership bid rather than attempting to analyse the reactions of the Six to all of the applications submitted in 1961 and 1962. In so doing this research mirrors the decision of the Six to devote most of their attention to the British application, since not only did they regard the question of British membership as the most important and complex aspect of enlargement, but they also felt (correctly as it turned out) that the fate of all of the other membership bids hinged upon the fortunes of the British application. Only occasional references will thus be made to the Community's view of the Danish, Irish and Norwegian applications or to the complex arguments which developed about the desirability of numerous association agreements.

Second, this account will concentrate exclusively on the British negotiations to enter the EEC, and will ignore the parallel talks about UK membership of the European Coal and Steel Community (ECSC) and of Euratom. The latter are not without interest or importance, but they had neither progressed as far by January 1963 as those relating to EEC membership, nor were they likely to exercise a decisive influence on the success or failure of the British bid. At most they might have affected the timing of the British entry.[4] And third, the book will focus primarily on the behaviour of the six member states as they met in Brussels, on the way in which they interacted and on the role played in their deliberations by the Community institutions, rather than on the public and bureaucratic debates which the prospect of enlargement provoked within each individual Community member state. It will not ignore the numerous contacts amongst the member states away from Brussels nor the bilateral meetings between British negotiators and their counterparts from each of the Six. The summit meetings between Macmillan and de Gaulle, and de Gaulle and Adenauer will also be covered. Where relevant there will be some discussion of the state of opinion within each of the six Community member states. But no apology is made for the concentration on events in the Belgian capital since it is the contention of this study that the fate of the British application, and with it the fate of Community enlargement, was determined primarily in the Brussels negotiations.

This Community-centred approach also distinguishes this study from much of the previous academic discussion of the 1961–3 application which has tended to fall into one of two categories. A great deal of the work done on the first, unsuccessful, attempt to enlarge the EEC has focused on the concerns, ambitions and behaviour of individual countries, whether applicants or Community members. Miriam Camps' *Britain and the European Community 1955–1963*, although the most thorough previous study of the negotiations, is one obvious example of this first tendency, since, as the title implies, the book is primarily devoted to the formulation of British policy towards the EEC. The politics and policies of the Six are a secondary concern.[5]

---

[4] The best existing account of the ECSC negotiations is in Dirk Spierenburg and Raymond Poidevin, *Histoire de la Haute Autorité de la Communauté Européenne du Charbon et de l'Acier: Une Expérience Supranationale* (Brussels: Bruylant, 1993), pp. 743–9.

[5] Miriam Camps, *Britain and the European Community 1955–1963* (Oxford University Press, 1964).

Likewise, nearly all of the research papers presented to the succession of recent conferences about the 1961–3 enlargement negotiations adopted a strictly national approach, examining the policy of individual governments and the trends of national public opinion rather than attempting to assess developments throughout the Community.[6] Anne Deighton's work on British policy falls into the same category. [7] Alternatively, some authors have tried to all but ignore the technicalities discussed in Brussels and have instead analysed the events of 1961–3 as an element in a long-running strategic debate about the organisation of the Atlantic Alliance and, more specifically, about the control and possession of nuclear weapons. John Newhouse, for instance, treats the unsuccessful British membership bid as part of a wider crisis between de Gaulle and the Anglo-Saxons.[8] Françoise de La Serre adopts a slightly different approach, discussing the application as a purely Franco-British affair, but once again great emphasis is placed upon defence policy questions in general and nuclear politics in particular.[9] Similarly, a recent article by Wolfram Kaiser has focused exclusively on Macmillan's attempt to strike a nuclear bargain with the French.[10]

Both of these approaches have their merits. Detailed national

---

[6] The principal papers of the 1994 Florence conference are published in Richard Griffiths and Stuart Ward (eds.), *Courting the Common Market: The First Attempt to Enlarge the European Community 1961–1963* (London: Lothian Foundation Press, 1996); those of the 1993 Cambridge conference are due to appear in George Wilkes (ed.), *Britain's First Failure to Enter the European Community, 1961–63: Crises in European Atlantic and Commonwealth Relations* (London: Frank Cass, 1997) and those of the 1996 Oxford conference will appear in Anne Deighton and Alan Milward (eds.), *Acceleration, Deepening and Enlarging: The European Economic Community, 1957–1963* (Brussels: Nomos/Giuffrè/LGDJ/Bruylant, 1997).

[7] Anne Deighton, 'La Grande-Bretagne et la Communauté économique européenne (1958–1963)', *Histoire, Economie et Société*, 13:1 (1994); Deighton and N. P. Ludlow, '"A Conditional Application": British Management of the First Attempt to Seek Membership of the EEC, 1961–3' in Deighton (ed.), *Building Postwar Europe: National Decision-Makers and European Institutions, 1948–1963* (London: Macmillan, 1995), pp. 107–26.

[8] John Newhouse, *De Gaulle and the Anglo-Saxons* (London: André Deutsch, 1970). A more recent piece of work concentrating on France, the United States and Britain during the first enlargement episode is Simona Toschi, 'Washington – London – Paris, an Untenable Triangle (1960–3)', *Journal of European Integration History*, 1:2 (1995).

[9] Françoise de La Serre, 'De Gaulle et la candidature britannique à la Communauté européenne' in Institut Charles de Gaulle, *De Gaulle en son siècle* (Paris: Plon, 1992), vol. V, pp. 192–202.

[10] Wolfram Kaiser, 'The Bomb and Europe. Britain, France and the EEC Entry Negotiations (1961–1963)', *Journal of European Integration History*, 1:1 (1995).

studies can bring out the intricacies of policy debate and the effect of domestic political factors in a manner which a multinational work cannot emulate, while Newhouse, de La Serre or Kaiser raise issues which, it is clear from the British records at least, were extensively discussed at the highest levels of government. But neither capture the full significance of the 1961–3 enlargement negotiations, for they overlook the way in which the membership applications submitted by Britain, Ireland, Denmark and Norway posed a challenge not simply to France, West Germany or Italy individually, but to the Community as a whole, and that the way in which the Six responded consequently reveals much about their attitudes towards each other and towards European integration in the early 1960s. An examination of the 1961–3 negotiations from this perspective also constitutes a valuable case-study of the early Community at work on a complex and potentially divisive issue, as well as a first indication of how the EEC reacted to the challenge of enlargement – an issue which has recurred at intervals throughout the Community's subsequent history. This book is thus intended as a contribution to the very young but fast-growing field of European Community history.

Most of the study is organised in chronological fashion. Such an arrangement allows the variations of mood, atmosphere and expectation that characterised the negotiations to be accurately charted and highlights the importance of momentum and confidence to the success of intergovernmental discussions. There are, however, two important exceptions to this rule. First, chapter 3, which explains the various economic and commercial issues raised by British membership of the EEC, is not arranged chronologically, but thematically. This allows all the details about each issue discussed to be grouped together, rather than being spread out over the six-month period during which the two sides set out their opening stances. Second, subsequent chapters, although largely following the order of events, will on occasion pull together *prises de position* that were separated by several weeks in order to permit a more comprehensive explanation of certain problems or controversies. Chapter 6, for instance, analyses the impasse that occurred over British domestic agriculture in a single section, despite the fact that this dispute spanned three months and several ministerial meetings.

The opening chapter will first recall why Britain and the Six found themselves economically and politically separated in the early 1960s.

The decision by the Six to proceed without Britain in 1950 and again in 1955 will be discussed. Second, the short but highly successful history of the EEC before 1961 will be reviewed. And third, there will be a brief examination of the gradual reversal of British policy towards the Six, starting with the unsuccessful 1956 free trade area proposal which, it had been hoped, would lessen the division between the United Kingdom and its Western European neighbours, and culminating in the July 1961 membership bid.

Chapter 2 will concentrate on the Community's reaction to Macmillan's announcement. After a brief review of the initial attitude of each member state towards British membership, it will focus on the efforts of the Six between August and December 1961 to decide how the negotiations with the applicants should be conducted. This examination of the lengthy procedural debate will introduce at an early stage one of the recurrent themes of the book, namely the way in which most of the Community members sought to reconcile a desire to see the Community enlarged with a concern that the admission of new members might undermine what they had already achieved and impede future progress. It will also explain why the negotiating method adopted was one which was not ideally suited to the needs of the applicants.

Chapter 3 will highlight the technical problems raised by British membership. Taking as its starting-point Edward Heath's speech in Paris on 10 October 1961, in the course of which the conditions Britain attached to membership were explained, the chapter will provide the technical background necessary to understand the chronological chapters which follow. It will also explain why so many of the issues raised by British membership were extremely controversial. In particular, it will highlight the potential incompatibility between Macmillan's pledge to safeguard both the interests of Commonwealth exporters and British farmers and the Community's attempt to establish a uniform common external tariff and a common agricultural policy. The final part of the chapter will address the political union negotiations among the Six and the US drive for greater free trade – two issues which, while not officially on the Brussels agenda, nevertheless became entangled with the enlargement negotiations.

The near crisis atmosphere of late April and early May 1962 constitutes the starting-point for chapter 4. In the ten months since the British application had been announced and the seven months of actual negotiations, very little progress appeared to have been made.

There was thus growing pressure from many of those most eager to see Britain join for a radical change in the way in which the negotiations were conducted. Others, by contrast, pinned their hopes on the meeting at Château de Champs in early June between Macmillan and de Gaulle. Agreement between the two statesmen, it was believed, might lead to a more cooperative French stance in the Brussels negotiations, thereby permitting much faster advance. The chapter will explain, however, that while a crisis in Brussels was averted and the first agreement between the Six and the British was initialled in May 1962, this improvement owed little to either procedural reform or the Champs meeting, but was instead largely due to a new and more flexible attitude adopted by the British. This paved the way for two months of significant progress, during which time several issues were satisfactorily settled and numerous others advanced. There remained, however, an enormous amount of ground still to cover if the British hope of reaching a comprehensive overview of the likely membership terms by September was to be attained.

The first half of chapter 5 focuses primarily on the vital tenth ministerial meeting of late July and early August 1962 when a sustained attempt was made to reach this goal. The progress made in this highly charged meeting will be described, as will the acrimonious circumstances in which the meeting ended. There will then be an attempt to assess the behaviour of the different member state delegations during the negotiations up to this date and, especially, the crucial July–August period. French tactics in particular will be examined in the light of newly released evidence about internal ministerial discussions in Paris. These discussions underline the extent to which de Gaulle's behaviour towards Britain was constrained by his government's refusal to provoke a crisis which might seriously damage the EEC, and with it, French national interests.

Chapter 6 will analyse the deadlock reached by the negotiations in the final months of 1962. By way of background it will also look at two developments away from Brussels which threatened to worsen Britain's negotiating position. The first of these was the growing antipathy towards Community enlargement of Konrad Adenauer, the German Chancellor – a development which will be charted using a variety of recently released German official documents. The second disappointment for Macmillan's government was the Commonwealth Prime Ministers' Conference held in London in September which, while acknowledging Britain's right to join the European Community, gave only the most grudging approval to the terms so far agreed. Both Adenauer's views and Commonwealth discontent were to contribute significantly to the difficulties encountered when the Brussels negotiations resumed in October. The key impasse, however, arose over agriculture, and it is therefore on the symptoms and underlying causes of this disagreement that the central portion of chapter 6 will focus. The chapter will conclude with an account of the Rambouillet meeting between the French and British leaders. The records of this last emphasise the extent to which de Gaulle had decided to block British membership before the Nassau agreement between Macmillan and Kennedy.

De Gaulle's 14 January 1963 press conference and the premature end of the Brussels negotiations dominate chapter 7. Before examining either the French President's intervention or the frantic diplomatic manoeuvres that followed, the chapter will analyse the state of the negotiations in January 1963. This is an important task given the contradictory French and British claims that the negotiations were either fatally becalmed or on the very threshold of success. It will then examine in some detail the final weeks of the British application and conclude by assessing some of the longer-term repercussions of the failure of the first British application.

This book is based on five principal archival sources.[11] The first of these is the records of the EEC Council of Ministers. The negotiations between Britain and the Six were not officially serviced by the Council secretariat: one of the procedural decisions taken in the autumn of 1961 was to establish a separate *ad hoc* secretariat for the international conference. In practice, however, most of the staff of this newly created body were drawn from the Council secretariat – augmented by a few British officials – and it was therefore natural that the papers relating to the British application should be stored in the Council of Ministers' archive. A sizeable and multilingual collection of highly varied documents ranging from the detailed reports of the many technical working groups to the minutes of ministerial meetings was thus preserved in Brussels, and constitutes much of the raw material

---

[11] One important additional source of information was shown to the author on condition that it not be cited directly. Where this has been used, an effort has usually been made to cite open sources which corroborate the information found. Nevertheless, there unavoidably remain passages which contain a more detailed account of certain meetings than would seem possible from the sources to which reference has been made.

out of which the pages that follow were fashioned. Equally important were the idiosyncratic holdings of the European Commission archives which include, amongst much else, reports on all but one of the ministerial meetings between the British and the Six (and vitally among the Six themselves) and all of the deputy-level gatherings. Written by Walter Hallstein and Jean-François Deniau for the weekly meetings of the European Commission, these reports provide important insights both into those aspects of the negotiations which the Council minute-takers chose to ignore and into the Commission's own view of developments. A third source was a range of German official papers preserved in the historical archives of the Foreign Ministry in Bonn and the *Bundesarchiv* at Koblenz. These offer only a rather patchy coverage of the negotiations themselves (a large number of the files relating to the actual technical negotiations are missing from the archives) but they do reveal much about German attitudes in the months before Britain applied, about the evolution of the Chancellor's view throughout the 1961–3 period and about the German role in the crisis of January 1963. Of still greater value were the French Foreign Ministry (Quai d'Orsay) records of the negotiations. The papers of the *Service de Coopération Economique* proved to be particularly revealing, containing not only regular reports from the French negotiators in Brussels, but also numerous memos examining French tactics and highlighting the interdepartmental discussions underway in Paris. Most unusually, the Quai d'Orsay papers also include a detailed account of the July 1962 Cabinet-level discussion between General de Gaulle and his ministers. Last but not least, extensive use was made of a wide variety of the British government documents available through the Public Record Office at Kew. Although primarily useful in determining the development of British policy, these UK holdings also contain countless reports from Brussels and from the various capitals of the Six detailing conversations and agreements with diplomats and negotiators on the Community side. They thus represent an important complement to the other four archival collections used.

These official papers were supplemented by material from the Conservative Party archive in the Bodleian Library, Oxford, and by a comprehensive reading of the press: *Agence Europe*, *Le Monde* and *The Economist* were surveyed for the whole of the July 1961 to January 1963 period, while the Chatham House collection of newspaper cuttings provided relevant material from a wide array of British, US and continental newspapers.[12] The fast-growing body of English, French, German and Italian secondary literature on the origins of European integration and on the relations between Britain and the continent was also consulted, as were the biographies and memoirs of some of the key protagonists. Finally, a few of the participants in the negotiations were kind enough to share some of their reminiscences. A full list of those interviewed, a comprehensive bibliography and a more detailed description of the official papers used are included at the end of the book.

[12] The primary evidence upon which this book is based was found in the English, French, Italian, German and Dutch languages. Most of this has been translated by the author. Nevertheless, a small minority of the quotations used are drawn from the official translations (usually into French or English) produced by the Community institutions.

1 From separation to application
May 1950 – July 1961

Harold Macmillan's announcement on 31 July 1961 that Britain planned to open negotiations with the European Economic Community (EEC) with a view to full membership was widely hailed as an historic turning-point. It signalled the culmination of a lengthy British policy change stretching back to the mid-1950s and marked the end of a period during which the six member states of the EEC had felt that they alone were ready to participate in the integration of Europe. By way of setting the scene, therefore, this first chapter will have three central tasks. First, it will briefly recall the initial separation between the British and the Six in 1950, the subsequent widening of this division and the abrupt end of this gulf in 1954. Second, it will look at the reappearance in 1955 of integration *à six*, the success of the Treaty of Rome negotiations and the unexpectedly smooth start which the Six made in the implementation of their wide-ranging agreement. And third, it will review British reactions to the *relance européenne*, starting with the United Kingdom's brief and half-hearted involvement in the work of the Spaak committee, proceeding through the period of tension between the British and the Six which followed, and ending with the post-1958 policy review which was to lead to Macmillan's 1961 application.

The Schuman Plan and the initial division of Western Europe

The 'Six' first appeared as a political grouping in June 1950, when, as a result of a French initiative, negotiations began in Paris about the creation of the European Coal and Steel Community (ECSC).[1] Robert Schuman, the French Foreign Minister, had announced his intention of creating a supranational organisation to oversee European production of coal and steel a month earlier; in doing so, he had demonstrated a new determination to rescue French foreign policy after half a decade of humiliating retreat. Contrary to French wishes, an independent and potentially powerful West Germany had come into being; it was in response to this defeat that French policy makers turned to European integration in an attempt to find a formula which would prevent a resurgent Germany from once again posing a threat – economic or political – to France.

The sector in which the French chose to act was partly symbolic – coal and steel were central to the production of armaments – and partly a response to a specific economic crisis. The end of Allied controls on German steel production threatened to interrupt the deliveries of German coke upon which French steel production, and with it the whole planned recovery of the French economy, depended.[2] But the Schuman Plan was also a highly political gesture, signalling the willingness on the part of the French government to confront its fear of Germany in a constructive manner, and overtly linking narrow sectoral integration to the political unification of Europe. It also marked a new readiness on the part of the French to go beyond the intergovernmental cooperation which had characterised all of the European institutions formed during the previous five years and experiment with a powerful and supranational High Authority.

This last was a key development. Although the powers which the French originally intended to give to the High Authority were substantially eroded in the course of the ECSC negotiations, the institutional structure of the new Community was significantly different from anything that had gone before. A quartet of institutions – a

---

[1] Klaus Schwabe (ed.), *Die Anfänge des Schuman-Plans 1950/1* (Baden-Baden: Nomos Verlag, 1988); Dirk Spierenburg and Raymond Poidevin, *Histoire de la Haute Autorité de la Communauté Européenne du Charbon et de l'Acier* (Brussels: Bruylant, 1993); Poidevin, *Robert Schuman: homme d'Etat, 1886–1963* (Paris: Imprimerie Nationale, 1986); Alan Milward, *The Reconstruction of Western Europe 1945–51* (London: Methuen, 1984); John Gillingham, *Coal, Steel and the Rebirth of Europe, 1945–55* (Cambridge University Press, 1991); François Duchêne, *Jean Monnet. The First Statesman of Interdependence* (New York: Norton, 1994), pp. 181–225; Eric Roussel, *Jean Monnet* (Paris: Fayard, 1996), pp. 512–66.
[2] Milward, *The Reconstruction*, pp. 392–5; Jean Monnet, *Mémoires* (Paris: Fayard, 1976), p. 346.

High Authority, a Council of Ministers, a Parliamentary Assembly and a Court of Justice – had been established which, in somewhat modified form, continues to stand at the heart of the Community today. Furthermore, the decision by the French government to make the acceptance of supranationality a precondition of participation in the ECSC negotiations prevented the British from attending the Paris conference. This was highly controversial. Even within the French government, the decision to start integrating Europe with Germany but without Britain was felt by many to be extremely unwise. Doubters ranged from President Vincent Auriol to Alexandre Parodi, the head of the Quai d'Orsay.[3] But such was Schuman's determination to create a strong and effective framework within which Germany could be contained and not to allow the scepticism of the British to weaken his proposed structure, that the French government defied domestic criticism and proceeded with the plan.[4]

The new French policy was enthusiastically welcomed by the West German government. Konrad Adenauer, the German Chancellor, had long been an exponent of greater ties between France and Germany – in March 1950 Adenauer had spoken of the need for a Franco-German union – and he thus had no hesitation in accepting the French proposal.[5] Membership of a European coal and steel organisation would not only remove one source of Franco-German tension but would also, much more fundamentally, start the international re-habilitation of Germany. Within the new organisation, the Federal Republic would be the equal of France.

Britain's absence, moreover, was more than compensated for by the American endorsement of the plan. As a result, Germany participated fully in the ECSC negotiations and was able to ratify the resultant Treaty of Paris by a comfortable margin, despite SPD unhappiness with both the exclusion of Labour-led Britain and the obstacles which, it was argued, German participation would place in the way of eventual reunification.[6]

Italy was also attracted more by the political aspects of the plan

[3] René Massigli, *Une comédie des erreurs 1943–1956: Souvenirs et réflexions sur une étape de la construction européenne* (Paris: Plon, 1978), pp. 199 ff.

[4] Schuman told the Foreign Affairs Committee of the National Assembly in June 1950: 'Nous n'avons pas cru devoir faire dépendre de cette adhésion préalable de la Grande-Bretagne le sort de notre initiative.' Cited in Poidevin, *Schuman*, p. 277.

[5] Konrad Adenauer, *Erinnerungen 1945–53* (Stuttgart: Deutsche Verlags-Anstalt, 1965), pp. 295–331.

[6] Spierenburg and Poidevin, *Histoire de la Haute Autorité*, p. 41.

than by its economic implications. Post-war Italian diplomacy had been characterised by a succession of disappointments and the government of Alcide De Gasperi had become an advocate of European integration largely in order to redress Italy's rather marginal role on the European and Western stage.[7] Previous Italian efforts to increase cooperation had admittedly been focused on the Organisation for European Economic Cooperation (OEEC) – in August 1948, for instance, Count Sforza, the Italian Foreign Minister, had proposed a significant increase in the OEEC's powers – but the Italians were not sufficiently wedded to the wider OEEC framework to spurn an opportunity to integrate more closely with a more limited number of European states.[8] Adherence to European initiatives such as the Schuman Plan and the European Defence Community project that followed had the additional advantage of acting as a politically popular 'smokescreen' for the more controversial Atlantic alignment sought by De Gasperi's government.[9]

The decision to join 'Little Europe' proved hardest for the Benelux countries. In Belgium, political reaction was generally favourable to the basic idea of a European coal and steel organisation, but sceptical and anxious about some of the more detailed aspects of the French plan. Politicians were divided as to whether the scheme would help or threaten Belgium's large coal and steel industries and there was great anxiety about the far-ranging powers that the French planned to give to the High Authority. Once the negotiation was complete, moreover, the owners of the Belgian coal mines launched a vociferous and well-funded campaign to obstruct the ratification of the Treaty of Paris. But this was insufficient to overcome the pragmatic awareness that Belgium could ill afford to stand aloof from a Community which included both France and Germany. In January and February 1953 both chambers of the Belgian Parliament ratified the Treaty.[10]

---

[7] Antonio Varsori, 'L'Italia e l'integrazione europea dal Piano Marshall al Piano Pleven' in Varsori (ed.), *La politica estera Italiana nel secondo dopoguerra (1943–1957)* (Milan: LED, 1993), pp. 343–4.

[8] Sergio Romano, *Guida alla politica estera italiana* (Milan: Rizzoli, 1993), pp. 64–7.

[9] Varsori (ed.), *La politica estera*, p. 18.

[10] Michel Dumoulin, 'La Belgique et les débuts du Plan Schuman (mai 1950–février 1952)' in Schwabe (ed.), *Die Anfänge*, pp. 271–84; Dumoulin (ed.), *La Belgique et les débuts de la construction européenne: De la guerre aux traités de Rome* (Louvain-la-Neuve: CIACO, 1987), pp. 20–5; Spierenburg and Poidevin, *Histoire de la Haute Autorité*, p. 39.

Similarly, Luxembourg, while again unhappy at the High Authority's 'dictatorial' powers, resigned itself to accepting the ECSC.[11]

The Dutch shared many of their Benelux partners' misgivings about the High Authority. In the Paris negotiations they thus emerged as the staunchest supporters of a Council of Ministers which would temper the High Authority's power. But the still more fundamental problem which the Schuman Plan posed to the Netherlands was the question of whether its continental position and its commercial links with Germany and Belgium should outweigh its traditional foreign policy ties with Britain. At the 1 July 1950 Cabinet meeting called to decide the Netherlands' response to the French plan, both Dirk Stikker, the Foreign Minister, and the Finance Minister Pieter Lieftinck argued strongly that Dutch participation should be made conditional on Britain also attending the Paris conference. They argued in vain, however. Aware of the great economic and political dangers which the Dutch would face if excluded from a strong continental grouping, the Cabinet decided that a delegation from the Netherlands should go to the ECSC negotiations, albeit it with instructions to query the proposed supranational arrangements, and once involved, the relative success of the Dutch delegation in obtaining both economic and institutional safeguards made it all but impossible for the Netherlands to repudiate the Treaty.[12]

For Britain, by contrast, a close involvement with a supranational coal and steel organisation was impossible to accept. Despite the amount of historical attention devoted to the exact circumstances in which the British opted not to attend the Paris conference, this decision was not primarily a result of either the brusque behaviour of the French or negligence and inattention on the part of the Labour government.[13] Instead, it reflected a profound difference in both economic and political circumstances between Britain and the Six as

---

[11] Spierenburg and Poidevin, *Histoire de la Haute Autorité*, pp. 38–9.

[12] Bernard Bouwman, 'The British Dimension of Dutch European Policy (1950–1963)', D.Phil. thesis, Oxford (1993), pp. 101–36; Richard Griffiths, 'The Schuman Plan' in Griffiths (ed.), *The Netherlands and the Integration of Europe 1945–1957* (Amsterdam: NEHA, 1990), pp. 113–35; Albert Kerstens, 'A Welcome Surprise? The Netherlands and the Schuman Plan Negotiations' in Schwabe (ed.), *Die Anfänge*, pp. 285–304.

[13] The classic work denouncing Schuman and Monnet's tactics is Massigli, *Une comédie des erreurs*, esp. pp. 185–238. There are echoes of the same approach and criticism of the British government in Michael Charlton, *The Price of Victory* (London: BBC, 1983), pp. 90–120 and in Roger Bullen, 'The British Government and the Schuman Plan May 1950–March 1951' in Schwabe (ed.), *Die Anfänge*, pp. 199–210.

the 1950s began. Economically, the fortunes of the main continental countries had become steadily more entwined in the late 1940s, while Britain remained much more closely linked to the Commonwealth and American markets. The United Kingdom was thus all but immune to the economic pressures which played so important a part in the Low Countries' decisions to join the ECSC.[14] And politically, Britain was prey to none of the foreign policy dissatisfaction which characterised France, Germany and Italy. On the contrary, with the creation of NATO in 1949, Britain's hope of a Europe protected and stabilised by an American guarantee had been attained. Britain in 1950 thus felt no need for European experiments, especially if they involved, as did the Schuman Plan, a sacrifice of sovereignty over two of the most politically sensitive sectors of the British economy.

The creation of a 'Little Europe' which did not include Britain was an important psychological step for the Six. It was not immediately clear, however, that the split between the British and the Six would apply to anything other than the ECSC or that it would last. Indeed, had the seriousness and longevity of the division been suspected in 1950, it is extremely doubtful that the Dutch would have been able to accept Britain's absence.[15] But in the years that followed the gap did grow and attitudes on both sides of the Channel hardened. In the autumn of 1950 Britain declined a French invitation to join negotiations about a European Defence Community (EDC). This, in turn, meant that the British were not involved in the debate about a political community and a customs union which became attached to the EDC project. And even in the discussions which UK representatives did join, such as the series of conferences about agricultural cooperation in Europe held in the early 1950s, there appeared to be an important distinction between the enthusiasm of some of the continental countries and the scepticism of the British. Lessons began to be drawn. Paul-Henri Spaak, for instance, in his capacity as the President of the Council of Europe Consultative Assembly, was brutally clear:

> There is a simple choice facing Europeans. Either we must line up with Great Britain and renounce the attempt to create a united Europe, or we must endeavour to create Europe without Great Britain. For my part, I choose the second alternative, despite the risks and all the dangers involved, because, reckoning all the possibilities,

[14] Milward, *The Reconstruction,* pp. 335–61.
[15] Bouwman, 'The British Dimension', pp. 130–1.

> I think the risks are less great and the dangers less serious than those
> which inaction and renunciation would inevitably imply.[16]

Not all European statesmen were prepared to put matters quite so simply. By 1952, however, even a critic of the 1950 split such as Stikker had conceded that the chances of building a united Europe in which Britain could be included were very slim.[17]

This was also the view of the United States. Well before the launch of the Schuman Plan, Washington had begun to feel that its hope of seeing a more united and therefore stronger Europe emerge was always likely to be frustrated by the British.[18] Thus in October 1949, Dean Acheson, the US Secretary of State, had urged France to assume the leadership of European integration.[19] With the declaration of 9 May 1950 this appeared to have happened. The launch of the Schuman Plan therefore signalled the start of enduring American support for tight integration between the Six as against wider cooperation including Britain. This preference for the Six persisted throughout the 1950s: deeply disappointed with the failure of the EDC, the US was to be an enthusiastic backer of the Treaty of Rome negotiations and, by contrast, highly ambivalent about the British-inspired free trade area discussions.[20] The assurance of American support thus greatly bolstered the willingness of the Six to press ahead without Britain.

All seemed to change, however, when in August 1954 the French National Assembly failed to ratify the EDC Treaty. The Parliamentary vote was widely interpreted as a sign that the French had lost faith in the integration process which they themselves had launched; as the Italian Ambassador to Paris observed, the EDC was not the sole casualty: 'also buried, I fear, is the idea of Europe being built by

[16] Spaak's resignation speech to the Council of Europe, December 1951. Cited in Dirk Stikker, *Men of Responsibility* (London: John Murray, 1966), p. 250.

[17] Stikker, *Men of Responsibility*, p. 188.

[18] Pierre Melandri, *Les Etats-Unis face à l'unification de l'Europe 1945–54* (Paris: Editions A. Pedone, 1980), pp. 221–8.

[19] Milward, *The Reconstruction*, pp. 391–2.

[20] Pascaline Winand, *Eisenhower, Kennedy and the United States of Europe* (London: Macmillan, 1993), pp. 25–82 and 109–37; Klaus Schwabe, 'Die Vereinigten Staaten und die Europäische Integration: Alternativen der amerikanischen Außenpolitik (1950–1955)' in Gilbert Trausch (ed.), *Die Europäische Integration vom Schuman-Plan bis zu den Verträgen von Rom* (Brussels: Nomos/Giuffrè/LGDJ/Bruylant, 1993), pp. 41–54; Melandri, *Les Etats-Unis*, pp. 263 ff.

means of specialised supranational authorities'.[21] He was one of many to draw this conclusion.[22] That it was the British Prime Minister, Anthony Eden, who defused the crisis caused by the EDC's collapse, masterminding the creation of the Western European Union (WEU) and so permitting a limited and controlled German rearmament, only reinforced the impression that the experiment with integration *à six* which had begun in 1950 had reached an unexpected end by 1954.

The revival of the Six and the creation of the EEC

All too quickly, however, the limitations of the WEU and more generally of British involvement in the integration process became apparent.[23] The British initiative had solved the problem of German rearmament; it had done little, by contrast, to address either the German or the Italian desire to use European integration to reestablish a role on the international stage, or the aspirations of the Benelux countries in particular, to press ahead with greater economic cooperation. American pressure for further integration also persisted. In the year that followed the EDC vote a wide variety of ideas for a revival of European cooperation were hence discussed by the Belgian, Dutch and German governments.[24] Whitehall, by contrast, seemed totally uninterested. It was thus a meeting of the ECSC members and not the WEU which served as a launching pad for a new series of initiatives. At Messina in June 1955 it was decided to appoint a committee of experts, chaired by a political personality, which would examine a range of ideas about possible new fields for joint action.[25]

With the memory of the EDC debacle still fresh in their minds, the representatives of the Six who met at Messina deliberately chose very different tactics from those adopted in 1950. First, much less emphasis

---

[21] 'Con essa, temo, è sepolto l'idea dell'Europa realizzata attraverso le agenzie sopranazionali specializzate.' My translation. Cited in Enrico Serra, 'L'Italia e la conferenza di Messina' in Serra (ed.), *Il rilancio dell'Europa e i trattati di Roma* (Brussels: Bruylant, 1989), pp. 93–4.

[22] See also Roberto Ducci, *I capintesta* (Milan: Rusconi, 1982), pp. 200–1; Melandri, *Les Etats-Unis*, p. 488; Robert Marjolin, *Le travail d'une vie: Mémoires 1911–1986* (Paris: Robert Laffond, 1986), p. 274.

[23] Benelux frustration is well documented in A. G. Harryvan and A. E. Kerstens, 'Benelux and the *relance européenne*' in Serra (ed.), *Il rilancio*, pp. 125–58.

[24] For an account of the Belgian planning see Joseph van Tichelen, 'Souvenirs de la négociation du Traité de Rome', *Studia Diplomatica*, 34 (1981), 332.

[25] Hanns Jürgen Küsters, *Fondements de la Communauté Economique Européenne* (Brussels: Editions Labor, 1990), pp. 64–8.

was placed on the divisive notion of supranationality. Second, the various plans selected for further study raised fewer problems of sovereignty than the EDC had done. Neither atomic energy nor customs barriers were as sensitive a topic as military self-determination. And third, the participating governments would initially limit themselves to studying the feasibility of the different plans rather than starting at once to draft binding treaties. It was thus possible for the French government to become involved in the process without immediately confronting those who had been instrumental in the defeat of the EDC.

Of the four projects studied by the Spaak committee, that for a European common market enjoyed the most widespread support. Originally a Dutch proposal, the idea of eliminating all tariffs and quotas between member states promised to consolidate the existing boom in trade between the nations of Western Europe. An irreversible set of tariff reductions would eliminate the danger that, when Western Europe next underwent a cyclical economic downturn, economic nationalism of the sort that had scarred the 1930s would reappear.[26] Belgium, Germany, Italy and, of course, the Netherlands all supported this idea. The French, however, were wary of any such scheme which, it was feared, would encounter the same economic and political opposition which had scuppered several of the customs union plans discussed in the late 1940s. All but a small côterie of politicians and officials grouped around the Prime Minister therefore opposed the customs union plan.[27] What did attract much greater political support in France, by contrast, was another of the projects under study, namely the proposal for a joint European effort to develop nuclear power for civilian purposes. As a result, Germany, Italy and the Benelux countries, while relatively unenthusiastic about cooperation in the nuclear field, agreed to pursue both projects. This enabled the French government to direct public and political attention towards the more popular scheme but to employ the Parliamentary sanction given to the atomic energy proposals to continue discussion of the common

[26] Griffiths (ed.), *The Netherlands*, p. 184.
[27] Gérard Bossuat, 'The French Administrative Elite and the Unification of Western Europe, 1947–58' in Anne Deighton (ed.), *Building Postwar Europe: National Decision-Makers and European Institutions, 1948–1963* (London: Macmillan, 1995), pp. 21–37; Marjolin, *Le travail*, p. 283; Pierre Guillen, 'Europe as a Cure for French Impotence? The Guy Mollet Government and the Negotiation of the Treaties of Rome' in Ennio di Nolfo (ed.), *Power in Europe? vol. II: Great Britain, France, Germany and Italy and the Origins of the EEC, 1952–1957* (Berlin: Walter de Gruyter, 1992), pp. 505–16.

market as well.[28] The fate of two very diverse schemes thus became inextricably linked – for so long as both survived, the intergovernmental discussions were able to continue.[29]

A similar willingness by the 'Five' to be flexible towards the French characterised many other stages of the negotiations. To counter French anxieties about the difference in social costs between its industry and that of its future partners, the Germans and the Dutch reluctantly agreed that the Treaty of Rome should contain provisions for the harmonisation of social costs.[30] Similarly, the French were able to insist on the inclusion of a string of safeguard clauses in the Treaty, which would allow a member state to postpone implementation in the case of economic difficulties.[31] And most fundamentally of all, a whole section was added to the Treaty of Rome to address the problems of France's overseas territories. Backed initially only by Belgium, the French pushed successfully for the Community member states to agree not only to allow the produce of France's (mainly African) colonies to enter the whole Community free of tariffs, but also to provide development aid through the European Development Fund.[32] Part IV of the Treaty of Rome thus stands as a monument to the Five's readiness to give way to French demands.

Such French success was only in part a tribute to the skill of her negotiators. Rather more significant was the twin realisation by the Five that France was both the country most likely to reject the Treaty of Rome, and the partner they could least afford to do without. European integration without Britain had already been shown to work; likewise, Europe could be built without the presence of Italy or the Netherlands. But in the absence of the Franco-German pairing, the political and economic *raison d'être* of the initiative would disappear. As a senior Italian diplomat explained: 'Europe cannot organize

---

[28] Andrew Moravcsik, 'Why the European Community Strengthens the State: Domestic Politics and International Cooperation', unpublished paper presented to the Conference of Europeanists, Chicago, April 1994, p. 26; Christian Pineau and Christiane Rimbaud speak of Euratom representing an 'écran de fumée'. *Le grand pari. L'aventure du traité de Rome* (Paris: Fayard, 1991), p. 197.

[29] Hanns Jürgen Küsters, 'The Treaties of Rome (1955–7)' in Roy Pryce (ed.), *The Dynamics of European Union* (London: Routledge, 1989), p. 89.

[30] Küsters, *Fondaments de la CEE*, pp. 213–15; Alan Milward, *The European Rescue of the Nation-State* (London: Routledge, 1992), pp. 212–16.

[31] Van Tichelen, 'Souvenirs', pp. 335–6.

[32] Küsters, *Fondaments de la CEE*, pp. 257–68; Milward, *The European Rescue*, pp. 218–20; Marjolin, *Le travail*, pp. 293 and 298.

without France and, to get her in, prices must be paid which may seem exorbitant. As the soldiers say, France has the geography.'[33] The Treaty of Rome negotiations thus underlined the centrality of France. It was a position which General de Gaulle was fully to exploit.

Despite the concessions which they had been obliged to make to the French, the Five remained constant in their determination to establish a European Community. In Germany, the Minister of Economic Affairs, Ludwig Erhard, and many officials at the Ministry of Economic Affairs were unhappy with the number of protectionist and *dirigiste* measures which had been allowed to distort the original conception of the common market.[34] Likewise, there were many in the Netherlands who felt that the Dutch vision of an open and liberal Europe had been tainted.[35] And in Belgium, Spaak and several other ministers had to threaten to resign, before van Acker, the Prime Minister, sanctioned the final Treaty.[36] But in the end the recognition that the conclusion of the Treaties of Rome was not merely a vital economic and political development, but also an achievement which might well prove impossible to repeat, prevailed in both Cabinet and Parliamentary debates – by 4 December 1957 the Treaties had been ratified by all six national Parliaments. The European Economic Community and Euratom started operation on 1 January 1958.

The honeymoon years

The return to power of Charles de Gaulle in June 1958 seemed initially to endanger the newly formed Communities. While out of government, the General had been fiercely critical of supranational integration and many of his associates and supporters had been amongst the most vociferous opponents of the EDC and related projects.[37] Michel Debré, for instance, had been the sole member of the international committee established to draw up a treaty for a European political community to vote against the preliminary draft in February 1953.[38]

[33] Cited in Milward, *The European Rescue*, p. 223; see also Marjolin, *Le travail*, p. 279.
[34] Küsters, *Fondaments de la CEE*, pp. 294–7.
[35] Willem Drees, the Dutch Prime Minister, was reported to have complained: 'In signing this Treaty the Netherlands has joined a relatively small and protectionist group.' Cited in Griffiths (ed.), *The Netherlands*, p. 202.
[36] Küsters, *Fondaments de la CEE*, p. 299; Dumoulin (ed.), *La Belgique*, p. 31.
[37] Roger Massip, *De Gaulle et l'Europe* (Paris: Flammarion, 1963), pp. 25–6 and 32–6.
[38] Rita Cardozo, 'The Project for a Political Community (1952–4)' in Pryce (ed.), *The Dynamics*, p. 57.

But while the new French leader reportedly commented that had he been in power when it had been negotiated the Treaty of Rome would have been organised 'in a rather different fashion', he chose to respect France's international obligations. As he put it to Macmillan in June 1958, 'one cannot tear up that which has been agreed'.[39] Indeed, the new French regime quickly confirmed its commitment to the Treaty of Rome, not merely through rhetorical assent, but much more significantly by launching a series of economic reforms which allowed France to confound the widespread expectation that it would have to employ the Treaty of Rome's safeguard clauses and implement the first stage of tariff disarmament on time and in full.[40]

This unanticipated success was mirrored in other aspects of the Treaty's implementation. So few were the problems encountered in carrying out the first tranche of tariff reductions, that in March 1960 the European Commission was able to propose that the liberalisation schedule mapped out in the Treaty of Rome be speeded up. It was also suggested that the planned Common External Tariff (CET) be introduced more rapidly. Despite some Dutch and German qualms about this latter aspect, in July 1960 the Council of Ministers agreed on the so-called 'acceleration'.[41] The implementation of the commercial aspects of the Treaty of Rome was further advanced when the Six managed, faster than might have been expected, to settle the dispute about the CET level for the so-called List G commodities – products that had proved so sensitive during the original Treaty negotiations, that it had only been possible to agree to postpone a decision on their tariff level.[42] Internal tariff cuts combined with the rapid creation of a working external tariff increased both the economic advantages of EEC membership and, conversely, the penalties of exclusion. Likewise progress towards the creation of a Common Agricultural Policy (CAP) was more encouraging than many had anticipated. The Stresa

---

[39] 'De manière assez différente' and 'on ne peut pas déchirer ce qui a été fait'. My translations. Cited in Raymond Poidevin, 'De Gaulle et l'Europe en 1958' in Institut Charles de Gaulle, *De Gaulle en son siècle* (Paris: Plon, 1992), vol. V, p. 81.

[40] Jean-Marc Boegner, '1958, le général de Gaulle et l'acceptation du traité de Rome', *Espoir*, 87 (1992), 28–30.

[41] Miriam Camps, *Britain and the European Community 1955–1963* (Oxford University Press, 1964), pp. 253–62; Hans von der Groeben, *Combat pour l'Europe. La construction de la Communauté européenne de 1958 à 1966* (Brussels: CECA–CEE–CEEA, 1985), p. 110.

[42] Küsters, *Fondaments de la CEE*, pp. 226–7; van Tichelen, 'Souvenirs', pp. 337–8; von der Groeben, *Combat pour l'Europe*, p. 61.

conference of July 1958, convened by the European Commission and bringing together agricultural experts from each of the member states, revealed a wide divergence of views about how European agriculture should be integrated. The unanimous final resolution recognising the importance of a CAP, however, provided the Commission with the mandate to develop its own plans for a CAP. These were ready by November 1959. A year later, a revised set of proposals formed the basis for the Council's approval of the general principles of the CAP and in December 1960 the idea of an import levy system was given Council support.[43] Much remained to be done before a CAP was fully established, but the early progress of discussions suggested that agreement *à six* was much more attainable than earlier attempts to establish European agricultural arrangements spanning all sixteen OEEC member states.[44] And finally, the setting up of the Community institutions had proceeded smoothly, with the Commission in particular quickly proving its effectiveness, not least in the free trade area discussions.[45] As Robert Marjolin was to note in his memoirs, the years between 1958 and 1962 seemed with hindsight to constitute the 'honeymoon stage' of the European Community's existence.[46]

The successful implementation of the Treaty of Rome also encouraged some of Europe's leaders to turn their thoughts towards new fields in which European cooperation might be developed. Of particular importance for the period which followed was the start of discussions amongst the Six about political union. These have been extensively examined elsewhere.[47] For the purposes of this study, it is enough to explain that with the appearance of an alliance of convenience between, on one side, de Gaulle and Adenauer – both of

[43] Michael Tracy, *Government and Agriculture in Western Europe, 1880–1988*, 3rd edn. (London: Harvester Wheatsheaf, 1989), pp. 252–4; Jacques Bourrinet, *Le problème agricole dans l'intégration européenne* (Montpellier: Editions CUJAS, 1964), pp. 144–54; von der Groeben, *Combat pour l'Europe*, pp. 75–84.
[44] For a discussion of these earlier, abortive attempts see Milward, *The European Rescue*, pp. 224–317; Gilbert Noël, *Du pool vert à la politique agricole commune. Les tentatives de Communauté agricole européenne entre 1945 et 1955* (Paris: Economica, 1988).
[45] Camps, *Britain and the EC*, p. 169.
[46] Marjolin, *Le travail*, p. 305.
[47] Robert Bloes, *Le 'Plan Fouchet' et le problème de l'Europe politique* (Bruges: College of Europe, 1970); Pierre Gerbet, 'In Search of Political Union: The Fouchet Plan Negotiations (1960–62)' in Pryce (ed.), *The Dynamics*, pp. 105–29; Georges-Henri Soutou, 'Le général de Gaulle, le plan Fouchet et l'Europe', *Commentaire*, 13:52 (Winter 1990–1), 757–66.

whom regarded intergovernmental cooperation between the Six on foreign policy and security issues as a worthwhile goal in its own right – and, on the other side, those such as the Italian Prime Minister Amintore Fanfani, Paul-Henri Spaak and Jean Monnet – who perceived a system of intergovernmental consultation as a useful first step towards genuine political integration – the successful establishment of some form of European political union looked feasible. Admittedly, fundamental disagreements over Europe's relations with the United States remained, as did deep disputes about the best relationship between any new political institutions and the existing Communities. The Dutch, moreover, remained implacably opposed to any political cooperation which did not involve the British.[48] But none of these obstacles were insurmountable. The question of Europe's international alignment did not have to be settled, one way or the other, before the establishment of mechanisms for foreign policy coordination, nor was it necessary to find anything more than a temporary compromise about the links between the proposed political secretariat and the Community institutions. And the Dutch would find it hard to hold out indefinitely. The confidence with which Jean-Marie Soutou, the French representative on the Fouchet committee, looked towards the imminent conclusion of a successful political union treaty was, by late 1961, fully comprehensible.[49]

It was thus a confident and optimistic Community to which Britain applied in August 1961. There were, of course, difficulties aplenty which would have to be overcome before the ambitious targets set by the Treaty of Rome could be attained. Important disagreements remained, moreover, particularly about the speed and direction of future progress. But the successes of the previous five years had created a widespread belief that most divisions of opinion among the Six could be bridged.[50] Only the Netherlands dissented strongly from this confident outlook.[51] And even Dutch gloom, whether about the Community's incipient protectionism or about the challenge which political union would pose to the Atlantic status quo, was born of the belief that cooperation amongst the Six, in both political and economic spheres, was likely to grow and intensify rather than to stagnate.

[48] Bouwman, 'The British Dimension', pp. 222–62.
[49] Interview with the author, 20.11.1991.
[50] Von der Groeben, *Combat pour l'Europe*, pp. 94–6.
[51] Bouwman, 'The British Dimension', pp. 220 ff.

Confronted by such dynamism, British European policy had gradually and painfully to adapt.

The end of detachment

Britain's initial reaction to the Messina meeting of June 1955 and the attempted relaunch of the Six was a strange combination of non-chalance and scepticism. 'Rab' Butler, the Chancellor of the Exchequer, described the Messina Declaration to Cabinet colleagues as 'weak and uninteresting': atomic energy cooperation was of scant interest to the UK as the Six had 'much to gain and little to give', while the idea of British involvement in a European customs union had been 'repeat-edly' rejected. Britain should, he recommended, respond positively to the invitation to send a representative to the expert discussions, but only because to refuse outright would be 'misunderstood'.[52] A Board of Trade official was thus sent to the initial Spaak committee meetings, although he was of much more junior rank than the representatives of the Six.

British doubts about the viability of a European common market were to persist until the ratification process of the Treaty of Rome was complete.[53] But the lack of concern that had characterised the first reaction gradually gave way to growing alarm at the possibility of Britain being excluded from a powerful economic grouping among the Six.[54] Thus the withdrawal of the British representative from the Spaak committee in November 1955 was followed by a series of *démarches* towards the Six which were inept at best, and at worst constituted an attempt to prevent the Common Market from coming into existence.[55] For many on the continent, the latter interpretation appeared more probable. By February 1956, Spaak had been prompted to write in pained terms to Eden; regretting the disappearance of the tolerant attitude with which Britain had regarded earlier attempts to

---

[52] Simon Burgess and Geoffrey Edwards, 'The Six plus One: British Policy-Making and the Question of European Economic Integration, 1955', *International Affairs*, 64 (1988).

[53] Richard Griffiths and Stuart Ward, ' "The End of a Thousand Years of History": The Origins of Britain's Decision to Join the European Community, 1955–1961' in Griffiths and Ward (eds.), *Courting the Common Market: The First Attempt to Enlarge the European Community 1961–1963* (London: Lothian Foundation Press, 1996), pp. 7–38.

[54] Burgess and Edwards, 'Six plus One', p. 406; Roger Bullen, 'Britain and Europe 1950–57' in Serra (ed.), *Il rilancio*, p. 330.

[55] John W. Young takes a charitable view in Michael Dockrill and John Young (eds.), *British Foreign Policy, 1945–56* (London: Macmillan, 1989), pp. 210–15.

integrate Little Europe he observed: 'It is no longer a case of somewhat sceptical but benevolent neutrality; it is outright hostility, clearly
expressed.'[56]

Under pressure from the US, Britain soon altered course.[57] Confrontation gave way to the search for an alternative European framework
which would either replace the Common Market should it fail (which
the Foreign Office still deemed likely) or, if a six-member customs
union did materialise, render it less harmful to those Western European countries who felt unable to take part.[58] The outcome, publicly
announced in July 1956, was Plan G – a proposal to create a free trade
area linking all seventeen member states of the OEEC. This would, the
British maintained, prevent the creation of the EEC from leading to a
harmful economic division of Europe.

The British suggestion was appealing to some of the Six. For the
Netherlands an OEEC free trade area would both limit the negative
effects of too high an EEC common external tariff and safeguard
political links between Britain and the Six.[59] Similarly, those in
Germany like Erhard who questioned the wisdom of German participation in a small economic bloc were attracted by the prospect of a
much larger tariff-free zone.[60] Erhard, in fact, tried unsuccessfully in
October 1956 to persuade the German Cabinet to suspend the Treaty
of Rome negotiations in favour of a more sustained effort to establish
a free trade zone. He was overruled by Adenauer and Hallstein.[61] The
Belgian government also could see the merits of the scheme.[62] But

[56] 'Il ne s'agit plus pour elle d'une neutralité un peu sceptique mais bienveillante, il
s'agit d'une hostilité clairement exprimée.' My translation. Paul-Henri Spaak,
Combats inachevés, de l'espoir aux déceptions (Paris: Fayard, 1969), p. 77.

[57] Camps, *Britain and the EC*, pp. 51–2.

[58] See Elizabeth Kane, 'Tilting To Europe? British Responses to Developments in
European Integration (1955–1958)', D.Phil. thesis, Oxford (1996); James Ellison,
'Harold Macmillan's Fear of "Little Europe" Britain, the Six and the European Free
Trade Area' (University of Leicester, Centre for Federal Studies, Discussion Papers on
Britain and Europe, No. BE95/5, October 1995); Ellison, 'Perfidious Albion? Britain,
Plan G and European Integration, 1955–57' in Iain Hampshire-Monk and Jeffrey
Stanyer (eds.), *Contemporary Political Studies, 1996* (Belfast: The Political Studies
Association, 1996), vol. I, pp. 21–32.

[59] Bouwman, 'The British Dimension', pp. 202–5.

[60] Küsters, *Fondaments de la CEE*, pp. 294–5.

[61] *Ibid.*, p. 197; see also Martin Schaad, 'Anglo-German Relations During the Formative
Years of the European Community, 1955–1961', D.Phil. thesis, Oxford (1995), esp.
pp. 106–16.

[62] Jean-Charles Snoy et d'Oppuers, *Rebâtir l'Europe* (Paris: Duculot, 1989), pp. 116–33.

alongside such enthusiasm there were persistent doubts about both the motivation of the British initiative and about its compatibility with the Treaty of Rome.[63] Following on so soon from a period of perceived British opposition to the Messina proposals, the free trade area plan was suspected by some as being nothing more than a manoeuvre, designed to throttle the Community at birth,[64] and even those such as Spaak who were ready to believe in the sincerity of the British proposal saw a danger that 'if it had been accepted [the British plan] would have drowned the Common Market in a free trade zone'.[65] Furthermore, the French government was highly reluctant to undermine its success in incorporating provisions for fiscal and social harmonisation in the Treaty of Rome and in maintaining an acceptable level of tariff protection vis-à-vis third countries, by allowing free trade with OEEC members who had not agreed to accept so many common rules and standards and who did not apply the CET.[66] However appealing to France were closer political ties to Britain, the proposed OEEC grouping could only become acceptable if it became much more similar to the Community itself.[67] As a member of the Foreign Minister's private office put it in March 1958: 'the free trade zone is politically necessary (because of our close ties of friendship with Great Britain), but economically impossible'.[68]

With the Six so torn by the free trade area proposals, the British initiative needed to be pursued with the utmost energy if it were to have any chance of success. This did not happen. Instead, discussions in the OEEC committee entrusted with the study of the proposal were allowed to become entangled in highly technical disputes which totally obscured the ultimate objective.[69] More damaging still was the failure of the British to reinforce their drive for a free trade area with

---

[63] Camps, *Britain and the EC*, pp. 166–7.
[64] Even the Swiss, among the most enthusiastic backers of the free trade area, were uncertain about British motives. See A. Fleury's comments in Serra, *Il rilancio*, p. 417.
[65] 'S'il était accepté, [le plan Britannique] aurait noyé le Marché commun dans une zone de libre échange.' My translation. Spaak, *Combats inachevés*, p. 82.
[66] Pineau and Rimbaud, *Le grand pari*, p. 198.
[67] Serge Bernier, 'Aspects des relations politiques anglo-françaises 1947–1958', PhD thesis, Ottawa (1981), p. 246.
[68] 'La zone de libre échange est politiquement nécessaire (en raison de nos liens d'amitié avec la Grande-Bretagne), mais économiquement impossible.' My translation. Robert Marjolin cited in 'La zone de libre échange devant l'opinion française', *Revue du Marché Commun*, 1 (1958), 32.
[69] Spaak, *Combats inachevés*, p. 83; Camps, *Britain and the EC*, notes the 'air of unreality' which pervaded the free trade area discussions (p. 169).

other policies designed to show that the United Kingdom had now recognised its need for strong European ties. In fact, the period between 1956 and 1958 was marked by a series of British decisions which seemed to highlight the divergence of interests between the UK and the Six rather than to narrow the divide. This was true at a political level, where, in marked contrast to the French, the British response to the Suez crisis was first and foremost to seek to repair relations with the United States; in the economic field where Britain continued to prefer full sterling convertibility to the continuation of the European Payments Union and where, in 1957, proposals for an Anglo-Canadian free trade area were discussed; and in the defence sphere where the increase in British nuclear collaboration with the US coincided with a significant reduction in the number of British troops stationed in Germany.[70] None of these policies suggested that Britain had yet started a fundamental reassessment of its attitude towards the continent.

As a result, the free trade area was never able to gather wide enough political support to overcome the sceptics. Indeed, Reginald Maudling, the chairman of the OEEC committee, was himself close to admitting defeat by June 1958.[71] The negotiations were not definitively ended, however, until a French government which was prepared to risk a lessening of ties between Britain and the continent came to power. On 14 November 1958, Jacques Soustelle, General de Gaulle's spokesman, announced that the French government had decided that it was impossible to create a free trade area without a common external tariff and measures to harmonise economic and social policy. A seventeen nation grouping, as envisaged by the British, was therefore not feasible.[72]

De Gaulle's action caused considerable anger amongst the Northern European members of the Community. The fury of Erhard and of the German Ministry of Economic Affairs was exceeded only by the anguish of the Dutch. But the political value of Franco-German conciliation was to prevail. Less than two weeks after Soustelle's announcement, de Gaulle travelled to Bad Kreuznach, where he and Adenauer agreed that free trade area talks posed a danger to the EEC.

---

[70] Ellison, 'Harold Macmillan', pp. 14–19.
[71] Snoy, *Rebâtir l'Europe*, p. 130.
[72] Gérard Bossuat, 'The Choice of "La Petite Europe" by France, 1957–1963: An Ambition for France and for Europe' in Griffiths and Ward (eds.), *Courting the Common Market*, p. 65.

In order to mitigate the damage to commercial links between the Six and their neighbours, the French and German leaders decided that the 10 per cent cut in tariffs between the Six, scheduled for 1 January 1959, should be extended to all third countries. They also agreed that the Commission should be entrusted with a study of future relations between the Six and the rest of Europe. But the free trade area discussions as such were not to resume.[73] This Franco-German deal, reinforced by strong indications from Washington that the Americans favoured the EEC rather than the free trade area, was enough to force all of the Six into line.[74] Great irritation remained – for the Dutch in particular, the fact that the Germans and the Commission had rallied to the French line only heightened their feeling that without Britain the Community was doomed to become a narrow and protectionist bloc[75] – but when confronted with the choice between the existing Community *à six* and the uncertain prospect of wider European cooperation including the British, all of the Six had opted to retain what they had and forsake wider ties.

In the months that followed there were a few Benelux-inspired attempts to revive discussions. But these were obstructed not only by the continued hostility of the French to the idea of a free trade area, but also by the European Commission, which from February 1959 was advocating a global liberalisation under the auspices of GATT as the solution to the problem of European trade.[76] Thus as the 1950s came to a close Britain was ever more clearly faced with the choice of remaining economically and politically isolated from its geographical neighbours or of turning once more towards the Six to seek either association with the Community or, as the majority of the Six hoped, full membership.

The decision to seek full membership

A far-reaching reassessment of British European policy began almost as soon as the free trade area negotiations collapsed. At first, the focus was on the establishment of a free trade association linking the United

---

[73] Bossuat, 'The Choice of "La Petite Europe"', pp. 65–6; Hans-Peter Schwarz, *Adenauer: Der Staatsmann, 1952–1967* (Stuttgart: Deutsche Verlags-Anstalt, 1991), pp. 465–7.

[74] The United States refused to mediate between the Six and the rest of the OEEC and made its preference for the former quite clear. Winand, *Eisenhower*, p. 119.

[75] Bouwman, 'The British Dimension', pp. 212–20.

[76] Camps, *Britain and the EC*, pp. 184–200.

Kingdom to Portugal, Switzerland and Austria plus the three Scandinavian countries. This led, in November 1959, to the signature of the Stockholm Convention and the formation of the European Free Trade Association (EFTA).[77] EFTA, it was hoped, would provide a limited European outlet for British exporters and strengthen the collective bargaining position of the Seven in any future negotiations with the Community. But it was immediately accepted that EFTA was not a long-term solution.[78] Britain apart, none of its members were major players, economically or politically; the Seven, moreover, had highly diverse political and economic systems and were geographically scattered. As a Foreign Office memo noted acerbically, all that really linked the members of the free trade association were 'ties of common funk' – in other words, a shared inability to sign the Treaty of Rome and accept the obligations and privileges of full Community membership.[79] It was thus predictable that by October 1959 – before the Stockholm Convention had even been signed – Whitehall was once more giving thought to Britain's relationship with the Six.[80]

Details of the British policy reassessment which ultimately led to a membership application are beyond the scope of this chapter. They have, moreover, been the subject of several studies.[81] A few of the salient moments are, however, worth mentioning. In March 1960, the Prime Minister put a series of questions about European policy to the Economic Steering (Europe) Committee – a body which, significantly, was chaired by Sir Frank Lee, Joint Permanent Secretary of the Treasury and a long-standing exponent of closer ties between Britain and the EEC. The committee's replies, which emerged in June, left open the exact form of relationship between the UK and the Six –

---

[77] The best published account of the formation of EFTA remains that contained in Camps, *Britain and the EC*, pp. 210–31.

[78] Maudling told the House of Commons in July 1960 that by forming EFTA 'we wanted to provide a more practical basis for future negotiations with the Six'. *Hansard* 1959–60, vol. 627, col. 1211.

[79] Cited in Griffiths and Ward, ' "The End of a Thousand Years of History" ', p. 20. An additional problem was the American dislike of EFTA: see Winand, *Eisenhower*, pp. 119–21.

[80] Griffiths and Ward, ' "The End of a Thousand Years of History" ', pp. 19–23.

[81] Camps, *Britain and the EC*, pp. 274–376; Charlton, *The Price*; Griffiths and Ward, ' "The End of a Thousand Years of History" '; Wolfram Kaiser, *Using Europe, Abusing the Europeans. Britain and European Integration 1945–63* (London: Macmillan, 1996); Alistair Horne, *Macmillan, 1957–1986* (London: Macmillan, 1989), pp. 256–62; Richard Lamb, *The Macmillan Years, 1957–1963. The Emerging Truth* (London: John Murray, 1995), pp. 126–57.

joining and 'close association' were the two options considered – but pointed unequivocally to the unsatisfactory nature of the status quo.[82] Deprived of access to the Community's markets, Britain's economy might face 'stagnation', the committee predicted.[83] More serious still, were the political costs of exclusion:

> If the Community succeeds in becoming a really effective political and economic force, it will become the dominating influence in Europe and the only Western bloc approaching in importance the big Two – the USSR and the United States. The influence of the United Kingdom in Europe, if left outside, will correspondingly decrease.[84]

Furthermore, the United States would increasingly attach greater importance to the views of the Six than to British opinions, while the UK's decline in status would also erode its leadership position in the Commonwealth.

> Quite apart, therefore, from the economic damage which we will suffer from the consolidation of the Six, if we try to remain aloof from them – bearing in mind that this will be happening simultaneously with the contraction of our overseas possessions – we shall run the risk of losing political influence and of ceasing to be able to exercise any claim to be a world Power.[85]

The Lee committee's conclusions were an important element in the background to the Cabinet's discussions of European policy in mid-July 1960. The political marginalisation foreseen by the Economic Steering Committee demanded a government response. It was, however, the numerous difficulties connected with British membership highlighted by the same report which appear to have shaped the Cabinet's cautious conclusions. A new approach to Europe was necessary, ministers recognised; the old free trade area proposals were dead and stood no chance of revival.[86] Permission was thus given to the Foreign Office to conduct bilateral discussions with individual Community member states. But the Foreign Office mandate for such contacts reflected ministerial anxiety about the effects that any new approach to the Six might have on the Commonwealth, on EFTA and on the British farming community. The diplomats involved were to enter into no commitments, to refuse to talk about agriculture, to insist that tariff-free entry of Commonwealth products into Britain must continue, and to demand that provision be made for Britain's

---

[82] PRO. Cabinet Office file (henceforward CAB) 134/1853; ES(E) Committee, June 1960.
[83] *Ibid.* Question 10.   [84] *Ibid.* Question 2.   [85] *Ibid.*
[86] PRO. CAB 128/34, CM(60), 31st meeting, 13.7.1960.

EFTA partners.[87] Furthermore, to avoid antagonising the Six, the Foreign Office was not to press the Community member states for discussions, but should instead wait to be invited.

Fortunately for Macmillan, the Germans were quick to respond to this new British attitude.[88] Only a fortnight after Selwyn Lloyd, the Foreign Secretary, had outlined the government's revised approach to the House of Commons, Adenauer suggested that British and German experts should meet in the autumn to discuss the 'Six/Seven problem'.[89] The first in a series of bilateral pre-negotiations thus took place on 3 November 1960. Later in the same month Macmillan visited Italy and was told by the new Prime Minister, Amintore Fanfani, that the Italians were also willing to explore possible solutions to the EEC/EFTA divide.[90] The opening round of Anglo-Italian talks was held in late December. By the end of 1960, therefore, the British were involved in exploratory discussions with two of the larger Community member states.

These first bilateral meetings were encouraging from a British point of view. Both the Germans and the Italians displayed great flexibility on the two most contentious issues – British domestic agriculture and Commonwealth trade. On the former it was recognised that British farmers constituted a special case; for this reason neither German nor Italian officials expected the British to participate in the CAP. And both countries also acknowledged the importance of Commonwealth trade. They could not go so far as to say that the tariff-free entry of Commonwealth goods into the United Kingdom should continue unchanged, but they appeared to accept that the Six would have to show understanding towards Britain's former colonies.[91] But these

[87] The details of the mandate were decided upon by the Economic Questions Committee. They are reported in PRO. Foreign Office General Correspondence (henceforward FO371) 158264; M634/12, Heath to Macmillan, 7.2.1961.

[88] The speed of the German reaction may have reflected the warning sent to the German Cabinet a month or so earlier by von Herwath, the Ambassador in London, that whilst a British change of heart on Europe was occurring, it remained fragile and would only survive if carefully nurtured and encouraged by the Six. AAA, Ref. 304, Bd. 104, 1959–60, Aufzeichnung 15.6.1960.

[89] *The Times* 11 and 12.8.1960; for Lloyd's speech see *Hansard* 1959–60, vol. 627, cols. 1099–1109.

[90] *The Times* 22.11.1960.

[91] The main points to emerge from the bilateral discussions are summarised in a draft FO note prepared for the Economic Steering (Europe) Committee. PRO. FO371 158264; M634/20, 7.3.1961. For more details on the German point of view: AAA, Ref. 200, Bd. 486, Groß-Britannien und die EWG, Juli 1960–Mai 1961.

discussions, while useful, suffered from two major deficiencies. The first was that the highly restrictive remit given to the Foreign Office made it very difficult to rise above narrow technical issues and discuss the best institutional and political framework for an EEC/ EFTA arrangement. It was therefore impossible for the Germans or Italians to determine whether the British were contemplating EEC membership, association or some other form of linkage. The second difficulty was that bilateral discussions offered an imperfect guide to the likely position of the Community as a whole. In particular, no pre-negotiation which excluded the French could be expected to give a realistic foretaste of the difficulties which the British would encounter if and when actual negotiations began. As Erhard commented percep-tively, there was a real risk that, unless the political issues were tackled head on and the French were persuaded that a Six/Seven settlement was desirable, 'we would talk indefinitely about building bridges without getting anywhere at all'.[92]

Macmillan's visit to France in January 1961 went some way towards addressing this second problem. The Prime Minister's discussions with de Gaulle about Britain and the Six were inconclusive: the French President seemed reluctant to admit that the issue of EEC/EFTA relations was of any great importance at all. Furthermore, de Gaulle was sceptical about Britain's ability to enter into any agreement with the Six without fatally undermining both its traditional links with the Commonwealth and its special relationship with the United States – a position which, as later chapters will show, the French leader never abandoned. Nevertheless, he was impressed by Macmillan's new determination to lessen Britain's separation from the continent, com-menting that the United Kingdom and Europe were about to open a new chapter in their relationship. The French President thus agreed that bilateral discussions between British and French officials would be useful.[93]

The Quai d'Orsay reacted to these signs of a new British approach with a mixture of confusion, mistrust and alarm.[94] Despite their success in ending the free trade area negotiations, the French were

[92] PRO. FO371 158185; M617/11, No. 16 Savings, Steel to FO, 19.1.1961.
[93] The relevant section of the minutes of this Rambouillet meeting is in PRO. FO371 158171; M615/33, 28.1.1961.
[94] All of these sentiments are very evident in the French Foreign Ministry files. Ministère des Affaires Etrangères (henceforward MAE), Série DE–CE 1961–6, Bte. 509.

well aware that several of their Community partners remained anxious to improve links with Britain. As a result, any new set of British proposals – something perhaps short of full Community membership but going beyond a simple free trade area – was likely to test the solidarity of the Six and impede rapid development within the Community.[95] At particular risk was the nascent CAP: if Germany was given the prospect of a wider free trade area limited to manufactured goods, the Federal Republic would be much less willing to accept a disadvantageous CAP as the price of commercial access to French markets. The senior group of French diplomats who visited London in late February 1961 thus came determined to dissuade the British from seeking any form of half-membership of the Community.

Led by Olivier Wormser, head of the Quai d'Orsay's Economic Affairs Division and a man that the British had come to fear and respect in the course of the free trade area discussions, the French team attacked many of the basic assumptions of the Anglo-Italian and Anglo-German talks.[96] The urgency of a Six/Seven solution was, for instance, queried, when Wormser declared that neither intellectually nor politically could he accept 'the idea that there was either a solution or a catastrophe'. [97] And the difficulty of any arrangement which was based on no more than a partial acceptance of the Treaty of Rome was underlined:

> The Treaty of Rome represents a compromise between the opening of national frontiers and the harmonisation of national policies, going towards a common policy in certain cases. Therefore, both politically and philosophically, to grant exceptions whether they be major as in the case of agriculture or minor . . . is to put the Six in a very difficult position.[98]

[95] A good example of the type of proposal which worried the French was the Müller-Armack plan. This scheme for a hybrid customs union/free trade area linking the Six and the Seven was devised in the German Economics Ministry and, while never adopted as official German policy, was known to enjoy widespread support. See *Financial Times* 4.1.1961 and Alfred Müller-Armack, *Auf dem Weg nach Europa. Erinnerungen und Ausblicke* (Tübingen and Stuttgart: Rainer Wunderlich Verlag/C. E. Poeschel, 1971), p. 234.

[96] PRO. FO371 158172; M615/60, French draft minutes of Anglo-French discussions, 3.3.1961.

[97] 'L'idée selon laquelle il n'y a qu'une solution ou la catastrophe.' My translation. *Ibid.*

[98] 'Le Traité de Rome se présente comme un compromis entre l'ouverture des frontières et un rapprochement des politiques nationales allant, dans certains cas, vers une politique commune. Donc philosophiquement et politiquement faire des réserves, qu'elles soient fondamentales comme dans le cas de l'agriculture ou mineures . . . cela revient à mettre les Six dans une position très difficile.' My translation. *Ibid.*

In no area was this more true than for agriculture. As Wormser put it bluntly; 'It is clear that if agriculture is excluded from an arrangement between the Six and the Seven, there will be no common agricultural policy.'[99]

By contrast, if the British ceased to search merely for an arrangement or association with the Community and sought instead to join the Six the whole situation would be transformed: 'If Britain said "we want to become members of the Treaty of Rome" it would then be easy to overcome all of the obstacles and to find a solution.'[100] When Sir Roderick Barclay, the senior Foreign Office representative present at the talks, objected that the basic problems would remain identical whether the British sought to join the Community or simply to associate, Wormser flatly contradicted this idea:

> The Six have reached a compromise amongst themselves which is the Treaty of Rome. They still have to implement it. There is a major difference between saying I want to be an associate for certain parts of the Treaty but do not want to participate in others, and saying that I want to be a member with all that the latter entails. It is a fundamental difference.[101]

Wormser's dismissal of any 'half-way house' between full membership and detachment was soon reinforced by the Americans. In late March 1961, George Ball, the US Under-Secretary of State responsible for European Affairs, visited London and was as outspoken as Wormser had been. The United States, he explained, would oppose any British attempt to secure the commercial advantages of membership without its obligations, but would, by contrast, consider a British decision to join the Community 'as a great contribution to the cohesion of the Free World'.[102] But if by demonstrating that only full membership was possible, the French had hoped to win a respite from

---

[99] 'Il est clair que si l'on exclut l'agriculture d'un arrangement avec les Six et les Sept, il n'y a pas de politique agricole commune.' My translation. *Ibid.*

[100] 'Si la Grande Bretagne disait "nous voulons devenir membres du Traité de Rome" alors il serait aisé de l'emporter sur tous les opposants et de trouver une solution.' My translation. *Ibid.*

[101] 'En effet les Six ont réussi entre eux un compromis qui est le Traité de Rome. Ils doivent encore le mettre en oeuvre. Il est très différent de dire, je veux être un associé pour une certaine part et ne pas participer aux autres activités, ou bien je veux être membre avec tout que cela comporte. C'est une distinction fondamentale.' My translation. *Ibid.*

[102] PRO. FO371 158162; M614/45, Draft record of talks with Mr Ball, 30.3.1961; for his own account of these talks and an explanation of the motives behind the US stance, see George Ball, *The Past Has Another Pattern* (New York: Norton, 1982), pp. 210–13.

'le problème anglais', they were to be disappointed. For the French and American stance was exactly what Macmillan and the other partisans of full British membership needed. Earlier in the year the Prime Minister had grown impatient with the slow advance of bilateral discussions and had told Edward Heath (as Lord Privy Seal the minister in charge of Britain's relations with the Six) that he was ready to hold a new Cabinet discussion of British policy towards Europe in order to permit a more positive approach. Heath, however, had successfully dissuaded Macmillan from such a course, arguing that domestic opposition to a major policy review – not least within the Cabinet – was such that an alteration of British strategy could only be contemplated once the inadequacy of the current approach had been conclusively demonstrated. As Heath wrote to the Prime Minister: 'If we are to persuade the Cabinet that they must take a major decision it will be necessary to show them that we have first done everything possible to achieve our object along the present lines.'[103] Wormser and Ball had, by April 1961, provided exactly the demonstration that Heath awaited.

On 20 April and again six days later the Cabinet debated the merits of a new and far-reaching approach to the Six. The case for change, as put forward by Macmillan, Heath and the other partisans of British membership, was primarily political.[104] Outside the Community, the Prime Minister and his allies predicted, the British would see their influence diminish. First EFTA and then the Commonwealth were likely to drift away and 'new world groupings would arise', marginalising the British in international affairs. Within a uniting Europe by contrast Britain could act as 'a bridge between Europe and North America', thereby both preserving the UK's world role and bolstering the unity of the West in the face of an ever-greater Soviet threat. Membership, moreover, would be fully consistent with Britain's long-established tradition of preventing the undue concentration of power within a small group of continental countries. It was in Britain's interest to acquire a powerful voice inside such a grouping rather than without. The economic damage which non-participation in the Common Market might do to the British economy and the possible commercial merits of membership were also highlighted. British

---

[103] PRO. FO371 158264; M634/12, Heath to Macmillan, 7.2.1961.
[104] Despite the release of Cabinet minutes confirming the political motivations of Macmillan, the myth persists that the British applied in 1961 first and foremost for economic reasons. See for instance Lamb, *The Macmillan Years*, p. 158.

membership was thus presented as an essentially defensive move, designed to preserve Britain's world role, to avoid the division of the West and to avert the economic penalties of exclusion.[105]

'Rab' Butler, the Home Secretary and the most senior of the ministers opposed to EEC membership, could do little to contest this high-political case. Instead, as had happened in July 1960, Butler and other sceptics drew attention to the costs of British membership, and in particular to the likely discontent of British farmers and the Commonwealth. Little had changed, the Home Secretary maintained, since the previous Cabinet discussion and much further thought about the Commonwealth and agricultural problems was required before any policy initiative could be taken. In 1961, however, unlike the previous year, the partisans of a new approach towards the Community were not prepared to allow this line of argument to dissuade them from their course. They thus countered Butler's warnings by pointing to the likelihood of Britain being able to negotiate special terms for the Commonwealth and farmers in the event of a full membership application. If such terms could be negotiated, most of the disadvantages to which the sceptics pointed were unlikely to arise. Britain, Heath suggested, could reserve final judgement on whether to join the Community until negotiations with the Six had revealed how many derogations and other special arrangements for the Commonwealth and British farmers would be on offer. Membership need only proceed if Britain's conditions had been fully met.[106]

The doubters had been outflanked. Their case against a British application was grounded on the practical difficulties which UK membership would cause. They could not mount much resistance to an approach to the Community which would only be carried through to membership if the damage to British and Commonwealth interests had been minimised. The Cabinet thus agreed that a new policy towards the EEC was desirable. It would not take effect, however, until full consultations had been carried out with all those groups liable to be affected by British membership of the EEC.[107]

The consultation process which followed only served to highlight the practical difficulties that British membership of the Community would pose. Ministerial envoys were dispatched to most Commonwealth capitals, to explain Britain's desire for change, but also to discover the extent of Commonwealth fears. On their return they were

[105] PRO. CAB 128/35 part 1; CC(61)24, 26.4.1961.   [106] *Ibid.*   [107] *Ibid.*

obliged to inform the Cabinet of 'the serious anxieties' harboured by Australia, New Zealand and Canada, of the political and economic misgivings felt by the Indian and Pakistani governments, and of the widespread belief amongst the leaders of the newly independent or almost independent states of Africa that the EEC's association regime constituted a retrograde and neo-colonial arrangement.[108] There was little indication that the Commonwealth would accept some economic losses so as to facilitate Britain's political aims. To avoid damaging Commonwealth criticism, British negotiators would have to arrange with the Six a wide variety of special arrangements to meet the myriad Commonwealth needs. Similarly the EFTA ministers who gathered in London for a Council meeting in June displayed little willingness to loosen Britain's obligations to its existing European partners in order to help the UK enter the EEC. Instead, as will be explained in chapter 3, the British were again forced to give undertakings which would prove problematical in the course of the Brussels negotiations. And finally, preliminary discussions with representatives of Britain's farming community suggested that they were deeply suspicious and sceptical about the planned CAP and highly reluctant to forsake the tried and tested British system of agricultural support. The pressure on the British government to seek innumerable safeguards in Brussels was therefore intense from all three of the special interest groups singled out for special attention.

Discussions did of course continue with the Six. Between April and June further talks were held with both French and German officials and a host of more informal meetings with the other member states took place. All served to build up a clearer picture of the likely negotiating stance of each of the Six. Furthermore, useful advice was received about both the need to couch Britain's application in the most positive terms possible and the impossibility of changing the Treaty of Rome – advice that significantly shaped the manner in which Edward Heath was to present the British case.[109] But two factors greatly reduced the utility of these pre-negotiations. The first was the impossibility of holding detailed bilateral discussions before the consultations with the Commonwealth, EFTA and British farmers had been completed and the British negotiating stance finalised. Few of the requests that Britain was to outline in Paris in October 1961 had

---

[108] PRO. CAB 128/35 part 2; CC(61)42, 21.7.1961.
[109] See, e.g., *Bundesarchiv*, Koblenz (henceforth BAK), Bd. 2560, Beitritt Großbritanniens zur EWG, FS 646 Thierfelder to AA, 23.7.1961.

thus been discussed in advance with the Six.[110] The second difficulty was that the manner in which Macmillan and the partisans of EEC membership had triumphed in April 1961 gave them little incentive to heed discouraging signals from the continent and every encouragement to overemphasise positive news. In early June, for instance, Wormser handed a British diplomat in Paris an informal note, which spelt out, in harsh terms, the French attitude towards British membership. The communication emphasised the impossibility of Commonwealth free entry continuing after Britain had joined, the absolute incompatibility of Britain's agricultural support system with the likely shape of the CAP, and the way in which no guarantees of access could be offered to Britain's EFTA partners.[111] The Foreign Office commentary attached to the 'Wormser note' as it was circulated within Whitehall sought to minimise its impact, however, noting that 'it probably represents [France's] maximum opening bid'.[112] In fact the note not only foreshadowed accurately the stance which the French would adopt in the forthcoming negotiations, but had also been seen and approved by a senior German minister.[113] But calls by opponents of British entry, such as Reginald Maudling, who suggested that the whole idea of a British application should be reexamined in the light of the French stance, were firmly ignored.[114] And great but unrealistic hopes were pinned on the ability of the Germans, the Dutch and the other Community members eager to see Britain join, to force the French to take a more conciliatory line.[115]

The proliferation of conditions and of special requests attached to Britain's application was hence barely tempered by contact with the Six. The outline of Britain's opening position, finalised at Chequers in late June 1961, owed considerably more to an estimate of how much British and Commonwealth opinion could accept, than to a prediction of what would be deemed negotiable by the Six. At the same time that Jean Monnet was advising the British to enter the Community without lengthy preliminary negotiations and to use their voice and their votes to obtain special treatment from within and de Gaulle was publicly

[110] The Foreign Office post-mortem on the negotiations was to admit as much: PRO. FO371 171441; M1091/539, April 1963.

[111] PRO. FO371 158177; M615/151, 1.6.1962.

[112] *Ibid.*, Gallagher memorandum, 14.6.1961.

[113] MAE. Série DE–CE 1961–6, Wormser to Bonn, 19.6.1961.

[114] PRO. FO371 158177; M615/158, Maudling to Macmillan, 15.6.1961.

[115] A further error which the Foreign Office retrospectively acknowledged: PRO. FO371 171441; M1091/539, April 1963.

insisting that Britain 'must join the Common Market; but without posing conditions', Macmillan's government was thus engaged in adding to its commitments and drastically reducing its room for manoeuvre.[116]

It was a highly conditional membership application which was given final Cabinet approval on 21 July 1961 and announced to the House of Commons ten days later.[117] As Macmillan explained:

> During the past nine months, we have had useful and frank discussions with the European Economic Community Governments. We have now reached the stage where we cannot make further progress without entering into formal negotiations. I believe that the great majority in the House and in the country will feel that they cannot fairly judge whether it is possible to join the European Economic Community until there is a clearer picture before them of the conditions on which we could join and the extent to which these could meet our special needs.
>
> Article 237 of the Treaty of Rome envisages that the conditions of admission of a new member and the changes in the Treaty necessitated thereby should be the subject of an agreement. Negotiations must, therefore, be held in order to establish the conditions on which we must join. In order to enter into these negotiations it is necessary, under the Treaty, to make a formal application to join the Community, although the ultimate decision whether to join or not must depend on the result of the negotiations.[118]

If the Six acceded to the British request, 'protracted' negotiations, dealing with 'delicate and difficult matters' would ensue. Only if and when these were successfully completed and the Commonwealth governments had again been consulted, would the British Parliament be asked to take a definitive decision on whether or not Britain should become a member of the EEC.[119] A major step to lessen the separation

---

[116] Monnet's advice was relayed in numerous conversations with the British; see e.g. PRO. FO371 158176–7 and 158179; M615/132, 136, 145, 148 and 188; for de Gaulle's speech see FO371 158178; M615/175, Dixon to FO, 3.7.1961.

[117] PRO. CAB 128/35 part 1; CC(61)42, 21.7.1961; *Hansard* 1960–1, vol. 645, cols. 928–31.

[118] *Hansard* 1960–1, vol. 645, col. 930. The full text of Macmillan's statement, plus that of Article 237 of the Treaty of Rome under which Britain had applied to the EEC, is reproduced in appendix 1.

[119] *The Economist* 5.8.1961 accurately described Macmillan's statement as being wreathed in 'a bower of "ifs" and "buts"'. George Ball was even more cutting, telling Kennedy that Macmillan was trying to 'slide sideways into the Common Market'. Cited in Ball, *The Past Has Another Pattern*, p. 218; see also David Dutton, 'Anticipating Maastricht: The Conservative Party and Britain's First Application to Join the European Community', *Contemporary Record*, 7:3 (Winter 1993), 524.

between Britain and the continent had been taken, but until the negotiations with the Six were brought to a successful conclusion, it was not certain that the gap which had developed since 1950 could be bridged.

2 Devising the rules of the game
August–December 1961

Continental reactions to the early news of the British application were overwhelmingly positive. Forewarned by a couple of days, Macmillan's fellow leaders were among the first to respond. Konrad Adenauer, the German Chancellor, expressed the hope that the course of the negotiations would be 'quick and good', the Italian Prime Minister Amintore Fanfani sent his 'warmest congratulations', while the Dutch Foreign Minister Joseph Luns and his Belgian and Luxembourg counterparts conveyed a similar welcome.[1] The European Commission followed suit, issuing a statement that described 31 July 1961 as 'a turning point in post-war European politics'.[2] Only the French gave sign of any reservations, General de Gaulle telling the British diplomat who delivered Macmillan's message that 'he feared that it would take a long time for the many difficulties to be settled'.[3] But even the French President soon wrote to inform Macmillan that 'my country warmly welcomes the intentions that you have just announced on behalf of yours'.[4]

These official reactions accurately reflected the warmth with which the vast majority of European opinion received news of Britain's application. In the Netherlands, in particular, most public comment was euphoric. The *Nieuwe Rotterdamse Courant* for instance claimed

---

[1] PRO. FO371 158278; M634/241, Adenauer to Macmillan, 29.7.1961; Sir Ashley Clarke to Philip de Zulueta, 28.7.1961; Sir Alexander Noble to the FO, 28.7.1961; Freese-Pennefather to the FO, 28.7.1961. Spaak's public response is in *Le Soir* 2.8.1961.

[2] *The Times* 2.8.1961.

[3] PRO. FO371 158179; M615/195, Sir A. Rumbold to FO, 28.7.1961.

[4] 'Mon pays accueille avec grande sympathie les intentions que vous annoncez de la part du vôtre.' My translation. PRO. Prime Minister's Files (henceforward PREM) 11 3559; de Gaulle to Macmillan, 3.8.1961.

that the prospect of Britain entering the EEC fulfilled one of the key priorities of post-war Dutch foreign policy.[5] Dutch misgivings about a small and restrictive Community, dominated by France and Germany, could be put aside and the likelihood savoured of an outward-looking and solidly Atlanticist European grouping. Similarly, most Belgian politicians and the majority of the press in Belgium welcomed Macmillan's announcement enthusiastically.[6] The Socialist Party, the Christian Democrats, *Volksunie*, and even the Walloon nationalists declared themselves in favour of enlargement, and foresaw a wide variety of probable benefits. Thus for Baron Jean-Charles Snoy et d'Oppuers, a leading Christian Democrat, British entry would bring to an end the damaging EEC/EFTA divide and allow the traditional economic and commercial links between Belgium and Britain to be revived, while for the Belgian Socialists, closer ties with the UK and Scandinavia, with their strong democratic traditions and well-respected Labour parties, would bolster the hopes of the left throughout Europe. According to one Belgian speaker at the 1962 Congress of European Socialist parties in Paris: 'Socialism will constitute the strongest political force in the enlarged European Community.'[7] A few interest groups in both countries harboured fears about the effects of British entry – both Dutch and Belgian farmers, for instance, were anxious about the fate of the CAP in an enlarged Community – but such qualms could only cautiously be advanced at a time when so many were so publicly delighted.[8]

In Germany also enlargement was seen as positive, in both economic and political terms. Prior to the appearance of the first tariff discrimination between the EEC and EFTA on 1 January 1959, West Germany had actually exported marginally more to the Seven than to the Six. The four most northern *Länder* – Bremen, Hamburg, Niedersachsen and Schleswig-Holstein – were particularly dependent on trade with Britain and Scandinavia: in 1958 33 per cent of their exports had gone to EFTA as compared to the 17 per cent sold to the five other

---

[5] Cited in the *Guardian* 2.8.1961.

[6] Daniel Paulus, *Les milieux dirigeants belges et les demandes d'adhésion du Royaume-Uni à la Communauté économique européenne* (Brussels: Université Libre de Bruxelles, 1971).

[7] 'Le socialisme représentera la force politique la plus importante d'une Communauté européenne élargie.' My translation. *Ibid.* pp. 109–12 and 138–9.

[8] *Ibid.* pp. 19–23; the strength of the pro-enlargement consensus is confirmed by Eliane Jacquemyns, *L'Europe des Six et la demande d'admission de la Grande-Bretagne au Marché Commun* (Brussels: Institut Universitaire d'Information Sociale et Economique, 1963).

EEC member states.[9] If the EEC/EFTA split persisted, it was feared that this volume of trade with EFTA would decline. Both the Bundes-verband der Deutschen Industrie (BDI) and the political representa-tives of the northern German regions had thus placed continuous pressure on the Federal Government to act so as to heal the economic division of Western Europe.[10] The British and Danish applications promised to facilitate this task. Also welcome in government circles would be an end to the long-running feud within the CDU between those who believed that Germany had erred in pressing ahead with the Six without Britain and the rest of EFTA – a group normally linked to Ludwig Erhard the Deputy Chancellor – and those, such as Adenauer, who felt that the political merits of close integration within the EEC outweighed any economic disadvantages. In March 1960, for instance, Erhard had publicly rejected the idea of an acceleration of the Treaty of Rome timetable for the establishment of the Common External Tariff, arguing that such a move would only aggravate the existing tension between the Six and the Seven; a little over two weeks later, however, a newspaper article by Dr van Scherpenberg, a State Secretary in the Ministry of Foreign Affairs, contradicted this thesis, pointing out that the existence of two trade blocs need not necessarily lead to trade friction. The EEC, van Scherpenberg maintained, was committed to a liberal trade policy which would minimise problems with EFTA.[11] A resolution of so public a dispute would benefit the CDU greatly. And finally, on a wider political level, British member-ship was expected to strengthen Western unity at a time of acute East–West tension. Even Josef Jansen, the German Ambassador in Paris and a renowned advocate of closer Franco-German ties, ac-knowledged that this would be highly welcome.[12]

In Italy, commercial ties with the Seven had been much less

[9] Figures cited in 7.11.1959 letter described in footnote 10 below; for a much more detailed analysis of Germany's trade with EFTA see Markus Schulte, 'Challenging the Common Market Project. German Industry, Britain and Europe 1956–63' in Anne Deighton and Alan Milward (eds.), *Acceleration, Deepening and Enlarging: The European Economic Community 1957–1963* (Brussels: Nomos/Giuffrè/LGDJ/Bruylant, 1997).

[10] BAK. BKA, B–136, vol. 2553, Verhältnis zwischen der EWG und der EFTA. See especially BDI report (30.9.1959), letter from the Senates of Hamburg, Bremen, Niedersachen and Schleswig-Holstein (7.11.1959) and letter from Fritz Berg, President of the BDI, to Adenauer (11.3.1960).

[11] Details of both Erhard's speech and van Scherpenberg's article in *Industriekurier* 24.3.1960 are in AAA, Ref. 200, Bd. 489.

[12] AAA, Ref. 200, Bd. 48, Jansen memo, 26.1.1961.

significant than for the Germans, and the political anguish caused by the EEC/EFTA divide had been correspondingly less acute. Nevertheless, the Italians too had good reasons to applaud the British approach. As was the case elsewhere, these ranged from the party political to the strategic. For the parties of the left, British membership was seen as a potential check on the unrestrained capitalism of the Six; for the right-wing MSI, by contrast, the inclusion of the UK within the Community would bolster the forces of anti-Communism.[13] More generally, British EEC membership was anticipated as a development which would strengthen the Community in both political and economic terms, increase the cohesion of the Western bloc and lessen Franco-German dominance within the EEC. Finally, and perhaps most simply, enlargement would reduce the discrepancy between the Europe which was striving to unite through the EEC and the broader Western European community. As one Italian Senator put it: 'Europe would not really have been itself without England's participation.'[14] All but the Italian Communist party thus declared themselves in favour of British membership.

In France, support for Community enlargement was less unanimous. Not only did de Gaulle have serious political misgivings about British participation in the EEC, but the French more generally had a series of commercial and economic anxieties about the possibility of Community enlargement.[15] Furthermore, many French diplomats feared that a British application to the Community might undermine all that they had achieved in the preceding years. As a Quai d'Orsay memo had noted in June 1961: 'Objectively, and irrespective of Britain's goodwill, UK membership of the Treaty of Rome threatens both the unity and the political standing of the Six. The negotiations will bristle with difficulties comparable to those which caused the free trade area negotiations to founder. But this time the Six may find it harder to escape blame for an eventual failure.'[16] The President's

---

[13] See e.g. *La Corriera della Sera* 7.9.1961.

[14] 'L'Europa non sarebbe stata veramente se stessa senza la presenza dell' Inghilterra.' My translation. *La Corriera della Sera* 1.8.1961.

[15] These will be explored in chapters 5 and 7.

[16] 'Objectivement, et quelle que soit la bonne volonté du Royaume-Uni, son adhésion au Traité de Rome fait peser une menace sur la cohésion et la consistence politique des Six. La négociation sera hérisée de périls analogues à ceux sur lesquels échouèrent naguère les pourparlers sur la zone de libre échange. Mais la responsabilité d'un échec éventuel serait peut-être, pour les Six, plus difficile à éluder que par le passé.' My translation. MAE. Série DE–CE 1961–6. Bte. 510. Direction des

guarded response to Macmillan's letter, described above, was thus representative of feelings within much of the government. Nevertheless, even in France there were many who welcomed Britain's application. Guy Mollet, the leader of the Socialist party and the man who had been Prime Minister during much of the Treaty of Rome negotiations, was one such, Jean Monnet another, and Paul Reynaud a third.[17] Much of the Mouvement Républicain Populaire (MRP), the centrist party upon which Michel Debré's coalition government still depended, also made clear their support for enlargement. And even prominent members of the French Cabinet, in particular Wilfrid Baumgartner, the Minister of Finance, had been privately encouraging to the British.[18] The cautious words of welcome issued by both de Gaulle and his Foreign Minister accurately reflected the political danger of overt opposition to enlargement.

In very similar fashion, the European Commission chose to keep silent about its doubts. A few senior figures in the Brussels institutions may have genuinely welcomed the British application. After all, as the Commissioner responsible for agriculture, Sicco Mansholt, commented to the European Parliament, Britain's change of heart constituted a dramatic endorsement of the path to integration which the Six had originally chosen.[19] But for most, the challenge of enlargement had arrived too early in the life of the Community.[20] There was 'no joy' at the first meeting of the Commission at which Macmillan's application was discussed.[21] Nevertheless the Commission could not be seen to oppose a development which so many in the Community endorsed. To do so would be to risk the wrath of the majority should the enlargement fail, or to be forced to work with a resentful new member state should Britain succeed in its application. The Commission hence had little choice other than to issue a formal welcome and

Affaires Politiques, Sous-Direction d'Europe Occidentale, Note 'L'Angleterre et l'Europe', 12.6.1961.

[17] *Le Monde* 2.8.1961 and 4.8.1961.

[18] PRO. FO371 158174; M615/85, Lee to Heath, 12.4.1961 and FO371 158176; M615/125, Heath note on conversation with M. Baumgartner, 15.5.1961.

[19] *Débats de l'Assemblée Parlémentaire Européenne 1961–2*, vol. II, p. 78.

[20] Marjolin made no secret of this in his memoirs. Robert Marjolin, *Le travail d'une vie. Mémoires 1911–1986* (Paris: Robert Laffond, 1986), pp. 332 and 336; that Hallstein felt very much the same is confirmed by my interviews with Karl-Heinz Narjes, his deputy *chef de cabinet*, and Jean-François Deniau, the Commission's chief negotiator at official level in the 1961–3 negotiations.

[21] Phrase used by Narjes. Interview with the author. The minutes of this meeting are in: ECHA. COM(61) PV 155 final, 2ème partie, 26.7.1961.

to approach the forthcoming negotiations with what Emile Noël, the Secretary-General of the organisation, has described as an attitude of 'constructive distrust'.[22]

Britain's prospects in the forthcoming negotiations thus looked encouraging. Most of Europe's political elite seemed to have put behind them the tensions and disputes between Britain and the Six which had scarred the late 1950s, and to have welcomed Britain's new approach with some enthusiasm. Those who did have misgivings felt it prudent to remain silent. The Community appeared likely to honour its pledge to remain open to all democratic European states willing to assume the obligations and responsibilities set out in the Treaty of Rome.[23] But with so many technical problems to be addressed before Britain's entry into the Community became a reality, warm words of welcome were not enough. As Macmillan had made clear, the UK would only enter the Community if its multiple conditions were met. It is thus to the delicate task of deciding how to approach the talks with Britain and the other applicants, and of selecting an appropriate procedure for the vital negotiations, that this chapter must now turn.

The formal response of the Community was surprisingly slow and guarded, given the political support for British membership described above. Ludwig Erhard, as President of the Council of Ministers, did not officially reply to Macmillan until late September and full negotiations only got underway in early November. This sluggish start owed much to the timing and the nature of the British application. Part of the problem was that while many in the Community had anticipated some British move towards closer relations with the EEC in the early part of the summer, their expectations had faded as reports filtered out of the rough reception received by the British government envoys dispatched to explain British thinking to the Commonwealth. Staff at the French Embassy in London, for instance, had informed their government in July that Parliamentary opinion had grown more hesitant about EEC membership in the light of Commonwealth complaints. This meant, the Embassy continued, that Macmillan's ability to announce a fresh policy initiative before the summer recess was being widely questioned.[24] Such reports, moreover, clearly

---

[22] 'Méfiance constructive'. My translation. Interview with the author.
[23] Preamble and Article 237 of the Treaty of Rome.
[24] MAE. Série DE–CE 1961–6, Bte. 509, Tel. No. 2223/24, Wapler to Couve de Murville, 12.7.1961.

reached the Elysée: the very next day, de Gaulle told the British Ambassador in Paris, Sir Pierson Dixon, that he had noticed that the British were having difficulties with the Commonwealth. 'He himself hoped that this question would eventually be solved but he thought it would take a long time.'[25] In Brussels too, there was a sense in mid-July, that the opportunity had passed – *Agence Europe*, normally a reliable indicator of the opinions prevalent within Community circles, suggested that the British government was so shaken by the Commonwealth reactions that no announcement was likely before the autumn.[26] As a result of such predictions, some among the Six may have been wrong-footed by Macmillan's statement.[27]

The second and more serious difficulty connected with the timing of the British application was that it occurred as the Community stood poised to enter an exceptionally intense and busy period of activity. With Stage II of the Community's transitional period due to start on 1 January 1962, a series of important decisions still remained to be made before this deadline could be met. First and foremost, the Six had to agree upon the first series of commodity regulations for the CAP; second they had to push on with the effort to harmonise certain basic social norms (although they were less insistent than they had been during the Treaty of Rome negotiations, the French still urged their partners to follow their example in harmonising male and female pay); and thirdly there were hopes that a new acceleration of the tariff dismantling timetable could be agreed. In addition, delicate negotiations were to start on the renewal of the association agreements linking the Six with their former colonies in Africa and the Caribbean. The small group of national and Community officials and ministers who would be most involved with this already full programme were also those who would have to respond to the British application. Time for the negotiations with the British would thus be hard to find before the New Year.[28]

A more short-term problem was that the British application was made at the start of the main continental holiday season. As Michael

---

[25] PRO. PREM 11 3337; Dixon to the FO, Tel. No.244, 13.7.1961.

[26] *Agence Europe* 13.7.1961.

[27] Chauvel told de Zulueta about the disarray over British membership he had found in Paris and explained that the French had been 'rather taken by surprise' by the British application. PRO. PREM 11 3560; de Zulueta to Michael Wilford, 1.9.1961; Hallstein also told Heath that he had been impressed by the 'vigour and rapidity' of the British move. FO371 158293; M634/528, Tandy to FO, Tel. No. 55 Savings, 9.10.1961.

[28] PRO. FO371 158298; M634/610, Tandy to FO, 30.10.1961.

Tandy, the British Representative to the European Communities, had warned, by the time the formal letter of application arrived in Brussels (on 10 August) there was virtually no one in the Community institutions senior enough to respond.[29] Detailed consideration of the British request, in both the member states' capitals and the Community institutions, was as a result very slow to begin. Any attempt to coordinate ideas about the way in which the negotiations should be conducted, or about the issues most urgently needing attention, was all but impossible at a national level, let alone between the six Community capitals. Karl-Heinz Narjes, the deputy *chef de cabinet* of Walter Hallstein, the President of the European Commission, exaggerated slightly in describing the mid-summer application as 'an unfriendly act' but it is undoubtedly the case that the prospect of a rapid start to the negotiations was worsened by the date on which the British chose to apply.[30]

All three factors go some way to explaining the sense of confusion that the British application generated and the two full months that elapsed between Macmillan's announcement and the opening of formal negotiations. A much greater source of difficulty, however, was the form of the British request. Article 237 of the Treaty of Rome, under which the British had applied, divided responsibility for assessing the membership request between the Community institutions and the member states.[31] To the Council, assisted by the Commission, went the task of deciding the basic eligibility of the candidate, while it was for the six member states, acting intergovernmentally rather than sitting as a Council, to negotiate with the British any necessary alterations to the Rome Treaty or special conditions of entry. The conditional nature of the British application, with the emphasis it placed on the terms of entry, meant that of these two roles it was the second that really mattered. As a result, if the Treaty was followed, the key phase of the application process would not be governed by the well-established rules of Community behaviour, but would instead be an intergovernmental negotiation the form of which had to be decided from scratch. The duties and influence of the Community institutions, the way in which the six member states would be represented, the very location of the negotiations and, most vitally of all, the extent to which the EEC participants would be bound by the notion of *esprit*

---

[29] PRO. FO371 158275; M634/195, FO minute, 5.6.1961.
[30] Interview with the author, 18.5.1992.
[31] For the text of the article, see appendix 1.

50

communautaire would all have to be determined before the negotiations proper could begin.

Both in Britain and among the Six it was agreed that negotiating arrangements chosen would have a decisive impact on the fate of the British application. A wise choice of procedure would minimise the dangers of the negotiations becoming trapped in detailed and technical arguments and reduce the risk that the British application would reawaken dormant tensions between the Six. It could also contribute to a constructive atmosphere, in which past tensions between the Six and the British were laid aside in order to concentrate on the future political and economic benefits which Community enlargement would bring. Conversely, an inept selection could lead to the wider political aims becoming submerged in excessively detailed discussions, or to the degeneration of the talks into mistrust and acrimony, as much between the Six themselves as between the Community members and the British. Furthermore, the debate about how the negotiations should be organised would give a first indication of how the Six intended to reconcile enlargement and the protection of the existing Community. Certain procedural choices would underline the EEC member states' professed desire to see the rapid and smooth entrance of Britain and some of her EFTA partners into the Community; others, by contrast, would emphasise the determination of the Six to protect the institutions, the procedures and the legislation which had been built up in the course of the previous six years. Finding a formula which would balance these two very different objectives would, however, be an exceedingly complex task.

In the absence of clear Treaty rules, the Six might have been expected to look to past experience for guidance. The 1955–7 negotiations which had led to the creation of the Community, the free trade area discussions between the Six and the rest of the OEEC member states and the association talks between the Community and the Greeks all constituted possible precedents. But none were ideal. Of the three, the most attractive and obvious model was the negotiation process which had led to the signature of the Treaty of Rome. The parallels were clear. In 1955–7 the Six had been obliged to overcome innumerable technical difficulties and narrow national interests in order to attain a political goal that they all felt was worth striving for; in 1961–3 similarly complex technical difficulties were anticipated, but once again the political gain seemed likely to outweigh sectional losses.

Moreover, the procedure chosen for the Treaty of Rome negotiations, in particular the use as the motor of discussions of a small committee of national representatives chaired by Paul-Henri Spaak, the Belgian Foreign Minister, was widely held to have been a major factor in their success.[32] The main difference, however, between 1955–7 and 1961–3 was that the British were applying to join a Community that already existed, rather than participating in the formation of a new entity. There was thus a danger that the creation of a new Spaak committee might lead the British and their fellow applicants to believe that the whole shape of the Community was open to renegotiation – something which all the governments of the Six had been at pains to deny.[33]

The second possible precedent, the 1957–8 negotiations about the creation of a seventeen–nation free trade area in Western Europe, conjured up less welcome memories. Not only had the British-led negotiations ultimately ended in failure, but they were also perceived as the central episode in the previous era of tension between the British and the Six. Thus, although the shadow of the Free Trade Area (FTA) project loomed large in the discussion between the British and the Community (there were at least two references to the 1957–8 talks in the course of the 25–7 September Council meeting at which the Six debated their response to the British application), the FTA negotiations were regarded primarily as an example of how not to proceed.[34] Similarly, the third 'precedent', the recently concluded association negotiations between Greece and the Community, was quickly dismissed. First, there was a huge difference between association under Article 238 of the type concluded with the Greeks and membership under Article 237 – no provision, for instance, was made by Article 238 for any 'adjustment' of the Treaty of Rome. Secondly, the negotiations provoked too many uncomfortable memories: several of the member states felt that the talks had been poorly handled by the

---

[32] A belief seemingly shared by the British government. See the report prepared, at Heath's request, by Bretherton, the British representative in the early stages of the Spaak committee's work. PRO. FO371 158301; M634/658, 18.9.1961.

[33] See e.g. Luns' comments to ITV on 28.8.1961; *Le Monde* 30.8.1961. Also speech of Emilio Colombo, the Italian Industry Minister, in Genoa. *La Corriera della Sera* 9.9.1961.

[34] Both Couve de Murville and Colombo referred to the earlier negotiations during the September Council meeting. CMA. S/490/61 (RU10) Extrait du Projet de Procès-Verbal de la réunion restreinte tenue à l'occasion de la 52ème session du Conseil de la CEE. 16.10.1961.

Commission, while the Commission itself resented the way in which the position that it had negotiated had been disowned by the Council.[35]

The COREPER discussions: August–September 1961

In early August 1961 it appeared likely that the procedural discussion would focus on two principal alternatives, one suggested by the Dutch and backed by at least three of the other member states, the other advocated by the French. The Dutch proposal was to form a new intergovernmental committee similar to that used in 1955–7, in which experts from all seven countries (plus the Commission) would gather and, spurred on by a prominent personality as chairman, seek to reconcile British needs with the existing Community system. The ideal chairman for the Dutch was, unsurprisingly, Spaak himself.[36] By mid-August the Belgian Foreign Minister had declared himself ready to do the job if asked, and there were indications that both the Italians and the Germans would support his selection.[37] Only the French registered their dissent, arguing that the Presidency or chair of the negotiations should rotate between the various participants, following the order established for the Council Presidency.[38] Tandy had, however, warned earlier that the various member states' thinking about the way in which the talks should be conducted was very 'fluid'.[39]

The Six had a first opportunity to coordinate their positions when the Committee of Permanent Representatives (COREPER) met on 23 August and Tandy's warning was immediately borne out. In place of a near consensus in favour of a seven-government negotiation, chaired throughout by a prominent political figure, the meeting registered general agreement that the negotiation should be bilateral – in other words between Britain and the Community acting as a unit. As the account of the meeting prepared by the Council Secretariat

[35] MAE. Direction d'Affaires Politiques, Série Europe 1961–5, Bte. 1975; Gorse to Quai, 28.1.1961. Interview with Narjes, 18.5.1992.
[36] PRO. FO371 158279; M634/258, Noble to Barclay, 1.8.1961.
[37] PRO. FO371 158281; M634/282, Heath memo, 2.8.1961; FO371 158287; M634/383, Godber minute, 18.8.1961; FO371 158284; M634/335, Tandy to Reilly, 10.8.1961.
[38] MAE. Série DE–CE 1961–6, Bte. 512; Tel. No. 2529–35, Wormser to Brussels, 8.8.1961.
[39] PRO. FO371 158278; M634/243, Tandy to FO, 30.7.1961.

noted: 'The main reason which makes it necessary to bring out clearly the bilateral character of this negotiation, springs from the dangers of a multilateral negotiation which might give the impression that the member States are ready to accept a renegotiation of the Treaty of Rome.'[40] Also ruled out were the idea of a Conference Presidency and a dedicated Conference Secretariat – 'the formation of Conference instruments of this sort risks strengthening the position of the applicant State from the outset'. In their place should be a Chairman for the Six (opinions were divided as to whether this post should be permanent or rotate), assisted by either the Council Secretariat or the Commission. Only the Dutch spoke out against a bilateral negotiation and in favour of a Treaty of Rome style arrangement.[41] Significantly, the initial tendency of the member states, once they met together, was to opt for a procedure that would protect the Community rather than facilitate the task of the applicants.[42]

Over the weeks that followed the divisions between the Six over procedure grew still more complex. By the time the Permanent Representatives had completed the report that they had been asked to submit to the 25–7 September Council meeting, there was a three-way split on the basic form of the negotiations. No longer isolated in their advocacy of the Spaak method, the Dutch had been joined by their two Benelux partners: the Belgians appear to have switched sides before the second COREPER gathering on 4 September, while the Luxemburgers rallied to the joint Low Country line after a meeting of Benelux Foreign Ministers in Brussels in early September.[43] The French had also changed their stance, rejecting the bilateral formula in favour of an intergovernmental conference between the seven states, but one chaired by the country holding the Council Presidency, not by

[40] 'La principale raison qui milite en faveur de la nécessité de marquer clairement ce caractère bilatérale de la négociation, tient au danger que recèle une négociation multilatérale qui pourrait donner l'impression que les Etats membres sont disposés à accepter une renégociation du Traité de Rome.' My translation. CMA. Aide-Mémoire: Résultats du premier échange de vues intervenu au sein de COREPER le 23.8.1961 au sujet des problèmes immédiats que posent les demandes d'association et d'adhésion à la Communauté.

[41] 'L'institution d'instruments de Conférence de cette nature risque plutôt d'entrainer, dès le départ, un renforcement de la position de négociation de l'Etat demandeur.' My translation. *Ibid.*

[42] Tandy noted this development with some disquiet. PRO. FO371 158285; M634/369, Tandy to FO, Tel. No. 37, 25.8.1961.

[43] PRO. FO371 158289; M634/413, Tandy to FO, 8.9.1961; FO371 158291; M634/453, Nicholls to Reilly, 15.9.1961.

a permanent chairman. Italy and Germany, meanwhile, remained faithful to the idea of a bilateral negotiation.[44] The position of the Dutch, Belgians and Luxemburgers seems to have been motivated in part by a desire to repeat the success of the earlier Spaak committee. This meant that the presence of Spaak himself was highly desirable. Baron van Tuyll, the Secretary-General of the Dutch Foreign Ministry, described the Belgian Foreign Minister as having 'a talent for putting through what he wanted' – a view which appears to have been widespread in the Low Countries.[45] As important, was the determination to prevent the adoption of any procedure that could hinder the negotiations and allow the French in particular to obstruct progress. A conference chaired by each member state in turn was one such format; not only would periodic changes of chairman disrupt the negotiation and slow the build up of momentum, but such a system would also leave the French in the chair during the January to June period during which the bulk of the negotiation would, it was hoped, be done.[46] And a negotiation conducted bilaterally between the British and the Community was also to be avoided, as the position of the Six would be dictated by the most rigid of the member states.[47]

Italian and German behaviour on this issue is harder to interpret. Both countries appear to have been torn between the desire to agree upon a negotiating method as quickly and as smoothly as possible, and the need to ensure that the system devised did not undermine the negotiating position of the Six. Equally, neither country wanted to antagonise the French. Thus in early August both seem to have been ready to accept the 'Spaak committee' option, only to abandon it, once it became clear that the French were resolutely opposed and that there was little prospect of a rapid agreement. Nevertheless, while neither Italy nor Germany held the question to be sufficiently important to delay the start of substantive negotiations, it would be wrong to assume that this readiness to compromise denoted an absence of

[44] CMA. S/442/1/61 (RU6), 22.9.1961; COREPER report to the Council on 'Problèmes soulevés par les démarches effectuées en vue d'une adhésion par les Gouvernements du Royaume-Uni, du Danemark et de l'Irlande'.

[45] PRO. FO371 158279; M634/258, Noble to Barclay, 1.8.1961; Baron Snoy said much the same thing: FO371 158278; M634/237, Barclay minute, 24.7.1961.

[46] PRO. FO371 158289; M634/427, FO to the Hague, Tel. No. 450, 7.9.1961; FO371 158291; M634/453, Nicholls to Reilly, 15.9.1961.

[47] PRO. FO371 158291; M634/454, Noble to FO, Tel. No. 229, 20.9.1961; FO371 158293; M634/515, Nicholls to FO, Tel. No. 269, 9.10.1961.

opinion.[48] There are strong indications that both states disliked the prospect of Spaak chairing the negotiations almost as much as did the French. As early as mid-August 1961, internal *Auswärtiges Amt* documents argued that a multilateral negotiation would increase 'the danger of a watering-down of the political content of the European Community'.[49] In Italy meanwhile, Attilio Cattani, the Secretary-General of the Farnesina, remarked somewhat maliciously to a British diplomat that he suspected the Belgian Foreign Minister wanted to chair the negotiations primarily to bolster his domestic prestige.[50] And both Emilio Colombo, the Italian Minister for Industry, and Rolf Lahr, the State Secretary in the Federal Foreign Ministry, demonstrated real conviction when speaking in favour of a bilateral negotiation at the 25–7 September Council meeting.[51] Moreover, support for a bilateral formula – the most *communautaire* of negotiating methods – would have fitted well both with the Italian and German stance on other procedural issues, and more generally, with the stress that both delegations laid throughout the negotiations on the maintenance of the Community fabric. In the case of Germany, the position appears to have been complicated by interministerial disagreements: as Heath was to find when he visited Bonn in early October, the views of Heinrich von Brentano, the Foreign Minister, differed markedly from those of Professor Alfred Müller-Armack, State Secretary in the Ministry of Economic Affairs.[52]

French antipathy to the appointment of Spaak as permanent chairman of the negotiations emerged very rapidly. In early August

[48] PRO. FO371 158291; M634/452; Quaroni, the Italian Ambassador in London, told Barclay that the Italians were ready to be very flexible about the chairmanship, 18.9.1961; FO371 158303; M634/709; Müller-Armack told Heath that he felt that the whole procedural debate had been allowed to take up much too much time, 9.11.1961.

[49] 'Die Gefahr der Verwässerung des politischen Gehaltes der Europäischen Gemeinschaften'. My translation. BAK. BKA, B–136, Bd. 2560; Abteilung 2, Aufzeichnung, 16.8.1961.

[50] PRO. FO371 158297; M634/573, Ashley Clarke to Barclay, 16.10.1961.

[51] Lahr argued: 'Il importe, en effet, avant tout d'éviter que les Six fassent apparaître en pleine négociation, leur éventuelles divergences d'opinion, car cela ne manquerait pas d'affaiblir considérablement leur position de négociation.' Colombo's line was very similar. CMA. S/490/61 (RU10). 16.10.1961.

[52] PRO. FO371 158293; M634/510, Steel to FO, Tel. No. 223 Savings, 7.10.1961. In general the Foreign Ministry was much more *communautaire* and sympathetic to the French line; the Economics Ministry tended to allow its desire to see Britain enter the Community override most other considerations.

Wormser instructed French diplomats in Brussels to do all that they could to avoid the formation of a new Spaak committee. Such a committee Wormser explained would rapidly expose the divergent views of the Six, lead to the isolation of the French and endanger the very essentials of the Community *acquis*:

> We are not ready to allow ourselves to be placed once more in the situation which characterised the 1957–8 negotiations, during which France found itself, even when alone with its Community partners, negotiating indirectly with Britain. If we repeated this mistake – which would amount to an acceptance that the starting point of the negotiation should be a series of compromises which would already include many of Britain's desiderata – what would be left of the Treaty of Rome by the end of the talks? [53]

Furthermore, Wormser warned that while Spaak himself was undoubtedly sincere in his determination to preserve intact the Treaty of Rome, the same could not necessarily be said for all of his subordinates. Once again the memory was invoked of the free trade area negotiations during which several Belgian officials had, according to Wormser, displayed greater enthusiasm for the seventeen-nation arrangement than they had for the EEC. Instead, the French representatives were to argue for an intergovernmental committee chaired by whosoever held the rotating Presidency of the Council.[54]

Such explicit instructions mean that Jean-Marc Boegner's initial advocacy during the COREPER discussions of a bilateral negotiation rather than an intergovernmental affair was almost certainly tactical. For the French the first overriding objective was to prevent the appointment of Spaak. To this end, a temporary alliance of convenience with the more *communautaire* Italians, Germans and Belgians was fully justifiable. By early September, however, once it had become clear that the Dutch idea was unlikely to prevail, the French could revert to type and advocate the type of negotiation which they had in reality supported from the outset.

---

[53] 'Nous ne serions pas disposés à nous replacer dans la situation de 1957–8 où la France se trouvait en fait, au sein même des Six, négocier par personne interposée avec la Grande-Bretagne. Si l'on revenait à ces errements – ce qui équivaudrait à prendre pour point de départ de la négociation avec les Britanniques des compromis qui incorporeraient en partie leur thèses – que resterait-il à la fin du compte du Traité de Rome?' My translation. MAE. Série DE–CE 1961–6, Bte. 512; Tel. No. 2529–35, Wormser to Brussels, 8.8.1961.
[54] *Ibid.*

The question of how far the Six wished to negotiate as a Community as opposed to six individual states also underlay much of the discussion about two further issues: the role of the Community institutions in the talks and the location of the negotiations. As explained above, a strict reading of the Treaty would have marginalised both the Council and the Commission during discussion of the British application. The Commission in particular, however, contested vehemently what it saw as 'an over-hasty reading' of Article 237, arguing that the Treaty framers had not anticipated a conditional application.[55] In August 1961 the Commission's most senior lawyer insisted that the negotiations should be conducted by the Council with the collaboration of the Commission. Only in this way would it be possible to avoid multilateral negotiations between the Six and the applicants 'which would have the result of weakening, if not destroying, the Community itself'.[56]

This line of argument did not survive for long in the COREPER meetings: as Axel Herbst, the deputy Secretary-General of the Commission who was present by right at the COREPER deliberations, noted ruefully, the member states were not ready to bind themselves with the rules of Community procedure.[57] There was no agreement as to what role, if any, the Council and the Commission should have, once they had expressed their opinion on the basic eligibility of the candidates. The French and initially the Dutch took the most legalistic approach, maintaining that the Treaty should be followed exactly, and that the Commission and Council should be totally excluded from the negotiations, unless called upon by the member states. By contrast, the other four countries acknowledged that a conditional application such as that submitted by the UK necessitated a departure from the rules set out in the Treaty, and that as a result both institutions should be allowed to play a significant part in the negotiations. The Council should thus be asked to express its opinion at the end of the negotiation when the membership conditions were known as well as at the beginning, while the Commission should not only have a

[55] 'Une lecture hâtive'. My translation. ECHA. BDT 38/84, No. 99. Letter from Jean Rey, Commissioner in charge of external relations to Michel Gaudet, Director-General of the Commission's Legal Service, 4.8.1961, S/04559/61.
[56] 'Qui auraient pour résultat d'affaiblir sinon de faire éclater la Communauté elle-même'. My translation. ECHA. Gaudet's reply to Rey. S/04559/61. Undated.
[57] Herbst's report on the 18.9.1961 COREPER meeting. S/04880/61. ECHA, BDT 38/84, No.99.

similar right, but should also be closely involved with the actual negotiations.[58]

The issue of where the negotiations were to be held was closely linked to the question of the involvement of the Community institutions in the application process. If Brussels was chosen, as the majority of member states hoped, the link between the Community and the negotiations would be symbolically affirmed. Furthermore, practical connections between the two would be encouraged; Commission expertise would be close at hand should it prove necessary, the Secretariat of the Council would be able to service the negotiations and frequent contact between those involved in the membership discussions and those working for the Community institutions would be inevitable. Conversely, a decision to site the negotiations elsewhere – Paris or Chantilly were the locations preferred by the French, but the possibility of Bonn or even Nice was also mentioned – would constitute, in both symbolic and practical terms, a distancing of the Community from the discussions between its member states and its would-be members.

The hard-line Dutch position on the Commission's participation was soon abandoned. As de Schacht, the Netherlands' Permanent Representative, admitted to Tandy, the Dutch had merely intended to scare the Commission and remind it that it had no 'prescriptive right to be present'.[59] By contrast the French, while sharing the Dutch view that the Commission needed reminding that it had only as much power as member states chose to allow it to have, maintained their opposition to Commission involvement up until the 25–7 September Council meeting. Even they, however, were unable to prevent the Commission from extricating itself from the demand that it submit its opinion on the application only once. Formally asked by the Council for its *avis* at the very end of August, the Commission replied in early September, explaining that:

> Given that the negotiations will deal with a series of issues of importance to the Community, the European Commission will express its opinion on these issues as and when they are raised during the negotiations. It will be on the basis of the final result of the discussions that the Commission will give the *avis* required by article 237 of the Treaty.[60]

---

[58] *Ibid.*   [59] PRO. FO371 158285; M634/369, Tandy to FO, 25.8.1961.

[60] 'Etant donné que les négociations porteront sur un ensemble de problèmes intéressant la Communauté, la Commission européenne exprimera son opinion sur ceux-

The Commission in other words would give its opinion of the applicants only as the membership negotiations unfolded and not before they began.

Also the subject of heated debate in the run up to the September Council meeting was the way in which the negotiations should be started. At the heart of the discussion was the suggestion that the Council, in its formal reply to the UK, should request that the British submit to the Six a comprehensive list of the various problems that would have to be addressed in the course of the negotiations and of the solutions which the British envisaged. The Six would then decide, on the basis of the British memorandum, whether or not it was worth starting membership negotiations. Born out of the feeling that the Six could not be expected to respond to a conditional application without knowing much more about those conditions, this idea appears to have originated in Community circles in Brussels but it was quickly fastened on to by the French.[61] In mid-September the French presented COREPER with a draft letter, setting out this request and suggesting that negotiations begin one month after the receipt by the Six of the British document.[62] This would bring home to France's partners the number and scale of the conditions which Britain sought, before the Six irrevocably committed themselves to any particular form or manner of negotiation.[63]

By 18 September when COREPER met to discuss the French draft, the other five member states had heeded British protests and turned against the idea. Instead they proposed a British-inspired compromise, whereby the Six would have an introductory meeting with the British delegation in the course of which a full statement of British requirements would be made orally, and would then adjourn for at least a fortnight in order to study the British position and prepare a joint response.[64] Nevertheless, the French proposal had struck a chord. In the days that preceded the COREPER meeting even Spaak had wavered, preaching the merits of what the press had quickly dubbed 'the shopping list' idea to his Benelux colleagues.[65] Once

ci au fur et à mesure du déroulement des négociations. C'est sur la base des résultats de celles-ci que la Commission donnera l'avis prévu par l'article 237 du Traité.' My translation. ECHA, BDT 38/84, No. 99. S/420/61 (RU4), Hallstein to Erhard, 8.9.1961.

[61] PRO. FO371 158285; M634/362; Tandy to Reilly, 22.8.1961.
[62] The text of the letter is reproduced as an annex to S/442/1/61 (RU/6). CMA.
[63] MAE. Série DE–CE 1961–6, Bte. 512; Wormser to Brussels, 4.9.1961.
[64] *Ibid.*   [65] PRO. FO371 158291; M634/453, Nicholls to Reilly, 15.9.1961.

again, therefore, a move that some angrily described as French sabotage was skilfully couched in a fashion that made the charge impossible to prove.[66]

Despite the success of British efforts to avoid being asked to submit their requests in written form, the procedural debate was in general frustrating for the British. Whitehall shared the view, prevalent on the continent, that the method of negotiation chosen could greatly influence the outcome of the application, and devoted much time and energy to the formulation of a British view about procedure. Following up its ideas was, however, difficult, as the British realised that the power of decision on procedural matters rested entirely with the Six. Any attempt to influence the member states' discussion directly might therefore be regarded as *non-communautaire* behaviour.

Foremost among British priorities was the appointment of a strong, permanent chairman. In London's eyes Spaak would have been ideal, but even a lesser figure was preferable to a rotating Presidency. Baron Snoy, a former Belgian minister, was one name mentioned. As to the site of the negotiation, the British felt that Brussels was 'in every way preferable' to Paris – partly because to accept Paris would be to rule out Spaak as chairman.[67] But at Heath's insistence, the guidance telegram sent to British embassies explaining Whitehall's views on procedure ended with a clear warning:

> It is, however, important that we should not get across [the] French at the start by seeming to lobby for Brussels or for any particular arrangement or individual for Chairmanship. [The] essential thing is that [the] atmosphere for negotiations should be as good as possible. You should therefore not, repeat not, volunteer any views on either point. [68]

Such was the care taken to follow these instructions, that when Sir Pierson Dixon, the British Ambassador to France, was appointed to head the British delegation (without relinquishing his Ambassadorial post), Tandy wrote to Christian Calmés, the Secretary-General of the

---

[66] Macmillan and Heath both chose to disregard Dutch warnings about French motives. Heath, while opposed to the idea, interpreted the French suggestion merely as a formula designed to help the negotiations get off to a good start. PRO. PREM 11 3560; FO to Bonn, Tel. No.2222, 22.9.1961 and Macmillan to Heath, 22.9.1961.

[67] PRO. FO371 158282; M634/314 and 315, Reilly minutes, 2.8.1961 and 8.8.1961. See also FO371 158284; M634/331, Barclay minute, 11.8.1961.

[68] PRO. FO371 158282; M634/315, FO to Brussels, Tel. No. 111, 10.8.1961.

Council of Ministers, to assure him that this decision was in no way designed to influence the Six in their choice of where the negotiations should take place.[69] British efforts to influence the Six were thus severely handicapped both by the fear of offending the French and, more fundamentally, by the unpredictable fashion in which debate amongst the Six evolved. Bilateral discussions with individual Community member states were a poor substitute for actual representation at the negotiating table.

The Council meeting: 25–7 September 1961

The 25–7 September Council meeting offered the unusual sight of Couve de Murville engaged in an orderly but none the less significant retreat. On the first point of the agenda – the form of the letter that the Council would send to Macmillan – the French Foreign Minister did initially push for the British to be asked to set out their requirements in writing. Couve de Murville gave way with surprising rapidity, however, when confronted by all other five member states, who while recognising the need for much more detailed information about British conditions felt that a request for written information might jeopardise the atmosphere in which the negotiations opened. After a brief adjournment, the French presented a compromise text, which toughened the letter's insistence that the British opening statement be detailed, but crucially dropped the requirement that it be circulated among the Six in advance of the first ministerial session.

French flexibility continued once the subject turned to the site of the negotiation. In a total departure from the previous French stance, Couve de Murville opened not by maintaining that the talks must be held in Paris, but simply by suggesting that the preliminary meeting, at which the British would state their terms, should be held in a different place from the rest of the negotiations. This cleared the way for a rapid compromise, with Brussels being confirmed as the main location of the talks, while Paris would host the opening ministerial session. As a gesture to German sensibilities, Bonn was chosen as the place in which any final agreement between the British and the Six would be signed. In similar fashion, the French appeared to have given ground even before discussion of the Commission's role began.

---

[69] CMA. 07.151. Composition de la délégation britannique aux négociations relatives à la demande d'adhésion au Marché commun présentée par le Royaume-Uni. Tandy to Calmés, 12.9.1961.

Replying to forceful speeches in favour of a significant Commission role from Hallstein, Colombo, Lahr and Spaak, Couve de Murville accepted that the Commission collaboration would be essential during the negotiations, but argued that, rather than deciding in advance on a formula about the Commission's functions, it would be better for the member states to decide as the situation developed. Encouraged by this new softening of the French line, Hallstein, Lahr and Spaak all put forward new compromise texts. After further discussion, it was agreed that the Commission would participate in the negotiations as a counsellor of the Six with the right to speak and, crucially, that when the Six met alone to coordinate their stance the Commission would participate fully. In return, the Belgians and the Dutch acknowledged that the negotiations were between the six Community member states and Britain and accepted that the Six would as far as possible present the British with a common point of view.

Only in the discussion of the form and chairmanship of the negotiations did the disagreements that had characterised the COREPER discussions reappear. On this issue the French were not prepared to give ground and their obstinacy was matched by that of the Benelux countries. With Lahr and Colombo intervening to make passionate speeches about the need for Community unity – something that both the Italian and the German ministers felt would be compromised by a multilateral negotiation – Ludwig Erhard, the chairman of the meeting, had little option other than to postpone discussion to a later date. The otherwise successful Council meeting thus fell short of agreement on probably the most important of the procedural decisions. In order to ensure that the opening session planned for 10 October in Paris could go ahead, however, an *ad hoc* formula was devised which left reponsibility for chairing the meeting to Erhard, the Council President.[70]

With attention focused on the contentious procedural issues described above, a series of other decisions discussed by the permanent representatives and sanctioned by the Council passed almost unnoticed. Despite their lower profile, however, some of these decisions were as important as those which had been hotly disputed. By opting for separate negotiations with all the applicants (Britain,

[70] CMA. S/490/61 (RU10). Extrait du Projet de Procès-Verbal de la réunion restreinte tenue à l'occasion de la 52ème session du Conseil de la CEE. 16.10.1961.

Denmark and Ireland initially; Norway was expected to follow at some point in the autumn) and by making clear that of these the British negotiations would be given *de facto* priority, the Six lessened their fear of being swamped.[71] By doing so, however, they were also storing up a future problem for the British, as the UK had promised its EFTA partners not to join the Community until satisfactory arrangements between the enlarged Community and the seven free trade area members had been made.[72] In similar fashion, the decision not to allow observers from third countries into any of the negotiating sessions was taken in a defensive frame of mind. During the weeks that followed the British application, the Australians, in particular, lobbied in several European capitals for the right to send observers to those parts of the discussions that directly involved Australian interests.[73] Moreover, the Danes expressed an interest in following at first hand any discussions between the British and the Six that concerned agriculture, a subject of immense significance to Denmark. The Six, however, were unenthusiastic, and decided at COREPER level to rule out any third-country participation, largely on the grounds that granting permission to one country to send observers would create a precedent and lead to a whole range of other countries, from the United States to the Community's own Associated Overseas Territories (AOTs), making similar requests.

A further decision approved by the 25–7 September Council was that the various membership applications should not be allowed to delay the Community's own progress.[74] This should not have come as a surprise to the applicants – it had been a major theme of many speeches by Community politicians in the months that preceded the

[71] There was agreement from the first COREPER meeting onward that the negotiations should be separate and that the British membership bid should be given priority. The possibility of a joint opening session for all three applicants was, however, initially kept open. CMA. Aide-Mémoire: Résultats du premier échange de vues intervenu au sein de COREPER le 23.8.1961 au sujet des problèmes immédiats que posent les demandes d'association et d'adhésion à la Communauté.
[72] The pledge was most clearly made in the so-called London agreement. See EFTA Bulletin, 2:7 (July 1961).
[73] PRO. FO371 158291; M634/453, Nicholls to Reilly, 15.9.1961; FO371 158180; M615/205, Harpham to Gallagher, 4.8.1961.
[74] COREPER had been unanimous from the outset of its discussions that it was 'indispensable que les travaux au sein de la Communauté se poursuivent au même rythme que précédemment'. CMA. Aide-Mémoire: Résultats du premier échange de vues intervenu au sein de COREPER le 23.8.1961 au sujet des problèmes immédiats que posent les demandes d'association et d'adhésion à la Communauté.

British application – but it was nevertheless a decision of crucial significance. For a start it greatly reduced the prospects of the British bid making much headway before January 1962 since, as noted above, the Community's own business was, until the year's end, likely to consume most of the time and energy of the senior officials and ministers who would have to deal with the enlargement negotiations. Second, it was a further blow to British hopes of being asked to participate as observers in some of the key discussions being conducted among the Six. Of particular importance to the British were the ongoing talks about the CAP and about the renewal of the arrangements between the Community and its African associates. Admittedly, the British had already decided – after at least one tentative approach to Spaak on this subject – that it was unwise to follow the Danish example and ask outright to be included in the CAP discussions.[75] Nevertheless, the British still appear to have clung to the possibility that 'the logic of events' would lead to their being invited to join in.[76] To have the Six decide that the applicants should not be permitted to delay progress – and the inclusion of the world's largest food importer, Britain, and a major agricultural exporter, Denmark, would inevitably complicate and delay the work of the Six – was a further blow to these hopes.[77]

The debate drags on: September–December 1961

The argument over the form of the negotiations continued, fitfully, for two and a half more months. Although from October onwards Heath's opening statement (outlined in chapter 3) gave the Six fresh topics to discuss and the procedural debate lost much of its intensity, there were still occasional flare-ups, notably on 10 October, when the

[75] For the approach to Spaak see PRO. FO371 158279; M634/246G, Heath to Spaak, 30.7.1961 and Pollock to FO, 31.7.1961. The Danish request was discussed in COREPER and finally refused by the 17–20 October meeting. CMA. 07.151 Préparation par le Conseil de la réunion ministérielle entre les états membres et le Royaume-Uni, ainsi que la déclaration commune des six devant être prononcée par le président du conseil CEE lors de cette réunion, tenue les 8/9 novembre 1961.

[76] PRO. CAB 134/1511; CMN(61)3, the General Negotiating Brief for the EEC negotiations noted the advantages that British participation would bring, but decided, in view of likely French opposition, that the British would be best advised to wait until invited rather than trying 'to stake a claim'.

[77] British aspirations of taking part in the internal discussions of the Six had already been reduced by Tandy's reports of the Permanent Representatives' views. PRO. FO371 158289; M634/427, Tandy to FO, Tel. No. 50, 12.9.1961.

Six gathered in Paris to hear Heath's speech.[78] Despite the first indications that cracks were appearing in their ranks, the Benelux countries used the opportunity to push once more for a new Spaak committee.[79] According to van Houten, the Dutch deputy Foreign Minister, they nearly succeeded: had it not been for the wavering of Erhard, France would have been totally isolated in its opposition.[80] This Dutch account may not be totally reliable, however. Von Brentano, whom van Houten grouped among the supporters of the Benelux line, had told Heath only a few days earlier of his continuing support for the bilateral formula and press reports confirm that the Germans probably sided with the French.[81] The Italians are also unlikely to have become committed partisans of a new Spaak committee. Such behaviour would not only have been inconsistent with their previous and subsequent approach to the issue of procedure, but would also jar with the Italian tendency throughout the negotiations to rally to the support of the French whenever Couve de Murville appeared in danger of isolation. Whatever happened, the whole meeting was ill-tempered and totally unsuccessful; with agreement no nearer, it had become much more likely that the *ad hoc* formula devised for the opening session would have to be extended to cover the first genuine negotiating encounter on 6–7 November.

Although there were signs that the despondency about the prospects of a new Spaak committee shown earlier by the Belgians was gradually spreading to the Dutch, the issue remained in a sterile deadlock for the rest of October and all of November.[82] Neither a German compromise proposal, based on a rotating chair but with the country holding the Council Presidency of the Six acting as a spokesman for the Community delegations, nor a suggestion by the British that a high-powered Secretary-General be appointed 'to help both the ministerial and official Chairmen with the conduct of the

[78] According to Heath, Erhard threatened to walkout, so unruly were the Six. PRO. PREM 11 3561; Heath to FO, Tel. No. 570, 10.10.1961.

[79] Only days before the meeting, Spaak was openly talking about the choice over the chair as being between two- and three-month rotations. PRO. FO371 158293; M634/515, Nicholls to FO, Tel. No. 369, 9.10.1961.

[80] PRO. FO371 158296; M634/563, Noble to FO, Tel. No. 243, 16.10.1961.

[81] PRO. FO371 158293; M634/510, Steel to FO, Tel. No. 223 Savings, 7.10.1961; *The Times* 24.10.1961.

[82] By late October Luns had all but given up hope. PRO. FO371 158302; M634/678, Noble to Barclay, 30.10.1961. FO371 158297; M634/585, Carey-Foster to FO, 23.10.1961, gives some indication of the tenacity of Dutch hopes.

meetings and to provide the necessary impetus and continuity to the discussions' made much headway.[83] By December, however, exhaustion and the need to agree on something before the negotiations progressed too far, led the Benelux countries to capitulate and accept a system in which the chair would move from one delegation to the next at three-month intervals. For the Six, the order of chairmanships would follow that used for the Council Presidency – this meant that the French would be in the chair from January 1962 until March – but the possibility of a British spell in charge was left open.[84] In giving way, however, some of the advocates of a permanent chairman appear to have comforted themselves with the thought that the system adopted would soon prove to be unworkable and would have to be replaced.[85] There was thus always the possibility that a few of the Six might disown the procedure agreed and, at some later stage of the application process, seek to revise the fashion in which the negotiations were being conducted.

The outcome

By the time that the question of chairmanship had been fully resolved substantive discussions between the British and the Six were already under way. It is therefore appropriate for the penultimate section of this chapter briefly to review how the procedural decisions outlined above translated into practical arrangements. In particular, the complex multi-level nature of the enlargement negotiations, and the way in which the Community's decision to negotiate on the basis of a unanimously agreed position slowed advance, will be explained. The final section will then underline some of the lessons which can be drawn from the manner in which the Six had decided to negotiate.

The main focus of public and press attention was the periodic

[83] CMA. S/516 f/61 (RU10), 07.151. Préparation par le Conseil de la réunion ministérielle entre les états membres et le Royaume-Uni, ainsi que la déclaration commune des six devant être prononcée par le président du conseil CEE lors de cette réunion, tenue les 8/9 novembre 1961. Heath's telegram proposing the Secretary-General idea is in PRO. FO371 158297; M634/585, FO to Bonn, Tel. No. 1318, 23.10.1961.

[84] CMA; RU/M/9/61; 07.151. Négociations en vue de l'adhésion du Royaume-Uni à la CEE: présidence de la conférence et de la délégation des six. A list of those who held the chair of the negotiations at both ministerial and deputy level is included in appendix 2.

[85] PRO. FO371 158307; M634/783, Lintott minute, 31.10.1961; FO371 158298; M634/610, Tandy to FO, 30.10.1961.

ministerial meetings. Held initially at an interval of one month, and lasting for two to three days, these brought together the principal ministers entrusted by Britain and the member states with responsibility for the enlargement negotiations, flanked when appropriate by other ministers whose departmental interests might be affected. Thus, for instance, Couve de Murville, the French Foreign Minister and the ministerial leader of the French delegation, was sometimes accompanied (and occasionally replaced) by Edgard Pisani, the Minister for Agriculture. If no minister was free to attend – a scenario which would become more common as the intensity of ministerial meetings rose – a senior official could act as stand-in. The European Commission, in its capacity as an observer, was usually represented by its President, Walter Hallstein, and by several other Commissioners.[86]

It was at these ministerial meetings that the most difficult political questions were expected to be resolved. In a negotiation as complex as that with Britain seemed likely to be, however, it was unrealistic to expect monthly ministerial encounters to solve all the problems which would arise. The ministerial discussions were hence preceded by much more frequent meetings at official level. Foremost amongst these were the weekly sittings of the Committee of Deputies. Every member state, Britain and the Commission each appointed a senior official as deputy head of their delegation, and it was between these officials that most of the preliminary negotiation took place.[87] Each ministerial discussion would start with a presentation from the deputy whose member state held the Presidency of the negotiations, setting out the progress made, highlighting points of contention and suggesting possible solutions. As a result, ministerial discussion could focus directly on those issues where disagreement remained; elsewhere, the text agreed at deputy level would be approved without debate. The deputies, in other words, performed a role equivalent to that of COREPER in the usual Community structure, with Ministers taking the place of the Council.

Not even the deputies had the time or the expertise to handle all the

---

[86] Appendix 2 lists the principal ministers involved with the Brussels negotiations and the members of the Commission who attended the talks regularly.

[87] The task of the British in persuading their domestic and Commonwealth audiences that they were being fairly treated in Brussels was not helped when certain sections of the press incorrectly translated the role of the deputy head of the British team, in French the *suppléant du ministre,* as the 'supplicant'! Lord Roll, talk at St Antony's College, Oxford. Appendix 2 lists all of the deputies.

problems raised by British membership. There was thus a third level of negotiation, in the form of the working groups. The exact number and role of these was a matter of some dispute. There was no dissent, however, from the notion that many of the highly technical issues thrown up by the prospect of enlargement needed to be analysed by national civil servants and Commission officials much better versed in the intricacies of Commonwealth trade, agricultural support systems or international commercial relations than either the deputies or still more the ministers. Discussions at a deputy level were thus often conducted on the basis of detailed reports compiled by working groups, much as in the normal Community business COREPER discussions built upon the preparation of Council working groups.

The real complexity of the British membership negotiations, however, sprang not from this three-level hierarchy, but from the decision by the Six to confront the British whenever possible with an agreed Community stance. This meant in practice that every meeting between the British and the Six, at whichever of the three levels described above, had to be preceded by an equivalent meeting among the Six. And it was at these gatherings *à six* that much of the real bargaining occurred. Only when a unanimous agreement had been reached – no small task in a negotiation involving so many controversial topics – could the British representatives be invited to join the discussions. The new Community stance would then be outlined by the Conference President and the British would be asked to respond. No real negotiation was possible, however, for if the British were unable to accept the revised Community offer and were unmoved by the attempts of the Six to convince them, the Community members had no option other than to closet themselves away once again and resume their internal negotiations in search of a new and more acceptable proposal. Progress it need hardly be said was not easy with so cumbersome a system.[88]

A first warning sign?

An uncharacteristically pessimistic comment to his Cabinet colleagues revealed some of the concern that Heath felt in watching the Six struggle for so long before agreeing to a satisfactory negotiating

---

[88] For a critical German view of the procedure adopted see Alfred Müller-Armack, *Auf dem Weg nach Europa. Erinnerungen und Ausblicke* (Tübingen and Stuttgart: Rainer Wunderlich Verlag/C. E. Poeschel, 1971), p. 236.

method. Shortly after the totally unsuccessful meeting of the Six in Paris, the Lord Privy Seal wrote to the Cabinet:

> This is not a good augury for the ability of the Six to agree among themselves on the many more important and substantial questions which must arise during the negotiations. It is, therefore, only realistic to suppose that the negotiations will be beset by delays of this kind.[89]

There were, however, other conclusions that can be drawn from the lengthy procedural debate, some of which were still more disturbing from a British point of view.

First, the very defensive attitude with which the Six approached the negotiations was underlined by the arrangements at length agreed upon. By deciding to coordinate their position before every meeting, by rejecting the appointment of a powerful Chairman or Secretary-General who could force through uncomfortable but necessary compromises, and by allowing the Commission to participate fully in the coordination of a Community position, the Six signalled their anxiety that the British application might awaken barely dormant divisions among the Community member states, but made clear their determination not to allow this to happen. By agreeing that the applicants should negotiate singly, and where possible successively rather than simultaneously, and by deciding to bar observers from third countries from attending, the Six revealed their concern that the integration process would be swamped by a sudden flood of membership and association requests. And by stating that the business of the Community must progress unhindered throughout the membership negotiations, the Six set down as a clear principle that the concerns and needs of the countries inside the Community took precedence over those of all others, including aspirant EEC members or associates. Such a Community-first attitude was of great significance at the start of a negotiation which would, to a great extent, depend upon how far the Community was prepared to go in preventing its system from damaging the economic concerns of another grouping, the Commonwealth.

Secondly, the gulf between what each member state told the British bilaterally and their behaviour once they were obliged to make a decision *à six* was highlighted. In part, this was a reflection of the fact that the views and perceptions of member states' representatives and diplomats in Brussels were not necessarily the same as the opinions of

---

[89] PRO. CAB134 1511; CMN(61)13; Heath memo, 20.10.1961.

their home-based colleagues, let alone their fellow diplomats in London embassies. But it was also a result of the way in which the Six had fallen into a habit of working together, a habit which was not necessarily amicable – the Foreign Office files abound with unflattering remarks made by French or Dutch diplomats about their colleagues among the Six – nor very fast, but one which did mean that the original policy intentions of each member state tended to emerge rather changed from the process of Community discussion. Thus the August indications that all bar the French would support a Spaak committee-type arrangement proved unreliable, with the Italians, Germans and initially even the Belgians giving their allegiance to a much more *communautaire* procedure. Admittedly COREPER, whose members after all worked together almost constantly, might be expected to be rather more prone to this phenomenon than delegations specially assembled for the British negotiations. Nevertheless, the episode should have given the British a warning against relying too heavily on promises given by individual members of the Six in the course of bilateral conversations.

Third, the very limited ability of the British to influence indirectly the decisions taken by the Six was underscored. The attempt, in October, to drum up support for a Secretary-General is a good example of this: despite having received favourable responses from three of the six Community capitals, the British failed even to have the idea discussed during the 24–7 October Council meeting.[90] From London's perspective, this too was disturbing at a time in which subjects being discussed among the Six – most notably the CAP but also the Association Convention – would have an immense bearing on the position of the British if they joined. The Italians and the Germans had both made helpful promises about keeping London informed about the progress of these discussions, but information alone was of little comfort, if the prospects of Britain being able to influence the direction taken by the talks were so negligible.[91]

Finally, the procedural discussion had produced conflicting signals about the influence of the French within the Community. On the surface, Couve de Murville's behaviour in the course of the 25–7

[90] PRO. FO371 158297; M634/585, Ashley Clarke to FO and Carey-Foster to FO, 23.10.1961; M634/588, Nicholls to FO, 24.10.1961; FO371 158298; M634/592, Tandy to FO, 24.10.1961; M634/594, Tandy to FO, 25.10.1961.
[91] PRO. FO371 158289; M634/416, Statham to Gallagher, 1.9.1961; FO371 158291; M634/452, Barclay minute, 18.9.1961.

September Council meeting could be interpreted as a healthy signal that the Five could control and indeed overcome French obstinacy.[92] Upon closer inspection, however, this picture becomes somewhat less clear. Of the three issues on which the French had given ground – the role of the Commission, the location of the negotiations and the 'shopping list' – only the last had been a priority for Paris. As early as 4 September, Wormser's note to the French Permanent Representation in Brussels admitted that France had little to fear and much to gain from Commission involvement in the negotiation.[93] The French, like the Dutch, only wanted to remind the Brussels institution of its subordinate status.[94] Likewise, French opposition to the membership discussions being held in Brussels was an expression of preference rather than a deeply held conviction. By early September Couve de Murville was willing to admit to Heath that Brussels would be more convenient as a location, and Quai d'Orsay dispatches to Brussels reveal that the French representatives only held their line on this issue until the 25 September Council meeting so as to ensure that a French concession on this would weigh in the 'final bargaining'.[95] Only on the question of whether Britain should outline its desiderata in writing did the French abandon an important goal. And even on this, the compromise agreed to among the Six fulfilled at least one of the French aims, in avoiding a situation in which the Six were obliged to respond at once to the opening of the British bid. The two weeks which would elapse between the British statement and the first ministerial meeting in Brussels would provide ample time for the French to influence the tone and content of the Six's reply.

In return for this one genuine concession and two symbolic retreats, the French had by contrast obtained three of their most cherished aims. First, they had blocked the formation of a new Spaak committee; the negotiations would not have a powerful and permanent chairman, able either to bully his partners into concessions, or publicly to condemn the obstructionism of a minority. Second, they had ensured that the Six were committed to maintaining a unified stance where possible. This would minimise British opportunities to play upon the

---

[92] Tandy saw it as such. PRO. FO371 158292; M634/487, Tandy to FO, 29.9.1961.

[93] MAE. Série DE–CE 1961–6, Bte. 512; Wormser to Brussels, 4.9.1961.

[94] *Ibid.* Wormser to Delfra, 13.9.61.

[95] PRO. FO371 158181; M615/225, Heath conversation with Couve de Murville, 11.9.1961; 'Marchandage final'. My translation. MAE. Série DE–CE 1961–6, Bte. 512; Wormser to Delfra, 13.9.1961.

serious divisions of opinion which existed among the Six. And third, the French had won the agreement of their partners that the normal business of the Community should progress unhindered by the membership applications. As a result the CAP timetable, to which the French attached such importance, still stood some chance of realisation. The outcome of the procedural debate should thus have reinforced rather than weakened the impression of French strength. It also illustrates how the French position was particularly strong when French diplomats were able to portray their stance as being designed to protect the Community as well as furthering French interests.

The British were understandably disappointed by the system devised.[96] The defensiveness of the Community and the determination of the Six to attach greater importance to their own internal unity than to the rapid and successful conclusion of the enlargement negotiations were an unwelcome surprise. Nevertheless, the British still had a great deal of influence on the length and duration of the negotiation, for it was they, and not the Six, who would largely decide on the number of issues to be discussed. It is therefore to the vital process of agenda setting and to the complex matter of how, and in what order, each item should be discussed, that the next chapter will turn.

[96] Eric Roll, *Crowded Hours* (London: Faber & Faber, 1985), pp. 118–19.

3   **Setting the agenda**
     October 1961–March 1962

On 10 October 1961, Edward Heath outlined Britain's opening position in the membership negotiations to his ministerial counterparts among the Six. The Lord Privy Seal's speech explained the overall British attitude towards the European Community and expanded upon the three special difficulties – the Commonwealth, British agriculture and the European Free Trade Association (EFTA) – which Macmillan's government was pledged to address in the course of discussions with the Six. Despite its length, however, Heath's Paris speech could do no more than set out the fundamentals of the British position. The Six limited their initial response to a simple acknowledgement of the British statement and did not reply in any detail until negotiations started in Brussels a month later. In seeking to explain the way in which both the tone and the agenda of the next sixteen months of negotiations were set, this chapter will hence range well beyond the Paris meeting and encompass many of the preliminary encounters between the British and the Community member states. Throughout, its purpose is to explain the substance of the negotiations and to bring out the political and economic issues at stake in the enlargement talks.

The spirit of the negotiations

The most striking feature of the Lord Privy Seal's speech in Paris was the warmth of its pro-European rhetoric. The cautious and almost apologetic tone in which Macmillan had announced his decision to apply to the EEC to the House of Commons was abandoned in favour of fulsome praise of the European Community and a whole-hearted declaration of the United Kingdom's desire to participate fully in all future integration. Britain, Heath stated, had always wanted to 'play a full part in the development of European institutions' and although, at one stage, it had felt unable to follow the Six in their attempt to move towards 'a more organic type of unity . . . it was never agreeable to us to find that we were no longer running with the stream towards European unity'.[1] British determination to end its separation from the Six was accentuated by the threat from the Communist world: 'Europe must unite or perish. The United Kingdom, being part of Europe, must not stand aside.'[2] Furthermore, Heath explained, his government had been swayed by 'the remarkable success of your Community . . . Our wish is to take part with you in this bold and imaginative venture; to unite our efforts with yours; and to join in promoting, through the EEC, the fullest possible measure of European unity.'[3] The British were thus applying in a 'positive spirit' and were determined to bring the negotiations to a successful conclusion.[4]

This positive spirit was quickly underlined as the Lord Privy Seal announced British willingness to accept most of the Treaty of Rome:

> Her Majesty's Government are ready to subscribe fully to the aims which you have set yourselves. In particular, we accept without qualification the objectives laid down in Articles 2 and 3 of the Treaty of Rome, including the elimination of internal tariffs, a common customs tariff, a common commercial policy, and a common agricultural policy.[5]

Those special difficulties which Britain would encounter could be dealt with entirely by means of protocols attached to the Treaty of Rome rather than through substantial amendments to the text of the Treaty. Moreover the British were ready to examine jointly the ways in which Community directives and regulations already passed by the Six – the so-called *acquis communautaire* – could be applied to the UK. On accession, Britain was also willing to make, in one operation, the same cuts in its tariffs towards Community member states as the Six had made by that date and to start the process of aligning its other most favoured nation (MFN) tariffs with the Community's common external tariff (CET).[6]

Alongside this willingness to accept most of that which the Community had already accomplished, the British declared themselves

[1] 'The United Kingdom and the European Economic Community'; HMSO, Cmnd 1565, November 1961, pp. 3–4.
[2] *Ibid.*   [3] *Ibid.*   [4] Cmnd 1565, p. 5.   [5] *Ibid.*
[6] Cmnd 1565, pp. 5–7.

ready to participate in all future integration. First and foremost, this meant agreement with the Bad Godesberg Declaration of 18 July 1961, in which the Community Heads of State and Government had stated their hope of moving swiftly towards greater political union.

> We [the British] fully share the aims and objectives, political and otherwise, of those who drew up this Declaration, and we shall be anxious, once we are members of the Community, to work with you in a positive spirit to reinforce the unity which you have already achieved . . . The more that we, the United Kingdom, can contribute to the unifying process of this great European Community, the more we shall feel that we are joining the historic enterprise which the genius of the European peoples has launched.[7]

But it also meant that Britain did not in any way intend to slow the pace of Community development in any field:

> I am convinced that we share the same essential interests and that the habit of working closely together, which you have learned over the past four years, and in which we should now like to join, will mean, not the slowing down of this process, but a continued advance and the development of closer unity.[8]

This emphasis on Britain's desire to play a constructive role in Europe was a deliberate tactical choice. In the months preceding the membership application, British ministers and officials had been repeatedly urged by their continental colleagues to present the British decision to approach the Community in the most pro-European fashion possible. Only in this way, they had been told, would the negative legacy of previous tension between the British and the Six be dispelled.[9] But however calculated, it was undoubtedly effective. The Germans, Dutch, Belgians and Italians were all complimentary about Heath's statement: Professor Alfred Müller-Armack, a Secretary of State in the German Ministry of Economics, for instance, described the Lord Privy Seal's comments as 'extraordinarily felicitous'.[10] Similarly the Commissioners present in Paris professed themselves pleased with Heath's tone.[11] And even the French, while more reserved, admitted to being impressed. De Gaulle told Sir Pierson Dixon, the

[7] Cmnd 1565, p. 7.   [8] *Ibid.*
[9] See e.g. PRO. FO371 158269; M634/131, Shuckburgh minute, 18.5.1961 and M634/140, Dixon to Reilly, 24.5.1961; also FO371 158278; M634/238, Barclay minute, 24.7.1961.
[10] PRO. FO371 158297; M634/589, Statham to Gallagher, 20.10.1961; see also M634/573, M634/578, M634/602, M634/606.
[11] PRO. PREM 11 3561; Lee to Macmillan, 11.10.1961.

British Ambassador in Paris, that the speech had been 'beautifully presented and cleverly drafted' while Olivier Wormser, the Directeur des Affaires Economiques et Financielles at the Quai d'Orsay and a veteran diplomat, maintained that he had never in his career seen a better prepared statement.[12] That such praise from the French was accompanied by a serious attempt to prevent the Six from making too hasty and too enthusiastic a reply was a still greater compliment to British tactics.[13]

As had become evident in the procedural discussions, however, Anglophile sentiments expressed by individual representatives of the Six did not necessarily lead to collective generosity on the part of the Community member states. And so it proved when the Six gathered in early November to decide upon their official answer to Heath's statement. Several draft replies were submitted, each indicative of individual national views about the spirit in which the negotiations should be conducted. Predictably perhaps, that put forward by the Dutch implied the greatest flexibility: the need to respect the Treaty of Rome was affirmed and it was made clear that the Imperial Preference system could not continue unchanged, but the importance of an accommodating approach towards the Commonwealth was acknowledged. Where feasible, the Dutch suggested, Commonwealth countries should be allowed to become associate members. If this proved impossible, 'it must be decided that Commonwealth countries should be guaranteed to maintain their exports to Britain at a reasonable level'.[14] At the other extreme, the French and Commission drafts were much less forthcoming. Both welcomed the British application – the Commission talked of a historic turning point – but neither hid the numerous difficulties that lay ahead. More importantly both Hallstein and the French insisted that the British should not be allowed to negotiate anything other than temporary and limited exceptions from the provisions of the Treaty of Rome. The British suggestion of using protocols rather than Treaty modifications was acknowledged, but it

[12] PRO. CAB 134/1511; CMN(61)17, 31.10.1961; FO371 158300; M634/640, Tel. No. 1170, Steel to FO, 6.11.1961.
[13] PRO. FO371 158300; M634/640, Tel. No. 1170, Steel to FO, 6.11.1961.
[14] 'Il doit être établi que les pays du Commonwealth doivent être assurés d'être en mesure de maintenir leurs importations sur le marché britannique à un niveau suffisament raisonnable.' My translation. CMA. 07.151 Préparation par le Conseil de la réunion ministérielle entre les états membres et le Royaume-Uni, ainsi que la déclaration commune des six devant être prononcée par le président du conseil CEE lors de cette réunion, tenue les 8/9 novembre. RU/INT/M3, Dutch draft, 7.11.1961.

was argued by the two delegations that this amounted to no more than a presentational device, and as such did not make it any more possible for the Six to allow long-term or wide-ranging exceptions to the Treaty regime.[15]

The German and Italian drafts represented an intermediate position. In both there was much praise for the British: Churchill's speech in Zurich in 1946 was recalled, as was the British role in the creation of the OEEC, the Council of Europe, NATO and the WEU. Moreover, the Germans went on: 'We have always been conscious of the fact that a Europe without Britain could not represent a complete Europe. It is therefore with all the more pleasure that we welcome the British decision to start negotiations with a view to joining the EEC.'[16] But beneath the flattery and the expressions of satisfaction at the British decision to apply, both the German and Italian drafts implied an approach much closer to the toughness of the French and the Commission than to the flexibility of the Dutch. The Italians, for instance, pointed to the need for the British to apply the Community's external tariff to all nations outside the EEC including those in the Commonwealth, while the German draft contained a powerful reminder that the EEC was primarily an organisation designed to promote and favour European interests:

> Our Community bears the name of 'European' Economic Community. This determines its mission, but also the limits which it must take account of when concluding special agreements. In the application of these limits we will not be narrow-minded . . . Nevertheless, in this field we cannot move too far from the marked path without running the risk of losing sight of our point of departure.[17]

The joint reply eventually presented on behalf of the Six by Rolf Lahr, the Secretary of State in the German Ministry of Foreign Affairs,

[15] *Ibid.* RU/INT/M1, French draft, 6.11.1961 and S/05701/61, Commission draft, 4.11.1961.

[16] 'Nous avons toujours été conscients du fait qu'une Europe sans la Grande-Bretagne ne peut constituer une Europe complète. C'est avec autant plus de satisfaction que nous accueillons maintenant la décision britannique d'entamer des négociations en vue de son adhésion à la CEE.' My translation. *Ibid.* S/555/61 (RU15), First German draft, 3.11.1961.

[17] 'Notre Communauté porte le nom de Communauté Economique "Européenne". Cela détermine sa mission, mais également ses limites dont il faut tenir compte pour les accords spéciaux. Dans l'application de ces limites, nous ne ferons pas preuve d'étroitesse d'esprit . . . Toutefois dans ce domaine, on ne peut s'écarter très loins du chemin tracé si nous ne voulons pas courir le risque de perdre de vue notre base de départ.' My translation. *Ibid.* RU/INT/M2, revised German draft, 6.11.1961.

at the first ministerial meeting on 8–9 November, retained much of the German and Italian language in the section complimenting the British on their decision to apply. Elsewhere, however, the dominant influence in the compromise text was the French draft. The key passage setting out the limits of EEC flexibility, for example, was drawn almost word for word from the French proposal:

> We have been assured that the United Kingdom's accession will, apart from the necessary adaptations, not require any amendments to the Treaty establishing the EEC and that it will be possible to settle by means of additional protocols the problems which will arise in connection with this accession. Nevertheless, we start from the principle that the protocols must not be allowed to modify the tenor and the spirit of the Treaty and must essentially concern transitional arrangements.
>
> In fact, however grave and important the problems facing the United Kingdom may be – and we are willing to recognise that they are in many cases grave and important – they need to be settled without exceptions becoming the rule and vice versa. Exceptions made must not be of such scope and duration as to call into question the rules themselves or impair the possibilities of applying these rules within the Community. The accession of new members must take place in such a way that they may subsequently share fully in the working out of common decisions in a Community spirit.[18]

The opening statement by the Six was thus a clear illustration of the influence the French continued to wield within the Community and of the defensive spirit with which most of the EEC members had decided to approach the enlargement negotiations.

Three major problems

This defensiveness on the part of the Community might have appeared unreasonable had the enthusiastically pro-European passages of Heath's speech cited above been representative of the whole British statement. But in fact less than a third of Heath's speech was devoted to such sentiments; most of the remainder, by contrast, was spent outlining the very formidable range of issues which the British hoped would be addressed in the course of the membership talks. Once the volume of British desiderata is taken into account, the cautious response by the Six is much more comprehensible. It is

---

[18] Cited in Frances Nicholson and Roger East, *From the Six to the Twelve, the Enlargement of the European Communities* (Harlow: Longman, 1987), p. 12.

therefore necessary to look more closely at 'the three major problems' which, according to Heath, EEC membership would pose for Britain, at the first possible solutions suggested by the Lord Privy Seal, and at the basic issues raised by these British requests.

The Commonwealth

The British request that special provisions be made to safeguard Commonwealth trade rested upon two general arguments. The first centred on the importance of the Commonwealth – important to the Free World in general, but more particularly to Britain and to the British public. Trade links, Heath argued, were essential to the health and vitality of the Commonwealth; an enforced severance of these ties might provoke a political reorientation of many Commonwealth countries and would sully the EEC's reputation across the world. As a result: 'I am sure that you will understand that Britain could not join the EEC under conditions in which this trade connection was cut with grave loss and even ruin for some of the Commonwealth countries.'[19] Second, Heath drew a parallel between the treatment of the Commonwealth and the fashion in which the needs of French, Italian, Dutch and Belgian colonies and dependencies had been accommodated during the Treaty of Rome negotiations. 'It is a striking fact, and very relevant to the Commonwealth problem, that in no case was a tariff imposed on trade where one had not been in force before the Treaty was signed.'[20] Instead, Heath recalled, the colonies of the Six had either become Associated Overseas Territories enjoying free access to all Community markets or – as had been the case for a few of the French territories in North Africa – had been granted special protocols which allowed unhindered entry into the French market.[21]

That the Commonwealth was of political and economic importance, both to Britain and to the whole of the West, was not contested by the Six. Neither the French nor the Commission – the two delegations which from the very outset of the negotiations took the toughest line towards British requests – sought in any way to deny this.[22] But the

---

[19] Cmnd 1565, pp. 7–8.   [20] *Ibid.*   [21] *Ibid.*

[22] CMA. RU/INT/M1 and 07.151. Premier document de travail de la Commission CEE contenant une analyse des propositions contenues dans la déclaration de M. Heath faite lors de la session ministérielle à Paris, tenue le 10 octobre 1961. S/05700/61. For French analyses see MAE. Série DE–CE 1961–6, Bte. 517; Note, 30.10.1961 and Ulrich to Dejean de la Batie, 13.10.1961.

general recognition that a serious problem existed did not lead to any agreement about the manner in which the difficulty should be addressed. On the contrary, Heath's analogy between the situation of the Commonwealth and that of the colonies and former colonies of the Six was strongly rejected. The Commission's analysis of Heath's speech, for instance, noted that the volume and diversity of Commonwealth exports to Britain made any such comparison meaningless. The Community's Associated Overseas Territories, the working document noted, had been producers of tropical products and raw materials.

> As a result, granting access to the Common Market did not, in general, lead to any serious problems of origin . . . or to direct competition with Community produce. By contrast, Commonwealth exports towards Britain are highly diverse. They are not composed exclusively of tropical agricultural products, but also of temperate zone agricultural produce. They also include manufactured products, whether finished or half finished. Therefore the problems which could safely be neglected when the Treaty of Rome was negotiated must inescapably be confronted.[23]

As a result, there could be no simple repetition of the Treaty of Rome formula. A variety of different approaches would be necessary to tackle the Commonwealth problem.

Heath's speech had admittedly gone some way in this direction. The section outlining the general nature of the Commonwealth problem was followed by separate passages addressing, on the one hand, the needs of the developing Commonwealth countries in Asia, Africa and the Caribbean, and, on the other, the problems which EEC membership would cause to the old Dominions.[24] This subdivision of the Commonwealth problem into two distinct categories was not, however, sufficient to please the Six. Led by the French, the Community member states were initially wary of the very idea of regional solutions to the Commonwealth problem. Instead they foresaw Commonwealth needs being met primarily by a series of special arrange-

---

[23] 'Il en résulte qu'en règle générale l'accès au marché commun n'entraînerait pas de grave problème d'origine . . . ou de concurrence directe par rapport aux productions de la Communauté. En revanche, les exportations du Commonwealth vers la Grande-Bretagne sont d'une diversité extrême. Il s'agit non seulement de produits agricoles tropicaux mais aussi de produits agricoles tempérés. Il s'agit aussi de produits industriels soit finis, soit demi-finis. Les problèmes qui avaient pu être négligés lors du Traité de Rome se posent alors de façon indéniable.' My translation. CMA. S/05700/61. Document de Travail no. 1, 2.11.1961.

[24] Cmnd 1565, pp. 9–12.

ments for individual sensitive commodities.[25] This would mean, for example, that the problem of Ceylon would not be solved by a general waiver of the CET for the produce of developing countries within the Commonwealth, but rather by a limited deal reducing or eliminating the Community's tariff on tea, Ceylon's principal export. By December, the two sides had relented slightly. Unwilling to see the negotiations immediately paralysed, both the British and the Six felt able to accept a compromise approach suggested by the Commission which divided the developing Commonwealth into a series of categories defined partly by region, but also by the type of produce exported.[26] It is these three subdivisions – intended to permit further work, not to prejudge eventual solutions – which this chapter must now examine more closely.

The easiest group of developing Commonwealth members and territories to deal with were those in Africa and the West Indies. Politically and economically similar to the countries and territories already associated with the Community under Part IV of the Treaty of Rome, Nigeria, Tanganyika, Kenya and the other countries that had made up former British Africa as well as several of the Caribbean islands were obvious candidates to be included in the Community's existing system. Such an arrangement, if agreed, would shield Commonwealth members in Africa and the Caribbean from any ill-effects resulting from British membership and bring a variety of benefits: association with the Community would provide these countries not merely with continued access to the British market, but also with tariff-free entry into the markets of all the other EEC member states.[27] In addition, the association agreement contained provisions for Community development aid. *The Economist*'s claim, made within days of the British application, that Part IV association offered the ideal solution to most of the problems facing Britain's former and actual colonies in Africa, thus seemed highly plausible.[28]

Despite such optimism, however, there were a variety of problems. The first was that the whole association system linking the Six and

[25] CMA. 07.51. Compte rendu de la première session ministérielle de la Conférence entre les Etats membres des communautés européennes et le Royaume-Uni, tenue à Bruxelles les 8/9.11.1961. RU/M/6/61.

[26] CMA. 07.151. Premier rapport du Comité des suppléants aux Ministres, présenté le 8 décembre 1961. RU/S/10/61. Annex II.

[27] William Gorell Barnes, *Europe and the Developing World: Association under Part IV of the Treaty of Rome* (London: Chatham House/PEP, 1967), pp. 6–7.

[28] *The Economist* 12.8.1961.

their former colonies was being renegotiated, largely to accommodate the rapid transition by many of the associates from colonies to independent states. As a result, neither the British negotiators nor their Community counterparts could predict with any degree of certainty the exact shape of the system which, it was hoped, much of the Commonwealth would join.[29] Furthermore, the French – always alert to the possibility of the British exercising undue influence on an internal Community negotiation, but also conscious that many former French colonies feared that the British application might delay the new association arrangement[30] – tried hard to have all discussion of Commonwealth association postponed until after the Community and its eighteen associates had successfully concluded the new association convention.[31] Second, the status of the Commonwealth members on whose behalf the British were meant to negotiate was also evolving rapidly. Between 1961 and 1963 Nigeria, Kenya, Uganda and Tanganyika all gained their independence. There was thus considerable uncertainty on both sides of the negotiating table.

The third difficulty was more fundamental. As in any system based upon trade preference, the economic advantages of association with the Community were inversely proportional to the number of other countries enjoying the same status. British membership, if accompanied by the inclusion of much of the Commonwealth in the association preferential zone, would give those countries already associated with the EEC one new tariff-free market to sell in, but this gain would be more than outweighed by the arrival of numerous Commonwealth competitors enjoying equally privileged access to all the markets of the enlarged Community. This problem was particularly acute given the fact that exports from the African Commonwealth already performed well in Community markets despite not having preferential tariff concessions. According to Commission figures for 1958, Community associates had so far failed to take full advantage of their trade preference in any market other than that of their former colonial ruler; in all other EEC countries they sold consistently less than the developing members of the Commonwealth.[32] As this situation could only worsen if the current associates lost their tariff advantage over

---

[29] CMA. S/5700/61. Commission Working Document No. 1, 2.11.1961.
[30] *Agence Europe* 6.10.1961.
[31] PRO. CAB 134/1523; CMN(O)(62) 6th meeting, 26.1.1962.
[32] CMA. S/5700/61. Commission Working Document No. 1, 2.11.1961.

their Commonwealth rivals, the warning signals delivered to the Community by the associates were entirely predictable.[33]

A rise in the number of Community associates also threatened to increase third country objections to the whole association system. Countries that exported tropical products yet were neither actual Community associates, nor Commonwealth members likely to become EEC associates, were bound to look askance as still more of their competitors sought to gain a privileged trade relationship vis-à-vis the EEC. Many Latin American states had protested vociferously when the system had originally been proposed and were almost certain to redouble their objections if the Community's preferential area was expanded to include much of the Commonwealth.[34] Of still greater concern than Latin American discontent was US displeasure.[35] The Americans had never been happy about the discriminatory nature of the association system and were trying to use the renegotiation of the association arrangements as an opportunity to reduce this aspect of the scheme. In May 1961 Kennedy had raised the issue with Hallstein and a month later the Commission had received an American memorandum which had urged the EEC to adopt a more 'global' approach to the trade problems of the developing world. In February 1962, a new communication arrived, advising the Commission against any solution to the Commonwealth problem which increased trade discrimination against Latin America.[36] A simple extension of the association system to African and West Indian Commonwealth countries was therefore likely to provoke strong US protests.[37]

The final two problems concerned the financial cost of the association system and the political nature of some of the possible newcomers. Germany and the Benelux countries were already anxious about the financial burden of the existing scheme; any increase in the number of beneficiaries of Part IV of the Treaty of Rome would only aggravate the problem. As a result, those member states which might have been expected to be most well disposed towards British requests

---

[33] *The Economist* 18.11.1961.

[34] Enzo R. Grilli, *The European Community and the Developing Countries* (Cambridge University Press, 1993), pp. 11–12.

[35] Pascaline Winand, *Eisenhower, Kennedy and the United States of Europe* (London: Macmillan, 1993), pp. 286–7; see also *Foreign Relations of the United States, 1961–1963 West Europe and Canada* (Washington: United States Government Printing Office, 1994), vol. XIII, pp. 27–8.

[36] *Le Monde* 4–5.3.1962; Winand, *Eisenhower*, p. 286.

[37] Winand, *Eisenhower*, pp. 289–93.

remained wary about the expense of generosity towards the Commonwealth.[38] Finally, Ghana and Rhodesia, for very different reasons, made several member states and associates hesitate before allowing a rapid expansion of the association system. The French in particular were unhappy at the thought of outspoken representatives of Nkrumah's Ghanaian government participating in the planned Association Council, as such a development might encourage the spread of populist nationalism throughout francophone Africa.[39] Similarly, both member states and associates had serious qualms about allowing white-ruled Rhodesia to take a place alongside the many newly independent African regimes.

Despite all these difficulties, both the British and the Six agreed that association remained the ideal solution for much of the developing Commonwealth. Nevertheless, there were problems enough to guarantee that, notwithstanding this consensus, the task of producing a compromise which satisfied not only the Six and the British but also their respective African partners would be time consuming and very delicate.

A second group of developing Commonwealth countries comprised India, Pakistan, Ceylon and Hong Kong. All four had originally been mentioned by Heath as possible candidates for association, but it quickly became apparent that none of the Six were willing to contemplate this possibility.[40] The Commission analysis of Heath's speech, for instance, stressed that association should be restricted to those Commonwealth countries and territories comparable to the existing associates: this meant that African members, both independent and dependent, could associate, but that in Asia only non-industrialised dependencies should be allowed to join.[41] This criterion clearly ruled out both the independent countries of the Indian subcontinent and the highly industrialised colony of Hong Kong. Alternative remedies were therefore required.

The Community member states were in general well disposed towards the countries of the Indian sub-continent. The importance of

[38] PRO. FO371 164776; M641/22, Delmar 12, Robinson to FO, 18.1.1962.
[39] *Le Monde* 4–5.3.1962.   [40] Cmnd 1565, p. 9.
[41] CMA. S/5700/61. Commission Working Document No. 1, 2.11.1961. For confirmation that this was not just the opinion of the Commission, cf. e.g. PRO. FO371 158306; M634/757, Delmar 14, Barclay to FO, 27.11.1961 or FO371 164775; M641/11, Barclay minute, 10.1.1962.

foreign currency earnings for all three economies in the region was recognised, as was the political desirability of maintaining good relations, economic and political, with India, Pakistan and Ceylon. But the goodwill of the Six was significantly tempered by the fact that the key Indian and Pakistani exports to Britain, and therefore by extension the most probable exports towards the Community once Britain had joined, were textiles. In 1961 Britain imported over US $102 million worth of textiles. Of this just over a quarter came from India, slightly under a quarter from Hong Kong and US $3.4 million worth from Pakistan. From EEC countries by contrast Britain purchased textiles of a value of only US $4.7 million.[42] This made generosity much more difficult. The textile industry was not only important in virtually all EEC member states; it was also one of the most protectionist of sectors, acutely sensitive about competition from low-cost Asian producers. When the Treaty of Rome had been negotiated, textile producers among the Six had successfully combined to ensure that the Community's external tariff for cottons and other textile goods remained significantly above the CET average. Any attempt to change this would be bitterly resisted. Moreover, opening Community textile markets at the behest of the British would be particularly difficult, as the way in which the Lancashire mills had been 'sacrificed' to the needs of India had entered the mythology of the continental textile industry as the cautionary tale about the dangers of excessive liberalism.[43]

Throughout the negotiations, the Six were thus obliged to balance their desire not to penalise India, Pakistan and Ceylon against the danger of offending the powerful textile lobbies within the Community. This conflict is evident from the mandate given to the first working group to study the problems of the Indian sub-continent. After over three hours of intensive debate, it was finally agreed by the Six in February 1962 that the experts should be asked to seek solutions which, on the one hand, did not adversely affect the export opportunities of the three developing countries, but which, on the other hand, ensured that the market of the enlarged Community was neither

---

[42] *Foreign Trade – Trade by Commodities* (Paris: OECD, 1962), vol. II, January–December 1961, p. 10.

[43] See e.g. *L'industrie cottonière française devant la demande d'adhésion de la Grande-Bretagne au Marché commun*, Supplement to *Industrie cottonière française*, 43rd year, No. 2, February 1962.

disturbed nor broken up. Reconciling these two, very different aims, would be a lengthy and complex task.[44]

Hong Kong aroused much less sympathy. The British argument for special treatment rested, as it had done for the other three countries in this category, on the colony's need for continued export earnings. In Hong Kong's case this was particularly vital, the British maintained, as the colony had no natural resources of its own and was totally reliant on the export of manufactured products. Without such trade Hong Kong would be unable to provide employment for its large and expanding population.[45] But the Six appeared less impressed by these arguments than by Hong Kong's capacity to produce low-cost manufactures – especially textiles – which were in direct competition with European goods. According to the progress report drawn up by the deputies in late April, the colony 'did not seem to have all the usual characteristics of a developing country'.[46] As such, Hong Kong was considered a much less deserving object of Community flexibility than either the Indian sub-continent or the African and West Indian members of the Commonwealth.

The third category of developing Commonwealth members contained a strange assortment of 'problem' territories, that could not be satisfactorily fitted into either of the previous groups. It thus included the oil-producing territories of Aden and Trinidad; Singapore, North Borneo, Brunei and Sarawak, all of which were being considered for incorporation within the planned Greater Malaysian Federation; the two European dependencies of Gibraltar and Malta; and the three High Commission Territories land-locked by, and in customs union with, the Republic of South Africa. Individually, none of these was likely to prove a major stumbling-block; collectively, however, they had the potential to use up valuable time and resources and to distract attention away from the key issues separating the British and the Six.

---

[44] Schulte argues that the German textile industry was slow to perceive the threat of Commonwealth textiles, but highly vociferous once it did become aware of the danger. Markus Schulte, 'Challenging the Common Market Project. German Industry, Britain and Europe 1956–63', in Anne Deighton and Alan Milward (eds.), *Acceleration, Deepening and Enlarging: The European Economic Community, 1957–1963* (Brussels: Nomos/Giuffrè/LGDJ/Bruylant, 1997).

[45] CMA. 07.515. 7ème réunion du comité des suppléants (RU), tenue le 7 février 1962. RU/S/22/62. Statement by Sir Pierson Dixon.

[46] CMA. 07.15. Rapport sur l'état des négociations: texte définitif. RU/S/59/62. 12.4.1962.

For all their complexity, none of the problems posed by the developing members of the Commonwealth were politically as sensitive for the British government as the difficulties of the three old Dominions. Canada, Australia and New Zealand were, as an opinion poll conducted in March 1962 revealed, the Commonwealth countries which mattered most to the British public in general and to Conservative voters in particular.[47] The sentimental ties, the family links, the shared memories of the Second World War all made relations with the three white and English-speaking former Dominions – and indeed with South Africa which had only recently withdrawn from the Commonwealth – much more intense and emotional than the ties with the emerging nations of Africa, Asia and the Caribbean.[48] Appeals to Britain's links with the former Dominions, moreover, were a staple of those campaigning against British membership of the EEC.[49] Canadian, Australian and New Zealand reactions would thus be the principal yardstick by which any terms negotiated in Brussels would be measured and any Commonwealth discontent would be ruthlessly exploited by the government's political opponents. As Macmillan acknowledged, Robert Menzies, the Australian Prime Minister, John Diefenbaker, the Canadian Premier, and Keith Holyoake, the Prime Minister of New Zealand, had a power to endanger, if not totally destroy, the British application unrivalled by the likes of Jawaharlal Nehru, the Indian Prime Minister, or Dr Kwame Nkrumah, the Ghanaian leader.[50]

Among the Six there was substantial recognition that the former Dominions could not be totally abandoned. There was also a fairly widespread view that New Zealand, which was peculiarly dependent on agricultural exports to Britain, might need rather better treatment than the Commonwealth norm. Nevertheless, there was an equally strong feeling that, in marked contrast to the poorer developing members of the Commonwealth, the former Dominions were in little

---

[47] *Daily Telegraph* 19.3.1962; for a more detailed analysis of public opinion about the Commonwealth see Robert J. Lieber, *British Politics and European Unity: Parties, Elites and Pressure Groups* (Berkeley: University of California Press, 1970), p. 193.

[48] Philip Bell and Peter Morris contrast the Conservative Party affection for the 'white Commonwealth' with Labour's enthusiasm for a multiracial family of nations. 'Les "Europe" des Européens ou la notion d'Europe' in René Girault and Gérard Bossuat (eds.), *Les Europe des Européens* (Paris: Publications de la Sorbonne, 1993), pp. 72–4.

[49] See, for instance, the full-page advertisement, featuring Field Marshall Montgomery, which was placed at Lord Beaverbrook's expense in all the major dailies on 4.6.1962.

[50] Harold Macmillan, *At the End of the Day* (London: Macmillan, 1973), p. 129.

need of great generosity. In 1961 Canada, Australia and New Zealand were all countries whose per capita GNP was comparable to that of the richest Community member state, and whose agricultural sectors were more modern, efficient and prosperous than any in Europe. As one official involved in the negotiations remarked to a British journalist, New Zealand farmers were 'millionaires compared with the peasants of Calabria'.[51]

It was, however, the nature of Canadian, Australian and New Zealand exports, rather than the wealth of the three countries, that made the problem of the white Commonwealth particularly intractable. For, unlike the African and Asian Commonwealth, whose exports were only in direct competition with those of the Six in the textiles sector, the three former Dominions were regarded as rivals by the Six in the production of a range of industrial goods, several key raw materials, a variety of processed agricultural goods, and, most importantly, a wide array of temperate zone agricultural commodities. Liberality towards Canada, Australia and New Zealand was hence much more painful and difficult for the Six than benevolence towards India or Africa. Furthermore, several of the member states feared that concessions granted to the developed Commonwealth were liable to lead to requests for equal treatment from the United States, Japan and other advanced economies. They could thus imperil both the whole Common External Tariff – widely seen as an essential cohesive element in the Community – and the nascent Common Agricultural Policy, another *sine qua non* of the Community's development for several member states, most notably the French.

The volume of manufactured exports from the developed Commonwealth to the United Kingdom was not very high. In 1958 Canadian, Australian and New Zealand manufactures exported to the United Kingdom had been worth a mere £55.5 million – less than 10 per cent of the £670 million total of exports from the three countries to Britain. The overwhelming majority of these exports, moreover, came from Canada – of the three former Dominions, the state least dependent on trade with the United Kingdom. Canadian exports in 1958 had been worth £1,800 million, of which only £310 million had been sold on the British market.[52] It was thus difficult for the British to claim that the 'vital interests' of the Commonwealth were at stake. As a result, the case for continued free entry into Britain for Common-

[51] *Observer* 22.7.1962.   [52] *Agence Europe* 7.8.1961.

wealth manufactures outlined by the Lord Privy Seal on 10 October was amongst the weakest and most tentative of British pleas. Heath pointed out that Commonwealth industries had significantly bene-fited from their preferential position in the UK market but at once admitted that 'indefinite and unlimited continuation of free entry over the whole of this field may not be regarded as compatible with the development of the common market and we are willing to discuss ways of reconciling these two conflicting notions'.[53] Almost before the negotiations had begun, therefore, the British had conceded that the status quo on manufactured imports would no longer be viable once Britain joined the Community. The principal challenge of the months that followed would be to devise a system of managed change, which was acceptable to the Six but which could also be 'sold' to three Commonwealth leaders who were distinctly unenthusiastic about British EEC membership.

The tariff levied on raw materials imported from the Common-wealth was the object of a second British request.[54] Most such imports caused few problems, as the CET was already set at zero. Common-wealth free entry would therefore be able to continue as before. But for five important items – aluminium, lead, zinc, wood pulp and newsprint – the rate was, on the contrary, rather high. Since all five were of significant interest to the Commonwealth (primarily to Canada, but in the case of lead to Australia also) the British asked that this anomaly be corrected and that the CET for all five materials be reduced to zero.[55] Likewise the British asked that a zero tariff be applied to twenty-two other, less important, items.[56]

This British request was appealingly simple. It was also fully compatible with the Treaty of Rome. Unfortunately, it took little account of the Community's previous attitude towards these materials. For it was no accident that the CET for these five tariff positions was unusually high: all five were of some importance to one or more member states, and therefore benefited from a degree of protection which would not easily be relinquished. Furthermore, all were items about which the Six had been bitterly divided. Newsprint, wood pulp and the three metals had all been on the so-called 'List G' – the

---

[53] Cmnd 1565, p. 11.   [54] *Ibid.*
[55] For the importance of these raw materials to Canadian and Australian trade see United Nations, *Yearbook of International Trade Statistics, 1961* (New York: United Nations, 1963), pp. 58 and 128.
[56] For a full list see CMA. RU/S/59/62, Annex 1.

collective name for all those commodities the tariff level of which had proved impossible to settle during the actual Treaty of Rome negotiations and upon which a definitive agreement had only finally been reached, after lengthy negotiations, in 1960. Aluminium, for instance, had provoked fundamental differences of opinion between on one side France, a producer, and Italy, a country which hoped to develop domestic production, and on the other Germany and the Benelux countries, all of which were major importers attracted by cheap non-European supplies. The impasse had only been solved by setting the CET at a relatively high 10 per cent to satisfy the French and Italians and permitting Germany, Belgium and the Netherlands to import sizeable quotas at substantially reduced tariffs. In requesting zero tariffs for five such controversial raw materials, the British were thus asking the Six to reopen a dispute which had barely been settled and reexamine issues about which feelings still ran high.[57]

To complicate matters further, the British hopes of reducing the CET on these items also threatened to entangle the British membership negotiations with the parallel yet separate discussions with Norway and Sweden about membership and association respectively. Norway was a major producer of aluminium, wood pulp and newsprint, Sweden an exporter of the latter two, and together they supplied 80 per cent of Britain's needs for wood pulp and much of its newsprint.[58] The balance of supply and demand within the enlarged Community – a major factor in any decision about tariff levels – would therefore vary greatly according to whether the Norwegian membership bid succeeded and upon the terms of any association agreement between the Community and the Swedes. This meant that if the Six and the British did manage to struggle through to a compromise which satisfied all parties to the British membership negotiation, the whole equilibrium could still be upset by developments in the discussions between the Six and Britain's Nordic partners. The possibilities for impasse and delay were almost boundless.

The eleven types of processed agricultural produce for which the British requested a zero tariff were also likely to be problematic. Once more the difficulty lay less in the scale of the trade involved – although sales of canned fruit were not insignificant, the patterns of food consumption in Europe were unlikely to be altered by the free

---

[57] For German alarm at the prospect of tariff reductions and Commonwealth competition see Schulte, 'Challenging the Common Market Project'.
[58] CMA. S/05700/61. Commission Working document No. 1, 2.11.1961.

entry of tinned rabbit or canned kangaroo from Australia! – than in the individual national sensitivities liable to be upset. In Australia, the canning industry had been used to provide employment for numerous war veterans – any decline in exports to Britain might thus produce the very type of emotive story of Commonwealth hardship which the British government dreaded and which Macmillan's opponents would not hesitate to exploit. A liberal approach by the Community, however, would deny the Italians – the principal European producers of processed fruit – one of the most obvious commercial advantages of enlargement. Moreover, Community producers of canned fruit were fearful that tariff reductions designed to help Commonwealth exporters would in fact result in large portions of the EEC market being captured by American companies. This would be to the advantage of neither Britain nor the Six.

The trade in manufactured goods, raw materials and processed food all paled into relative insignificance, however, when placed alongside the principal Commonwealth concern: temperate foodstuffs. Almost universally seen as the most complicated and important commercial issue to be dealt with in the negotiations – *Le Monde* for instance described it as 'the most complex dossier' – the question of how to reconcile Britain's traditional purchase of grain, butter and meat from the Commonwealth with the new Common Agricultural Policy being set up among the Community member states was expected to be one of the key determinants of success or failure in the negotiations.[59] With a successful deal on temperate zone products, Macmillan's government could afford to give ground on Commonwealth manufactures or raw materials and still claim to have all but resolved the Commonwealth problem; without, no number of concessions won from the Six on lesser issues would conceal that the most vital of interests, for Australia and New Zealand at least, had not been protected.

British trade figures for 1961 reveal quite how much was at stake. Canada, the most industrialised of the Commonwealth countries, still exported over US $242 million worth of agricultural products – more than a quarter of all Canadian exports to the United Kingdom.[60] Canadian exports to the UK of wheat alone were valued at US $157

---

[59] 'Le dossier le plus complexe'. *Le Monde* 2.8.1961.
[60] OECD, *Foreign Trade*, pp. 3–4.

million.[61] For Australia, sales of food were even more important, US $275 million, out of a total value of exports to the UK amounting to US $503 million, while the figures for New Zealand amply justified Macmillan's description of the former Dominion as 'an English farm in the Pacific'.[62] In 1961 New Zealand's exports to Britain were worth US $449 million; of this total less than a quarter was accounted for by non-agricultural exports.[63] Sales to Britain of butter, worth US $108 million in 1961, cheese, valued at more than US $50 million, milk and fruit were essential to the well-being of the New Zealand economy.[64] Adopting the CAP would deal a double blow to this trade, firstly by abolishing the Imperial Preference enjoyed by many Commonwealth imports and secondly by subjecting Commonwealth produce to a tariff which European competitors would not face. French and Dutch producers could thus expect to capture a large part of the valuable British market and, even in sectors in which European production was insufficient, the ending of Imperial Preference would mean that Commonwealth suppliers would have to compete on equal terms with other third nations such as the United States and Argentina.

Any change to the British agricultural trade pattern would also have a significant domestic impact. British food imports were not subject to the high tariffs that were the European norm and most products thus reached the consumer at comparatively low prices.[65] Adoption of the CAP would put an end to this 'cheap food' policy and push upwards most food prices. Estimates varied widely as to how great the likely increases were: a study by D. T. Healey cited in *The Times* calculated that the average consumer would spend an extra £8 per annum on food; the fiercely anti-EEC *Daily Express*, by contrast, gave front-page treatment under the headline 'Housewives Beware!' to a prediction 'that every man, woman and child in the country' would pay over £20 more each year.[66] Accurate estimates, however, were almost impossible to make given the continuing uncertainty

---

[61] *Ibid.*, p. 31.

[62] *Agence Europe* 7.8.1961; PRO. PREM 11 4230; Record of a conversation at Rambouillet, 15.12.1962.

[63] OECD, *Foreign Trade*, pp. 1–4.   [64] *Ibid.*, pp. 22–4.

[65] Michael Butterwick and Edmund Neville Rolfe, *Food, Farming and the Common Market* (London: Oxford University Press, 1968), pp. 20–6 contains a full description of the UK agricultural support system.

[66] *The Times* 25.5.1962; *Daily Express* 18.12.1962. To put these figures in perspective, the average weekly pay of a manual worker in Britain in 1961 was £35 2s. *Social Trends* (London: CSO, 1971), p. 73.

over the common price levels to be used for the CAP. What was beyond dispute was that any movement in prices would be upwards and this was bound to be exploited by those against British membership of the Community. Once more, therefore, it was in the interests of the British government to minimise the extent of change.

Heath's opening statement did not ask for a total preservation of the status quo. Instead, the Lord Privy Seal spoke of seeking to reconcile Britain's obligations to its Commonwealth suppliers with the CAP as it evolved. The CAP proposals put forward by the Commission, Heath noted, emphasised the need for the CAP to take account of the interests of third countries. It was therefore to be hoped 'that we can reach agreement in principle that full regard should be paid to the interests of the Commonwealth producers, and that they should be given in the future the opportunity of outlets for their produce comparable to those they now enjoy'.[67] Britain, in other words, did not rule out change to its agricultural system and its approach to food imports. Any modification made, however, should not erode the access of Commonwealth exporters to the lucrative British market. It was this belief that lay at the heart of the 'comparable outlets' formula.

The Community did not respond immediately to this aspect of Heath's speech. With the lengthy negotiations between the Six about the shape of the CAP still not completed, it was both practically and politically difficult to comment systematically on British ideas. But by February 1962, when the Six and the British staged the first ministerial meeting devoted almost entirely to agriculture, this obstacle had disappeared. Following the marathon discussions over the entire New Year period and the eventual agreement of 14 January 1962, the basic framework of the CAP was now settled and it was possible for the Six to measure British requests against actual Community legislation rather than Commission proposals.[68] Once this process started, however, it quickly became apparent that, unfortunately for the British, the Six had strong incentives to preserve their new system intact and to insist that the onus of change lay fully with the applicants.

The first and most basic problem confronting the British was simply

[67] Cmnd 1565, p. 12.
[68] For an account of the final stages of the CAP discussions see Hans von der Groeben, *Combat pour l'Europe. La construction de la Communauté européenne de 1958 à 1966* (Brussels: CECA–CEE–CEEA, 1985), pp. 112–20.

that the Six were understandably reluctant to tamper with an agreement in which they placed great hopes but which had only been achieved at the cost of considerable time and political capital.[69] In the course of the CAP negotiations all the Community member states had been obliged to give ground and to make concessions. These had been justified domestically as a price worth paying for a European agricultural policy. With a common policy secured, however, it would be almost impossible to reopen these disputes and seek to untangle the complex web of compromises that lay at the heart of the 14 January deal for the benefit of the British and Danish newcomers. Doing so would jeopardise the prize which all had worked so hard to secure. It was thus no coincidence that the strongest warning to the British that it was they rather than the Six who would have to change their system of agricultural trade and support was delivered by Sicco Mansholt, the Commissioner responsible for agriculture, only a few days after 14 January. Addressing the European Parliamentary Assembly, he declared that Britain could not expect more than a few adaptations to be made to the CAP, adding: 'When I speak of adaptations to take account of the market situation, I am not contemplating allowing any change to the fundamentals or the essence of what we [the Six] have agreed. This cannot be negotiated all over again.'[70]

The nature of Britain's requests did nothing to encourage flexibility on the part of the Six. The very idea of granting Commonwealth exporters guaranteed access to British or indeed EEC markets was in fundamental contradiction with the concept of *préférence communautaire* – one of the three principles upon which the CAP was based.[71] This stipulated that producers within the Community should, in all cases, be given a commercial advantage over those outside of the EEC. British plans for 'comparable outlets' would do the exact opposite: not only would they limit the potential sales in the UK of European producers, but they would also give Commonwealth exporters a guaranteed market share – something which not even EEC producers

---

[69] This is discussed in N. Piers Ludlow, 'A Problem of Trust: British Agriculture and the Brussels Negotiations 1961–3' in George Wilkes (ed.), *Britain's First Failure to Enter the European Community, 1961–63* (London: Frank Cass, 1997).

[70] 'Lorsque je parle d'adaptations à la situation du marché, je ne conçois cependant pas que le fond ou l'essence de ce que nous avons convenu puisse être modifié. Cela ne peut pas être négocié une nouvelle fois.' *Débats de l'Assemblée Parlementaire Européenne 1961–2*, vol. I, pp. 78–82.

[71] Michael Tracy, *Food and Agriculture in a Market Economy: An Introduction to Theory, Practice and Policy* (La Hutte, Belgium: Agricultural Policy Studies, 1993), p. 166.

were meant to enjoy. To accede to the British proposals would thus mean that the Six were prepared to undermine significantly one of the key rules of their new system before it had even started to operate.

Community rigidity over the principle was reinforced by commercial self-interest. France and the Netherlands, the two EEC states which had been most eager to establish the CAP, were both significant agricultural exporters. They thus had every interest in displacing, as quickly as possible, Commonwealth suppliers from their entrenched position in the UK market. In 1961, Britain had imported US $3.75 billion worth of food, including wheat of a value of US $283 million and dairy products worth more than US $410 million.[72] The British market alone was thus a rich prize. But there was more than this at stake. For if Britain was given permission to continue to use its traditional suppliers of agricultural produce and to flout the principle of Community preference, Germany too might press to retain its custom of buying much of its food from the United States and other non-European producers. This would be anathema to the French. In French eyes, one of the principal merits of the CAP, indeed one of the main advantages of European integration in general, was the privileged access that French farmers would gain to the lucrative German markets. In 1961, West Germany had imported food of a value of US $2.3 billion, including US $196 million of wheat. Much of this, however, had been purchased from the US, Canada and Argentina.[73] It was this reliance on non-European suppliers that the French felt that the CAP should change. As de Gaulle had explained to Edgard Pisani, his Minister for Agriculture: '[an agricultural policy] is owed to us, in compensation of the serious risks which we have taken – perhaps incautiously or too early – in the industrial and commercial field'.[74] If Benelux, Italian and German industrial products were to

---

[72] OECD, *Foreign Trade*, pp. 22–4.

[73] With French sales of agricultural produce to the Germans totalling US $169 million in 1961 and Dutch exports to Germany worth US $340 million, EEC suppliers accounted for only a third of German food imports. Both the US and the Commonwealth outsold the French. OECD, *Foreign Trade*, pp. 3–4 and 31.

[74] '[Une politique agricole] nous est dû en contrepartie des risques graves que nous avons pris, peut-être imprudemment – ou trop tôt – en matière industrielle et commerciale.' My translation. Edgard Pisani, *Le Général indivis* (Paris: Albin Michel, 1974), p. 64. For a fuller discussion of French motives see John T. S. Keeler, 'De Gaulle et la politique agricole commune de l'Europe: logique et héritage de l'intégration nationaliste' in Institut Charles de Gaulle, *De Gaulle en son siècle* (Paris: Plon, 1992), vol. V, pp. 155–67.

enjoy free access to French markets, the French felt that they had the right to export their agricultural produce to the rest of the Community. To endanger this prospect was much too high a price to pay for British membership of the Community.

Britain's application and the Commonwealth trade problem also obliged the Community to face, earlier than might otherwise have been the case, the larger issue of its responsibility towards healthy world agricultural trade. An enlarged Community, including both Britain – the world's largest importer of food – and Denmark, would control over 60 per cent of world trade in cereals. EEC policy on cereals would thus have an impact felt far beyond the Community's borders. This, as Sicco Mansholt explained to the European Parliamentary Assembly, would provide the enlarged Community with both an opportunity and a challenge:

> British membership of the EEC will give birth to a large single market, both industrial and agricultural, which will have a decisive impact on world trade. [This will give us] a unique opportunity . . . to resolve a certain number of extremely difficult problems concerning world trade and the relations between our Community and third countries . . . We must not shrink from this grave responsibility. We cannot create a common market in the way in which we cultivate and tend our own gardens, without concerning ourselves with those who live and work beyond our walls but who depend upon us. [75]

Throughout the negotiations, those conscious of the danger that the Community might acquire a reputation as a protectionist and selfish trading bloc as far as agriculture was concerned – and alongside Mansholt, Spaak was an articulate exponent of this view – sought to use the British application to push the CAP in a more liberal direction. Equally, however, the French perceived the enlargement discussions as an opportunity to gain backing for their own rather different vision of the world agricultural market. The idea of a world-wide agreement, under which cereal prices would rise, the major producers would

---

[75] 'L'adhésion de la Grande Bretagne donnera naissance à un grand marché unique, industriel autant qu'agricole, qui aura une influence décisive sur le commerce mondial. [Ceci nous donnera] une occasion unique . . . de résoudre un certain nombre de problèmes très difficiles concernant les échanges mondiaux et les relations de notre Communauté avec les pays tiers . . . Nous ne pouvons pas nous dérober à cette grave responsabilité. Nous ne pouvons pas créer un marché commun comme nous aménageons et cultivons notre jardin, sans nous préoccuper de ceux qui vivent et travaillent au delà de l'enclos et dépendent de nous.' My translation. *Débats de l'Assemblée Parlementaire Européenne 1961–2*, vol. I, pp. 78–82.

cease to subsidise their exports, and would instead redirect their surplus production towards the starving of the Third World, was put forward by the French at several points in the negotiations.[76]

This tendency to view discussions with the British in a wider context was reinforced by American pressure. In 1962, as will be discussed in greater detail below, there was mounting US concern at its persistent trade deficit with the European Community. The CAP agreement of January 1962 had thus been greeted with dismay in Washington, as something liable to erode America's commercial position still further.[77] Orville Freeman, Kennedy's Secretary of State for Agriculture, lost no time in warning the EEC of the United States' alarm and his message was reinforced whenever Community officials met their American counterparts. Hallstein, for instance, was sternly warned that the Americans were unhappy with the prospect of falling farm exports to Europe. Against this background it became particularly difficult for the Community to devise arrangements which gave Commonwealth exporters a better chance of selling in EEC markets than their American competitors.

With so much at stake it was inevitable that the Community response would be extremely cautious. It quickly became clear that the range of palliatives and solutions which the Six were prepared to consider was of a very different type from that favoured by the British. On 22 February, for instance, the ministers of the Six ruled out any possible quantitative deals with the Commonwealth.[78] This, at a stroke, excluded the quotas, market-sharing agreements or long-term contracts referred to by Heath.[79] At the same meeting, the British were also told that there was no prospect of a permanent preferential position for Commonwealth exporters. Maurice Couve de Murville, the French Foreign Minister, speaking in his capacity as chairman of the Six, conceded that temporary measures might prove necessary to avoid excessive harm being done to the Commonwealth. But the solution which the Six envisaged for the longer term owed much more to the pressures described in the preceding paragraphs than to

[76] Wormser had realised that a British application might represent an opportunity to alter the whole system of world agricultural trade several months before the negotiations began. MAE. Série DE–CE 1961–6, Bte. 512; Note, 29.5.1961; for examples of the French actually putting forward this argument in the negotiation see chapter 5 below.

[77] Winand, *Eisenhower*, pp. 298–302; *Foreign Relations of the United States*, pp. 97–100, 113–116 and 128–34.

[78] *Agence Europe* 23.2.1962.   [79] Cmnd 1565, p. 12.

British thinking: 'The relations between Great Britain and the Commonwealth are just one part of the wider issue of relations with third
countries and as such it is clear that the long-term solutions [to the
Commonwealth problem] must probably be found within the framework of world-wide agreements.'[80] Such world-wide arrangements,
Couve de Murville explained, might include EEC commitments about
its agricultural price policy and about the volume of foodstuffs
purchased from non-European suppliers.[81] But they would evidently
be very different from the type of lasting deal between the enlarged
Community and the Commonwealth on which British hopes had
initially been based.[82]

Overall, the Commonwealth problem had ramifications for a wide
range of Community policies. Handled with intelligence and flexibility by all sides it could prove soluble. A sensible approach towards
the difficulty, moreover, might even encourage the Community to give
thorough consideration to the external impact of closer European
integration. But it also contained ample ingredients for dispute, delay
and even impasse. On both sides, commercial self-interest allied to
political sensitivity could easily deter that flexibility which, from the
outset, it was evident would be needed if the problems that British
membership of the Community posed for her former Empire were to
be satisfactorily resolved.

British domestic agriculture

British farmers had long been regarded as another group whose needs
would have to be addressed if Britain did seek an accommodation
with the Community.[83] They were also widely, if somewhat inaccu-

---

[80] 'Les relations de la Grande-Bretagne avec le Commonwealth sont une partie du
problème général des relations avec les pays tiers et il est évident qu'à cet égard, des
solutions à long terme devront probablement être trouvées dans le cadre d'arrangements mondiaux.' My translation. CMA. 07.51 Compte rendu de la 4ème session
ministérielle entre les états membres de la CEE et le Royaume-Uni, tenue les 22/23
février 1962. RU/M/13/62. Draft minutes. Annex III.

[81] *Ibid.*

[82] PRO. CAB 134/1511; CMN(61)2, Brief on the Commonwealth and the Common
Market. Annex B. 4.9.1961. The British did recognise that the methods by which
Commonwealth access was ensured might have to evolve. In 1961, however, they still
hoped that 'comparable outlets' would continue to be available after the Community's transitional period was over.

[83] See e.g. Selwyn Lloyd's speech to the House of Commons on 25 July 1960. *Hansard*
1959–60, vol. 627, col. 1102.

rately, seen as a group of voters whose support was essential for the electoral survival of a Conservative government.[84] It was thus no surprise that British domestic agriculture was the second category singled out by Heath as requiring special treatment. Britain, the Lord Privy Seal explained, could accept the objectives of the CAP. Implementing the policy would take time. Both UK farmers and consumers had grown accustomed to an agricultural system based on direct Exchequer grants to the farmers and on the tariff-free entry of food supplies. This enjoyed the trust of the farming community. Any change would have to be accomplished gradually – as foreseen by the Treaty of Rome – and in a fashion which maintained the standard of living of the farming community.[85] Similarly, the horticultural industry would need both time and help as the tariff protection upon which it had traditionally relied was slowly removed.[86]

A more detailed exposé of British needs could not be made until the Six had completed their own negotiations about the CAP. Nor was it possible for the Six to respond in anything other than very general terms before the exact rules of the new policy were settled. Discussion of domestic agriculture was hence left off the agenda until the New Year. But if this wait was frustrating for the agricultural experts involved with the British bid, the final outcome of the marathon CAP negotiations was considerably more disturbing.

The 14 January 1962 agreement confirmed that agricultural protection in the Community would be based on a radically different method from that employed in Britain. Under the CAP, a protected and unified market for each product would be created. Prices would be brought to the same artificially high level across the Community and would be sustained firstly by means of a variable levy imposed upon all imported foodstuffs – this would ensure that no import, however cheap, could undercut the EEC price for each particular product – and secondly by market intervention if the internal price seemed likely to fall below the designated floor. Within this managed market Community farmers would, after 1970, be able to trade freely, unimpeded by tariff barriers. Given the wide diversity of food prices among the various member states at the outset, however, this internal market would only be instituted progressively. During the years between July 1962 and 31 December 1969 – the so-called transitional

---

[84] The myth and reality of Conservative Party dependence on the farm vote is explored in Lieber, *British Politics*, pp. 195–8.

[85] Cmnd 1565, pp. 12–15.   [86] Cmnd 1565, pp. 15–16.

period – member states would be able to maintain a limited degree of protection against each other as their agricultural prices were gradually aligned. EEC countries would, however, be given a steadily increasing advantage over third country importers by means of the *abattement forfetaire* – a mechanism which each year would widen the margin between the levy charged to non-Community exporters and the tariff imposed upon imports from elsewhere in the EEC. This was designed to ensure that all Community farmers had some time to adapt, but that by 1970 exporting member states such as the French and the Dutch would have been able to establish a strong presence in other European markets.[87]

The British system, in total contrast, did not rely upon tariffs. As explained above, entry into the British market remained virtually barrier free for many agricultural commodities. This meant that the food prices paid by the British consumer were substantially below the European norm. British farmers were enabled to survive in this competitive market thanks to 'deficiency payments'. These were government grants paid directly to the farmer and designed to cover the shortfall between the low market price and the much higher producer price, set annually during consultations between the Ministry of Agriculture and the National Farmers' Union (NFU). The great merit of this system was that it satisfied consumer, importer and farmer alike. Its two principal drawbacks were first the high cost to the taxpayer and second its incompatibility with the Community system which the British were pledged to accept.[88]

The difficulty of introducing the CAP into Britain was accentuated by the details of the 14 January agreement. First amongst the problems posed was the brisk timetable set for movement towards a European common market for agricultural produce. Britain's task would have been substantially easier had Germany been successful in its quest for a significantly longer transitional period. The refusal by the Commission, backed by France and the Netherlands, to countenance a slower pace of development, however, meant that the newcomers as well as the original member states would be under pressure to meet the 1970

[87] *The Times* 5.11.1962; Butterwick and Rolfe, *Food, Farming*, pp. 3–16; John Marsh and Christopher Ritson, *Agricultural Policy and the Common Market* (London: Chatham House/PEP, 1971), pp. 9–12; T. K. Warley, *Agriculture: The Cost of Joining the Common Market* (London: Chatham House/PEP, 1967), pp. 8–17.
[88] *The Times* 2.11.1962; Butterwick and Rolfe, *Food, Farming*, pp. 20–6; Warley, *Agriculture*, pp. 27–32.

deadline. The second problem was similar. Also rejected during the CAP negotiations were the numerous national pleas for various underdeveloped and uncompetitive sectors to be given special dispensation from the general CAP rules. This greatly reduced the prospects of Britain securing special concessions for its less prosperous farmers. Agricultural ministries among the Six, not to mention farmers' organisations, which had been obliged to accept that no privileged arrangements were negotiable, would protest vigorously should the applicants be granted what they, the founder members, had been denied. Third, the mechanics of some of the specific regulations did not appear adequate, in the eyes of British experts, to cope with the requirements of an expanded Community market. The absence of provisions for EEC intervention into the market for eggs, for instance, would, the Ministry of Agriculture predicted, lead to great price instability once Britain and Denmark – both large producers – had joined the EEC.

Those areas in which the CAP was less clear were equally problematic. The Six, in their frantic race to complete the CAP negotiations before the end of 1961, had postponed several important decisions to a later date and had allowed other issues to remain intentionally ambiguous. Price policy was the most important example of the former. Unable to resolve the conflict between France, a reasonably efficient producer eager to set EEC target prices at a moderate to low level, and the desperately inefficient German producers wedded to much higher agricultural prices, the Six had decided that the exact level of Community prices did not need to be determined until 1963. This 'solution' was not, however, welcome to the UK government: British attempts both to convince domestic farmers that the CAP would not cut their income and to reassure the Commonwealth that the CAP need not encourage European surpluses, were much less effective in the absence of a fixed Community price structure. Similarly the deliberately ambiguous phrasing of some of the new regulations added to British difficulties. A resolution of UK anxieties about the financing of the CAP was made much harder to attain by the inconclusive nature of cereals regulation number 25 – the so-called 'financial regulation'. This suggested that after 1970 all the proceeds from CAP levies imposed upon non-EEC agricultural imports should be given to the Community – an arrangement which would result in importers of foodstuffs such as Germany and Britain paying almost single-handedly for EEC agricultural policy – but permitted a degree of uncertainty as to whether these plans for the common market stage of the CAP would require unanimous Council approval before entering into force. If a new Council vote was required, Britain and Germany would have the opportunity to block or modify these provisions at a later date; by contrast, if, as the French maintained, no further deliberation was needed, British acceptance of the CAP would imply agreement to a financial arrangement which would heavily penalise the British if they continued to purchase much of their food from non-European suppliers. Setting out Britain's position on this issue, without reawakening the Franco-German dispute which had been the cause of the ambiguity, would be an all but impossible task.

British discomfort with the outcome of the CAP negotiations was particularly apparent on 22 February 1962, when agriculture was discussed for the first time at ministerial level. As usual, the two statements delivered by Heath and by Christopher Soames, the Minister of Agriculture, were couched in the most positive terms possible. Nevertheless, the section dealing with the 14 January agreement was careful rather than enthusiastic. Britain, Heath stated, could accept the basic principles upon which the deal was grounded. Furthermore, the UK did not seek 'changes just for the sake of change'.[89] It was clear from the lengthy list of difficulties that followed, however, that the British government had serious reservations about the whole shape of the new system and about its ability to safeguard the livelihood of British farmers. Several modifications to the CAP were proposed, a transitional period of twelve to fifteen years for British agriculture was requested, and the UK government sought permission to supplement from Treasury coffers whatever Community support British farmers received.[90] For all the effort to strike a pro-European tone, it was difficult to escape the conclusion that the statements by Heath and Soames amounted to an implicit vote of no confidence in the EEC's new agricultural policy.

The Community's response revealed that there was little common ground between the two sides. Both Couve de Murville and Mansholt underlined the impossibility of substantial changes being made to the CAP. Both speakers also explained the difficulties of granting any Community member state too long a transitional period.[91] Mansholt, moreover, pointed out that, as a member of the Community, Britain

[89] CMA. 07.51. Compte rendu de la 4ème session ministérielle entre les états membres de la CEE et le Royaume-Uni, tenue les 22/23 février 1962. RU/M/13/62. Annex II.
[90] *Ibid.*   [91] CMA. RU/M/13/62. Annexes III and IV.

would be able to use its voice in the Council and the Commission to press for any alterations that experience showed to be necessary.[92] The most fundamental challenge to the British case, however, was delivered by the French Foreign Minister, who cast doubt on the very idea that British farmers would have greater difficulty in adapting to the CAP than their continental counterparts: 'I must say frankly that we among the Six cannot really see the particular reasons why these adaptations which – I acknowledge – are in any event going to be painful and difficult will be significantly more uncomfortable in the British case than they are elsewhere.'[93] By early March, Community discontent at Britain's stance on domestic agriculture had been translated into an unwillingness even to discuss the issue. During one of the preparatory meetings of the Six, Bernard Clappier, the chairman of the deputies' committee between January and March, commented that the basic problem was that the British could not bring themselves to trust the mechanisms of the CAP. This made discussion fruitless. As a result, Clappier argued, the gap between the two sides was only likely to be bridged once Britain had grown more accustomed to the ways of the Community.[94] Debate about the likely impact of the CAP on British domestic agriculture was thus pushed down the agenda and all but ignored in the early phases of the negotiation. This lack of urgency, however, denoted total disagreement rather than insignificance. The issue would return to haunt the negotiators in the final stages of the British membership bid.

The European Free Trade Association

The third group for whom Heath requested special treatment were Britain's six partners in the European Free Trade Association (EFTA). Denmark, Norway, Sweden, Switzerland, Austria and Portugal were all in the process of reviewing their own relations with the Community, the Lord Privy Seal explained, and it would be some time before the most appropriate way in which Britain's ties to its free trade area

[92] CMA. RU/M/13/62. Annex IV.
[93] 'Je dois dire franchement que, du côté des Six, nous apercevons mal les raisons particulières qui feraient que ces adaptations qui – je le reconnais – sont de toute façon douloureuses et difficiles, seraient sensiblement plus malaisées dans le cas britannique que dans le cas des autres pays.' My translation. CMA. RU/M/13/62. Annex III.
[94] ECHA. S/01566/62, Report No. 10 on the 11th deputies' meeting (7/8.3.1962), BDT 145/88, No. 245.

partners could be preserved would emerge. Some of the EFTA countries might accompany the British in applying to join the Community;
others were likely to opt for association. Regardless of the choice made,
however, the British could not abandon the rest of EFTA.[95] To underline this point Heath quoted the communiqué issued by EFTA leaders
after their Council meeting in London in June 1961: '[Britain and
Denmark promised to maintain the Association] until satisfactory
arrangements have been worked out . . . to meet the various legitimate
interests of all members of EFTA, and thus enable them all to
participate from the same date in an integrated European market.'[96]
Britain, in other words, was not prepared to allow any form of tariff to
be placed on its trade with the EFTA members, whatever the outcome
of the various negotiations between the Six and the Seven.

The Six reacted with dismay to this British stance. Hallstein, in
particular, warned the UK against assuming that the outcome of
negotiations with the Seven would necessarily be 'an integrated
European market'. Association, the Commission President explained,
was a very flexible term which might involve the removal of all tariffs,
but it was unwise to base British policy on this assumption.[97] And it
was not even certain that all of the members of EFTA would be able to
become associates of the Community. Sweden, Switzerland and
Austria were all neutral states, a fact that gave partisans of a strongly
integrated Europe with a distinctive political orientation serious
qualms about any close relationship. Spaak, for instance, publicly
admitted to having grave doubts about associate membership for
neutral states as this might constitute 'an obstacle to the political
development of a United Europe'.[98] Other senior European statesmen
disagreed: Ludwig Erhard, the German Minister for Economic Affairs
and Deputy Chancellor, told Heath that 'the political aims of the EEC
were still too vague for the Six to be justified in excluding neutrals
from a wider association'.[99] Nevertheless, with clear indications that
the French, the United States and the Commission, not to mention Jean
Monnet's influential network of 'Europeans', all shared Spaak's point
of view there was a genuine risk that the association negotiations –

[95] Lieber, *British Politics*, pp. 190–1.   [96] Cmnd 1565, p. 16.
[97] CMA. 07.151. Réunion ministérielle de la Conférence entre les états membres de la
CEE et le Royaume-Uni, tenue à Bruxelles les 8/9 novembre 1961. Discours
prononcés. RU/M/3/61.
[98] 'Une entrave au développement politique d'une Europe Unie', *Le Monde* 27.1.1962.
[99] PRO. PREM 11 3561; Record of a meeting between Heath and Erhard, 9.10.1961.

not due to begin in any case until the talks with the British had reached an advanced stage – would be complex, lengthy and not guaranteed to end in success.[100] Tied by the London pledge, the British thus risked having the whole timetable of their entry into the Community put at risk by the unpredictable nature of talks between the Six and the UK's Nordic, Alpine and Portuguese partners.

Two external influences

The three problems described above were expected to form the heart of the Brussels negotiations. Apart from the discussion of some of the institutional implications of enlargement – something which was only anticipated in the latter stages of the negotiations – few other topics were likely to feature formally on the Brussels agenda. A chapter describing the issues at stake in the negotiations between the British and the Six would not be complete, however, without a brief reference to two other negotiations which, while proceeding totally independently, could not but affect and be affected by the progress of the British membership application. These were the attempt by the Kennedy administration to start a sweeping liberalisation of world trade and, geographically somewhat closer, the discussions among the Six about the establishment of a political union.

President Kennedy's desire to reduce tariff barriers was signalled at a press conference in November 1961.[101] From the outset, the President stressed that his foremost aim was to guarantee US access to the markets of the EEC:

> One third of our trade is in Western Europe and if the United States should be denied that market we will either find a flight of capital from this country to construct factories within that wall, or we will find ourselves in serious economic trouble . . . the people of this country must realise that the Common Market is going to present us with major economic challenges and, I hope, opportunities.[102]

The overt linkage of the campaign with developments in Europe

[100] *The Economist* 19.8.1961; *Débats de l'Assemblée Parlementaire Européenne 1961–2*, vol. II, pp. 93–6; PRO. CAB 134/1546, CMN(SC)(61)9, 10.11.1961; *Foreign Relations of the United States*, pp. 40–2; George Ball, *The Past Has Another Pattern*, (New York: Norton, 1982) pp. 218–20.

[101] The most recent examination of Kennedy's motives is in Winand, *Eisenhower*, pp. 168–88.

[102] Cited in John W. Evans, *The Kennedy Round in American Trade Policy* (Harvard University Press, 1971), p. 140. The linkage between Community enlargement and

continued in the New Year when the US administration presented its new trade legislation to Congress. Amongst the arguments presented by Kennedy to Congress was that the US President needed the power to carry out the same type of wide-ranging tariff cuts that the countries of Europe had employed while building the Common Market. Only in this way could the forces of competition allow new patterns of trade.[103] Still more striking was the way in which the text of the bill was designed to reap maximum benefits from EEC enlargement. In addition to a general authorisation to cut US tariffs by 50 per cent, the White House also sought permission to negotiate with the EEC a zero rate tariff for those products of which more than 80 per cent of the total world trade was supplied by the EEC and the US.[104] If Britain did join the EEC, this so-called 'dominant supplier' clause would enable the US and the Community to eliminate tariff protection on a wide range of items.[105] In the absence of Community enlargement, by contrast, EFTA production would be sufficiently high to ensure that, of the original list of product categories likely to be affected, only aircraft would fall within the terms of the legislative proposal.[106] The most radical section of Kennedy's trade plans was thus highly dependent upon the success of the Brussels negotiations.

European reactions to Kennedy's vision had been mixed. Predictably perhaps, Erhard, a long-standing campaigner for freer trade, announced that Germany was fully in favour of the proposed tariff cuts. Likewise the Dutch responded in a positive fashion, while the Commission – to whom the task of negotiating most of the tariff reductions would fall – was generally enthusiastic.[107] But on the part of the Commission, at least, there was a note of caution underlying the general welcome. Hallstein, while visiting the United States, questioned the feasibility of totally eliminating tariffs on a large number of products without a range of common rules and Robert Marjolin, a Vice-President of the Commission, expressed a certain amount of unhappiness at the dominant supplier clause.[108] The French meanwhile were still more reserved. Valéry Giscard d'Estaing, the Minister

the need for greater trade liberalisation was apparent as early as August 1961; see *Foreign Relations of the United States*, pp. 37–8.

[103] Evans, *The Kennedy Round*, p. 143.   [104] *Ibid.*, p. 142.

[105] Robert Kleiman, *Atlantic Crisis: American Diplomacy Confronts a Resurgent Europe* (London: Sidgwick and Jackson, 1965), p. 122.

[106] Evans, *The Kennedy Round*, p. 155.   [107] *Le Monde* 13.4.1962.

[108] *Le Monde* 13.4.1962; FO371 164776; M641/30, COMLEE(62)6, 22.1.1962; Monnet was also unhappy: see Winand, *Eisenhower*, p. 185.

of Finance, expressed some support for Kennedy's ideas, but used a speech to the American Club in Paris to emphasise the continued importance of the CET in preserving the unity of the EEC. Giscard also set out the French view that total free trade was not possible without some form of common economic organisation.[109] From a British point of view, however, these general reactions to the planned American legislation mattered less than the way in which the prospect of a new round of world tariff negotiations affected the Community's behaviour in the membership talks. For there was a real and alarming possibility that some of the Six might use the forthcoming Kennedy negotiations both as an additional reason not to grant special discriminatory terms to the Commonwealth – something which would anger the Americans – and as a justification for short-term rigidity over tariff levels in anticipation of the transatlantic bargaining that lay ahead.

The drive towards political union and Britain's membership bid were entangled in at least two important ways. First, as discussed in chapter 1, the prospect of a political Europe appearing alongside the European Economic Community had been an important factor in convincing Macmillan and the rest of the British government that separation from the Six was no longer in Britain's national interests. Even before the UK had decided to join the Community, Macmillan had demonstrated his concern by writing to de Gaulle and suggesting that Britain could be involved in some way with the political union negotiations, if the Six so desired.[110] Second, several of the Six reacted to these signs of British interest by pressing for the UK to be invited to play a full part in the discussions. Joseph Luns, the Dutch Foreign Minister, for instance, used the 'Little Summit' of the Six in February 1961 to insist that plans for a political union along the lines suggested by de Gaulle and Adenauer should only go ahead if the British were allowed to participate.[111]

This Dutch argument – soon dubbed *le préalable anglais* – reflected Benelux dissatisfaction with political union on the intergovernmental lines envisaged by the French. Such an arrangement, the Dutch and Belgians feared, would too easily be dominated by the bigger European powers, and in particular by the French and the Germans. It

---

[109] *Le Monde* 31.3.1961.

[110] PRO. FO371 158171; M615/27, Macmillan to de Gaulle, 7.2.1961.

[111] Miriam Camps, *Britain and the European Community 1955–1963* (Oxford University Press, 1964), pp. 328–9.

would thus become acceptable only if this Franco-German dominance could be balanced by the inclusion of another major power – Britain. UK participation would also reinforce the Atlantic orientation of Western Europe. Belgium, the Netherlands and Italy feared that, under French leadership, a political Europe might be tempted to seek an autonomous position, somewhere in between the two superpowers. With the Atlanticist British included, however, a scenario of this type was inconceivable.[112] The fact that British membership of a political union would render still more distant the prospects of a supranational political community of the type advocated by Belgium and Holland was recognised, but this postponement of long-term ambitions was accepted as a necessary price for medium-term stability.[113]

Britain's potential contribution to a European political union was also something which Macmillan chose to stress in his summit meetings with de Gaulle. The vital encounters of Champs and Rambouillet during which this tactic featured prominently will be discussed in later chapters. Nevertheless, as early as the Birch Grove meeting in November 1961, Macmillan had started to use the prospect of close Franco-British cooperation at the heart of a politically united Europe as a prize which might tempt the General from his frosty aloofness. Thus on 24 November the British Prime Minister assured de Gaulle that Britain fully shared the French preference for state-based cooperation on political matters and that he personally felt the Fouchet Plan to be 'a very good idea in its broad terms'.[114] Then the next day Macmillan went further, speaking of the danger that Europe might never unite unless France and Britain together assumed the leadership of the continent and hinting that the two countries might cooperate particularly closely in the field of defence: 'Europe could be organised in concentric circles. There could be a political and military core around which there would be an economic organisation.'[115] The French President's response was non-committal.[116]

---

[112] Bernard Bouwman, 'The British Dimension of Dutch European Policy (1950–1963)', D.Phil. thesis, Oxford (1993), pp. 222 ff.

[113] The best attempt to explain the contradiction which lay at the heart of the Benelux thesis was made by Spaak in an interview with *Opera Mundi* in April 1962. Reprinted in *Le Monde* 11.5.1962.

[114] PRO. PREM 11 3561; Record of a conversation at Birch Grove, 24.11.1961.

[115] PRO. PREM 11 3561; Record of a conversation at Birch Grove, 25.11.1961.

[116] The use and impact of this tactic by Macmillan is looked at in more detail in N. Piers Ludlow, 'Le paradoxe anglais: Britain and Political Union', *Revue d'Allemagne*, 2 (1997).

The debate about British participation in the political union negotiations and Macmillan's musings to de Gaulle brought out into the open some of the more fundamental arguments for and against British involvement in the integration process. It thus illustrated the way in which the technical issues about Commonwealth trade or British farmers discussed above were flanked by vital questions about Europe's future political organisation and its international alignment. But, paradoxically, such issues were marginalised in Brussels. The conditional nature of the British application, with its emphasis on the obstacles which had to be overcome before the British could decide to join, meant that the agenda for the negotiations between the British and the EEC member states was dominated by technical questions. As a result, political judgement, of the sort which might have been required had the British needed simply an affirmative or negative reply to their application, was postponed by the innumerable economic and commercial issues which had been raised in Heath's speech in Paris. It was possible, of course, that most of these preliminary matters, however complex, would eventually be cleared away, and the fundamental political choice between a Community of Six or an enlarged EEC confronted. At such a point, the British would be able to count upon a great deal of goodwill and a widespread view that the inclusion of Britain could only strengthen the existing Community. The enormous agenda to be covered before such a moment was reached, however, was likely severely to tax even those among the Six who were well disposed towards British membership and to provide ample opportunity for procrastination and obstructiveness by those less eager to see Community membership grow.

4 Learning to advance: the search for a fruitful method

January–July 1962

> Bill Gorell Barnes
> Spins the colonies yarns
> About how AOT-dom
> Is better than freedom [1]

The opening months of 1962 were a frustrating period for most of those involved in the British membership negotiations. In both the UK and on the continent, it had been confidently expected that once the lengthy CAP negotiations amongst the Six were successfully concluded – something which was accomplished in the second week of January 1962 – the pace of advance in the enlargement discussions would rapidly increase. Heath, for instance, told the press on 12 January that 'during these next few months we shall see negotiation greatly speeded up, and there will be a faster tempo in Brussels'.[2] But despite the widespread political desire to see Britain enter the Community, neither the Lord Privy Seal's prediction nor the many other, similar statements made by both British and EEC negotiators were borne out in practice. Throughout the winter and early spring of 1962 there was little substantive progress and few indications that faster advance was close at hand. The first part of this chapter is hence dominated by the search for an effective way of negotiating in Brussels. It will start by examining the way in which several of the member states pressed for a change in both the method

---

[1] The first of several poems written by members of the British delegation to wile away the hours while the Six struggled to reach internal agreement. William Gorell Barnes was a representative of the Colonial Office, and as such his tasks included persuading soon-to-be-independent countries of Africa that they should associate with the Community. With thanks to Peter Pooley.

[2] *Financial Times* 13.1.1962.

and the spirit of the negotiations, go on to look at the abortive search for an Anglo-French political solution, and then explain how a change of policy in London finally cleared the way for the first agreements of the 1961–3 negotiations.

A change of method?

As the sixth ministerial meeting of the British membership negotiations, scheduled for 8–9 May, approached, the atmosphere in Brussels was gloomy.[3] Nine months after Britain's desire to open talks with the Six had been announced, and six months into the negotiations themselves, both sides had set out their respective views in some detail, but no genuine bargaining had yet taken place. Indeed, the most tangible product of negotiations hitherto – the progress report compiled by the Committee of Deputies, which had been completed on 12 April – only underlined just how much remained to be done. On at least six of the eight major issues identified by the report, the British and the Six were separated not merely by technical differences but also by disagreement over fundamental principles.[4] The section dealing with British domestic agriculture, for instance, revealed that while the Six questioned whether British farmers needed any special provisions at all, the British government harboured clear misgivings about large portions of the newly agreed CAP.[5]

The widespread impatience and frustration resulting from this lack of progress was accentuated by at least two outside factors. One was the announcement by Macmillan that Commonwealth Prime Ministers would assemble in London in September to discuss the terms agreed between Britain and the Community.[6] This provided the negotiators with a clear deadline: unless a second Commonwealth conference was to be convened – something which the British were keen to avoid – at least the outlines of a settlement had to be established by the end of the summer. The other, potentially still more serious, factor was the breakdown in Paris of the political union discussions. It was widely rumoured that de Gaulle had been angered by Heath's speech to the WEU in April, interpreting the Lord Privy Seal's professed readiness to participate in the political union

[3] *Guardian* 11.5.1962.
[4] CMA. 07.15. Rapport sur l'état des négociations: texte définitif. RU/S/59/62. 12.4.1962.
[5] CMA. RU/S/59/62, pp. 34–40.   [6] *The Economist* 28.4.1961.

discussions as a veiled demand that the British be included.[7] Heath's speech, the French President allegedly felt, had triggered the Belgian and Dutch objections which had doomed the project.[8] It was thus feared that the French might retaliate by stalling in Brussels. But even if this did not happen, any deterioration of intra-Community relations seemed bound to be an additional obstacle to rapid progress towards British membership. As a senior Italian official explained to Heath in late April: 'If the Six remained in deadlock on the political front, gloom and disillusionment would spread and the climate would not be conducive to successful negotiations with [the British] in Brussels.'[9]

The sterility of discussions led several of the delegations openly to discuss ways in which a faster and more productive negotiating tempo could be assured. Numerous options and variations were pointed to, most falling into one of three broad categories. First and most radical were suggestions that the negotiating procedure, so arduously agreed upon the previous autumn, should be reassessed. Predictably, the member states most enthusiastic about procedural change were Belgium and the Netherlands – the principal losers in the September–December discussions – but there were also indications that the Germans would support a change of approach. In early January, Pierre Forthomme, the Belgian representative on the Committee of Deputies, had treated his five colleagues to an impassioned call for change. Not only did he suggest a radical transformation of the spirit in which the negotiations were conducted – these talks were not, he pointed out, a GATT negotiation in which every concession had to be accompanied by a corresponding gain – but he also proposed that the Six should strive less hard to maintain a common position. Such unity could only be ensured at the cost of much enforced silence on the part of the Six. Forthomme therefore suggested

---

[7] Dixon refers to these rumours in the Paris Embassy's history of the application. PRO. FO371 171449; M1092/129, Dixon to Home, 18.2.1963. The full text of Heath's speech was published as *European Political Union. Text of a statement by the Lord Privy Seal, the Right Honourable Edward Heath, MBE, MP, to the Ministerial Council of Western European Union in London on April 10, 1962* (HMSO: Cmnd 1720, May 1962).

[8] Couve de Murville also clearly suspected British sabotage, asking of Heath's speech: 'Etait-ce simple maladresse, prise de position à l'intention d'un Parlement réticent et susceptible, ou manoeuvre visant à peser sur les rapports entre les Six?' *Une politique étrangère, 1958–1969* (Paris: Plon, 1971), p. 374.

[9] PRO. FO371 164782; M641/153, Record of a conversation at the Ministry of Foreign Affairs in Rome, 26.4.1962; see also FO371 164781; M641/126, Delmar 61, Roll to FO, 13.4.1962.

that some of the EEC member states adopting a softer line towards the British should act as honest brokers between the applicant and the more rigid EEC partners. Two months later Paul-Henri Spaak, the Belgian Foreign Minister, was equally heretical, telling Heath that the only way forward was for the seven – in other words the Six and the British – to draw up a joint paper setting out 'the political options on all main points'.[10] This would have constituted a clear departure from the bilateral type of negotiation used hitherto.

The Dutch and Germans by contrast preferred to suggest more gradual change. As early as January 1962, Baron van Ittersum, the leader of the Dutch delegation at official level, had written to Bernard Clappier, his French opposite number and from January until March the chairman of the Committee of Deputies, suggesting a number of limited reforms. These included the drawing up of a list of priorities and the setting of a more detailed timetable. Van Ittersum implied that these innovations might rid the deputies of their tendency to steer clear of the 'big problems'.[11] Günther Harkort, the German deputy, took a similar line, arguing that the setting of interim deadlines plus the use of informal deputies' meetings might break the deadlock.[12]

Alongside suggestions that the negotiators should actually alter their method of work were calls, some of which were British inspired, for longer and more frequent meetings.[13] To a certain extent this reflected the belief that longer meetings would in themselves be beneficial. In April, for instance, Jan de Pous, the Dutch Minister of Economic Affairs, called for a marathon meeting at the end of June, arguing that this was the only means of instilling a degree of urgency into the negotiations.[14] But the frequent disputes over the conference timetable also indicated a deeper division among the conference participants between the British, Dutch, Belgians and Germans who felt that the British membership application deserved priority treatment, and the French, the Italians and the Commission officials who were determined to press ahead simultaneously with all other Com-

[10] PRO. FO371 164779; M641/83, COMLEE(62)30; Record of a conversation between the Lord Privy Seal and Spaak in Brussels, 8.3.1962.
[11] PRO. FO371 164776; M641/31, Delmar 11(62), Barclay to FO, 25.1.1962.
[12] PRO. FO371 164776; M641/40, Delmar 13(62), Barclay to FO, 25.1.1962.
[13] For a clear example of British impatience see PRO. FO371 164782; M641/146, CODEL 141, Dixon to FO, 3.5.1962.
[14] PRO. FO371 164781; M641/133, Noble to Barclay, 12.4.1962.

munity business.[15] Given the relatively small number of national officials qualified to handle Community affairs, the two positions were clearly incompatible.

A third method by which it was hoped that the British negotiations could be speeded up was to devise complicated package solutions. The Commission, the Germans and the Dutch all tried to circumvent lengthy bargaining over each concession to the British by drawing up draft agreements which, ideally, would contain enough of interest to each member state to secure general consent.[16] The limitations of this approach were revealed, however, when the package under preparation in Bonn fell foul of the long-standing rift between the *Auswärtiges Amt* and the Ministry of Economic Affairs.[17] If it proved impossible to satisfy the conflicting ambitions of two German government departments, it seemed unrealistic to hope that a package acceptable to all of the Six could be put together. None of the packages ever progressed as far as the negotiating table.[18]

Frustration at the lack of progress reached a climax at the sixth ministerial meeting, held three days later than planned, on 11–12 May, in Brussels.[19] The very fact that Spaak chose to attend rather than to send his usual stand-in, Henri Fayat, was an indication that the Belgians at least hoped that the meeting would break the deadlock. And the Belgian and Dutch behaviour in the meeting, particularly during the preparatory discussions held by the Six, confirmed this intention. The importance of the meeting, however, lies less in the substance of the Benelux case – passionate though this was – than in the way in which the pressure for change was overcome by a coalition of the Italians and the Commission.

---

[15] The deputies' meetings of 27.4.1962 and 3.5.1962 contain good examples of such disputes. See PRO. FO371 164782; M641/145, CODEL 140, 3.5.1962; or ECHA. S/02692/62, Report on the 18th meeting of deputies; BDT 145/88, No. 245.

[16] PRO. FO371 164783; M641/163, Delmar 63, Roll to FO, 28.4.1962; M641/167, Delmar 69, Roll to FO, 4.5.1962; FO371 164785; M641/217, Delmar 82, Robinson minute, 31.5.1962.

[17] PRO. FO371 164785; M641/217, Delmar 82, Robinson minute, 31.5.1962, notes the slow progress of the German package. Two weeks later it was decided to shelve the attempt, officially because the time was not ripe. FO371 164785; M641/237, Delmar 86, Robinson minute, 15.6.1962.

[18] The idea of a package deal stayed alive long enough, however, seriously to worry the French. In early May, Wormser urged his colleagues to 'tuer dans l'oeuf ces initiatives'. MAE. Série DE–CE 1961–6, Bte. 517, Wormser note, 8.5.1962.

[19] The postponement was the result of a political crisis in Italy. *The Times* 7.5.1962.

Emilio Colombo, the Italian Industry Minister, chairing the preparatory meeting of the Six for the first time since assuming the Presidency of the negotiations a month earlier, sought to pre-empt criticism by suggesting a limited number of reforms. First of Colombo's proposals was that more expert working groups be formed, so as to reduce the excessive workload of the Committee of Deputies. Second, the conference should adopt the end of July 1962 as a deadline, by which the overall shape of the final deal – or *vue d'ensemble* – had to be agreed. Third, and necessary in order to make this target date realistic, extra ministerial meetings should be scheduled for June and July.[20]

Such minor changes were insufficient to satisfy Luns and Spaak. Instead, the two Benelux ministers called for a fundamental alteration in the way in which the negotiations were handled. For Luns, this would involve the drawing up by the Six of a list of concessions which the Community should be prepared to make in order to facilitate British membership – a suggestion which was greeted with horror by Hallstein in particular.[21] Spaak was even more radical. Reacting angrily to an attempt by Colombo to steer the discussion away from high principle and towards the more mundane issue of the CET level on a list of twenty-one Commonwealth products, the Belgian Foreign Minister asked his colleagues whether they were really prepared to spend an hour debating customs tariffs when there were fundamental decisions which needed to be taken. The key question which the conference had to address, he argued, was how to devise a formula which could meet both British and Community requirements about Commonwealth trade – and such an overall aim would not be furthered by the discussion of twenty-one minor products. Once the general political principles had been decided, the experts could be given explicit instructions and then be left to devise the appropriate technical solutions. But general political decisions had to precede detailed technical discussions, not vice versa.[22]

The Italians, however, were not prepared to see the technical agenda of the meeting replaced by a general political discussion. In the first instance it was Attilio Cattani – Secretary-General of the Farnesina and with Colombo in the chair the most senior spokesman for Italy – who countered Spaak, persuading the Belgians and Dutch that to launch a debate about the fundamental principles at stake in

[20] ECHA. BDT 145/80, S/03057/62, Report No.19 on the 6th ministerial session (11–12 May).
[21] *Ibid.*   [22] *Ibid.*

the enlargement negotiations would be to waste rather than to save valuable time. This allowed the Six to press on with their discussion of substance and to agree on the common position necessary to confront the British.[23] Then, after the UK delegation had been invited to join the meeting, Colombo once more set out his very limited suggestions for change, ignoring both a series of pointed remarks by Heath about the need for greater flexibility on both sides and a British suggestion that it might help matters if both ministers and deputies were sometimes allowed to discuss matters without committing themselves.[24] The sixth ministerial meeting thus ended with remarkably little having been changed. The pressure for procedural reform had been temporarily thwarted.

Champs: a missed opportunity?

One possible – and far-reaching – alternative to procedural change in Brussels was for Britain to by-pass the Community-level discussions altogether and seek a high-level political agreement with France, the country which was generally felt to be least enthusiastic about UK membership. As a result, many observers reacted to the impasse of the March–April 1962 negotiations by turning their gaze towards the forthcoming Anglo-French summit, planned for the beginning of June. In early May, for instance, Baron Samuel van Tuyll, Secretary-General of the Dutch Foreign Ministry, assured the British Ambassador in the Hague that the technical problems associated with British membership were, of themselves, little obstacle. 'Given a political decision to reach agreement', the experts in Brussels could solve all the difficulties 'in a matter of weeks'. The French, however, were unlikely to permit such a development before de Gaulle and Macmillan met at the Château de Champs in June.[25] Only a summit meeting, in other words, could unblock the negotiations. Such hopes gathered force when the press began to carry stories that Macmillan would arrive in France bearing rather more than messages of goodwill. The Prime Minister, press reports in both London and Paris suggested, was ready to propose that once the membership negotiations were successfully

---

[23] *Ibid.*
[24] CMA. 07.51. Compte rendu de la 6ème session ministérielle entre les états membres des communautés et le Royaume-Uni, tenue les 11/12 mai 1962. RU/M/20/62.
[25] PRO. FO371 164782; M641/156, Tel. No. 228, Noble to FO, 7.5.1962.

completed, Britain and France might cooperate in the formation of a joint nuclear strike-force.[26]

There were solid grounds for these rumours. Macmillan had long believed that French acquiescence in British Community membership could be secured by an Anglo-French nuclear deal.[27] In 1961, however, he had been unable to test this belief due to American opposition to the French nuclear programme.[28] A year later, the British Prime Minister no longer felt it possible to respect this American veto. Only two days after receiving a message from President Kennedy which reaffirmed American dislike of any Anglo-French cooperation on nuclear matters, Macmillan treated Jean Chauvel, the outgoing French Ambassador in London, to a long and rambling discourse about the circumstances in which France and Britain could 'reach an understanding with a view to making the nuclear armament'.[29] Three weeks later he spoke in very similar terms to Geoffroy de Courcel, Chauvel's replacement, suggesting that Britain and France might jointly act as nuclear trustees for the whole of NATO.[30]

These two conversations appear to have caused considerable excitement in Paris.[31] Indeed Clappier warned Eric Roll, the deputy leader of the British delegation at official level, that the prospect of a nuclear deal might totally distract the British and French leaders from the more pressing problems being confronted in Brussels.[32] But de Gaulle himself appeared to be unimpressed by Macmillan's suggestions. On 22 May the French President told the British Ambassador in Paris that there could be no question of pooling British and French nuclear efforts, firstly as the British were in no position to do so without

---

[26] *Financial Times* 3.5.1962.

[27] Wolfram Kaiser, 'To Join or not to Join: The Appeasement Policy of Britain's first EEC Application' in Brian Brivati and Harriet Jones (eds.), *From Reconstruction to Integration: Britain and Europe since 1945* (Leicester University Press, 1993), pp. 150–1; the background to Macmillan's ideas and the American constraints on British nuclear cooperation with the French are extensively discussed in Ian Clark, *Nuclear Diplomacy and the Special Relationship. Britain's Deterrent and America, 1957–1962* (Oxford: Clarendon Press, 1994), esp. pp. 317–24.

[28] PRO. PREM 11 3311; Kennedy to Macmillan, 8.5.1961.

[29] PRO. PREM 11 3712; Ormsby-Gore to Macmillan, 17.5.1962; PREM 11 3792; French record of the conversation, 19.4.1962; no British record exists.

[30] PRO. PREM 11 3775; Record of a conversation between Macmillan and de Courcel, 9.5.1962.

[31] PRO. PREM 11 3712; Zuckerman to Watkinson, 25.5.1962; PREM 11 3775; Roll to Lee, 18.5.1962.

[32] PRO. PREM 11 3775; Roll to Lee, 18.5.1962.

express American permission, and secondly because France had to have its own, totally independent nuclear deterrent. Nothing else would guarantee French and European security or give France the status of a genuine world power.[33] On the eve of his meeting with de Gaulle, Macmillan seems thus to have once more shied away from a nuclear bargain with the French.[34]

Both the press at the time and subsequent academic literature on the first British application have perceived the Champs meeting as a success.[35] No dramatic breakthrough was made by de Gaulle and Macmillan, but a positive signal was sent to the Brussels negotiators, clearing the way for the fruitful discussions of June and July.[36] This view seems at odds with both the British and the French records of the encounter.[37] At Champs, Macmillan was able to set out the British case for membership much more effectively than he had done seven months earlier when he and the French leader had met at Birch Grove. He did not succeed, however, in persuading the French President that Britain was yet able to join the EEC without seriously undermining the organisation's European character. As a result, there is nothing to suggest that the instructions of French negotiators in Brussels underwent any substantial change nor that the two leaders were able to take the kind of 'political decision' in favour of enlargement which van Tuyll and many others awaited.

Macmillan and de Gaulle did briefly talk about agriculture. They did so, moreover, with a frankness often absent in Brussels. De Gaulle admitted that once the Community was fully established it might no longer import any temperate zone products and Macmillan conceded

---

[33] PRO. PREM 11 3775; Dixon to FO, Tel. No. 188 Savings, 22.5.1962.

[34] The illusions upon which the idea of a nuclear deal was based are explored in Wolfram Kaiser, 'The Bomb and Europe. Britain, France and the EEC Entry Negotiations (1961–1963)', *Journal of European Integration History*, 1:1 (1995).

[35] *Le Monde* 7.6.1962; Nora Beloff, *The General Says No* (London: Penguin, 1963), p. 133; Robert Kleiman, *Atlantic Crisis: American Diplomacy Confronts a Resurgent Europe* (New York: Norton, 1964), pp. 68–70; Constantine Pagedas, 'Troubled Partners: Anglo-American Diplomacy and the French Problem, 1960–1963' (PhD thesis, King's College, University of London, 1996), pp. 273–7.

[36] Miriam Camps, *Britain and the European Community 1955–1963* (London: Oxford University Press, 1964), pp. 398 and 428–9 and John Young, 'Britain and the EEC, 1956–1973: An Overview' in Brivati and Jones, *From Reconstruction to Integration*, p. 106.

[37] Details from the British record follow. The French record is not yet officially open, but both Françoise de La Serre and Maurice Vaïsse, who have been allowed to see it, confirm that it provides scant grounds for optimism.

that Commonwealth producers might have to be content with higher prices for a lower volume of imports. In addition each leader explained why their respective farming populations were so sensitive about change. But the technical issues debated so extensively in Brussels appeared of secondary importance at Champs; the dominant theme of the discussions was Britain's readiness to become fully European.[38]

Macmillan set the tone by stating, according to the French record, that 'Kipling's England is dead'.[39] Philip de Zulueta, the British minute taker, summarised the Prime Minister's words more prosaically but the thrust was identical: 'The younger generation felt much more European than the older people who had been brought up in the days of Kipling with the idea that their work in the world lay inside the British Empire. Now this was no longer the case and the European idea gave the young people an ideal to work for.'[40] The French President remained sceptical. After a brief outline of his hopes for some type of political union between France, Germany and perhaps Italy, de Gaulle went on:

> Now the suggestion was that the Common Market should be enlarged; this was perhaps conceivable but Britain was not quite in the same position as the Continental countries; she was not quite so menaced by the Russians. It was perhaps true that in reality the Channel was not much of a protection but it made a psychological difference to the people of Britain. Then again Britain was much more open to world influences than Europe and saw things differently from people on the Continent. Finally, there was the British liaison with the United States. This was naturally close because of a common language, common habits and joint engagements. Britain could join the Community but it would then become a different sort of organisation. Of course, Britain would bring considerable economic, political and military strength and would make the Community a larger reality but it would also change everything. That was why France had to look at this matter carefully.[41]

[38] PRO. PREM 11 3775; Record of a conversation at the Château de Champs, 2–3.6.1962.

[39] 'L'Angleterre de Kipling est morte.' My translation. Cited by M. Vaïsse in a paper delivered to a Cambridge Centre for International Studies/European University Institute conference on 'Breakdown in Brussels', St John's College Cambridge, 30.6–2.7.1993. The phrase is also used in Couve de Murville's account of the meeting, *Une politique étrangère*, p. 403, and in that by Alain Peyrefitte, *C'était de Gaulle* (Paris: Fayard, 1995), p. 302.

[40] PRO. PREM 11 3775; Record of a conversation at the Château de Champs, 2–3.6.1962.

[41] *Ibid.*

Macmillan responded vigorously, using every possible occasion to assure the General that Britain was ready to be European. He pointed to past mistakes caused by the lack of harmony between France and Britain – both world wars, he claimed, could have been averted had the two powers cooperated – and suggested that the Soviet Union would be the main beneficiary if the two once more failed to unite. The danger of British isolationism if the membership bid failed was also invoked, and the long-term importance of the special relationship with the United States was played down. And in a clear attempt to exploit de Gaulle's disappointment at the failure of the Fouchet negotiations, the Prime Minister suggested that the consensus on political issues which had proved so elusive among the Six might be easier to attain once the British had joined the Community.[42]

More radical still was Macmillan's readiness to contemplate Britain's military contribution to a united Europe. As argued above, this did not amount to a specific offer of Anglo-French nuclear cooperation in the short term. Nevertheless, Macmillan was prepared to amplify the comments he had first made at Birch Grove about the development of a genuine security dimension of European cooperation: 'There might be a European organisation allied to the United States. There would be a plan for the defence of Europe. The nuclear power of the European countries would be held as part of this European defence.'[43] With the advent of 'a solid European organisation', the Atlantic Alliance, Macmillan predicted, could become one based on an equal relationship between the United States and Europe.[44]

For all its vagueness, such speculation was a major departure from Britain's traditional Atlanticism and de Gaulle was obviously impressed. But, as the French record of the meeting makes clear, it was not yet enough. Summing up his tête-à-tête discussions with Macmillan for the benefit of Pompidou and Couve de Murville who joined the discussions on Sunday 3 June, de Gaulle explained:

> Overall you have shown us that you have evolved greatly and that you now understand how it would be in your interest to build Europe. But you are not yet ready to do this, since you remain attached to the world beyond Europe and because the idea of choosing between Europe and America is not yet ripe in your heart ... Great Britain is coming towards Europe, but it has not yet arrived. [45]

---

[42] *Ibid.* [43] *Ibid.* [44] *Ibid.*
[45] 'Au total vous nous faites l'effet d'avoir beaucoup évolué et de comprendre l'intérêt

Despite all Macmillan's efforts, there was no significant change in the French stance as a result of the Champs meeting.[46] No political decision had been taken and the hopes of all those in favour of British EEC membership had once more to focus on the hard grind of negotiation in Brussels.

A change of approach

Fortunately for the partisans of early British membership, the prospects of success in Brussels had been substantially increased by a little-noticed, but highly significant change in British policy. Over a month before Champs and days before the heated sixth ministerial meeting described above, the UK delegation to the Brussels negotiations had submitted revised position papers on three key issues to the Committee of Deputies. The full significance of this move may not have been realised immediately – hence the tension at the ministerial meeting itself – but this British flexibility signalled a new willingness on the part of the UK government to abandon its starting position and move towards the stance agreed upon among the Six. Over the following two months this decision was to transform the pace of the negotiations. Why this was so requires some additional explanation.

The fundamental problem confronting the British membership bid up until May 1962 was that the positions adopted by the two sides were too distant for real negotiation to be possible. Although both the British and the Six had set out their case in much more detail than had been possible in October 1961, their attitudes remained essentially unchanged since the Paris meeting. For the British, a large number of permanent exceptions to, if not changes of, the Treaty of Rome and the Community *acquis* remained the object; for the Six, any such special

que vous auriez à faire l'Europe. Mais vous n'êtes pas encore sur le point de la faire parce que vous demeurez encore attachés au monde extra-européen et parce que l'idée de choisir entre l'Europe et l'Amérique n'est pas encore mûre dans votre esprit . . . La Grande Bretagne est en train de venir à l'Europe mais n'y est pas encore venue.' My translation. Cited in Françoise de La Serre, 'De Gaulle et la candidature britannique aux communautés européennes' in Institut Charles de Gaulle, *De Gaulle en son siècle* (Paris: Plon, 1992), vol. V, p. 194.

[46] Peyrefitte's account of de Gaulle's comments to French ministers shortly after Champs confirms that while the President had been impressed by Macmillan's determination he did not feel that Britain had yet proved its readiness for Europe. As he claimed to have put it to the British Prime Minister, 'il faut que vous évoluiez encore'. Peyrefitte, *C'était de Gaulle*, pp. 299–303.

cases had to be limited in number, scope and duration. As a result, the British and the Six had spent the early ministerial meetings preaching at each other with much eloquence and conviction but with few concrete results. Until one or the other side moved, progress of any type would be hard while the rapid advance necessary to meet the July deadline was absolutely impossible.

In an unguarded moment during his visit to Canada in May, Macmillan is alleged to have commented somewhat bitterly that if the Six 'want us in, they will have to make it easy for us'.[47] And certainly it was hard for the British to do too much of the running. There were many in the Commonwealth as in the Conservative Party who had felt that Heath's Paris speech had given away too much to the Six before the negotiations had even begun. It was thus politically difficult for the British to abandon their opening position without either being forced to move or obtaining something tangible in return. Moreover, there seems also to have been a feeling, exemplified by Macmillan's remark, that Britain, having taken the courageous decision to apply to the EEC, could now legitimately wait until the Six translated their warm words of welcome into concessions in Brussels. Such hopes, however, while reinforced by the repeated promises of help from the Dutch and Belgians in particular, ignored the even stronger reasons for inflexibility on the part of the Six.[48]

Part of the problem was that some of the Six did not believe that it was the Community's responsibility to move first. As applicants to the EEC, it was the British who were clearly the *demandeurs* and as such the side most called upon to be flexible.[49] The EEC member states thus had only to bide their time until the would-be member summoned up the courage to accept the rules and treaties of the Community. But still more important than the belief that the Six should not make concessions too early were two factors that all but ensured that the Six could not be flexible before the British had narrowed the gap between the two sides. First, the opening stance of the Six was solidly grounded on the *acquis communautaire*, a set of agreements which themselves represented the fruits of lengthy and often arduous

---

[47] *Financial Times* 3.5.1962.
[48] For one such Belgian promise see PRO. FO371 158293; M634/515, Tel. No. 369, Nicholls to FO, 9.10.1961.
[49] For some of the attempts to persuade the British that they should move first, see PRO. FO371 164782; M641/153, Record of a conversation at the Ministry of Industry, 26.4.1962; or FO371 164781; M641/130, Statham to Gallagher, 5.4.1962.

previous negotiations. To depart radically from this was to risk reopening painful controversies among the Community member states. Any attempt, for example, to accede even partially to the British request that the CET level for lead be set at zero was likely to destroy the fragile truce which had temporarily been reached between France, Germany and Italy, who felt that their lead-processing industries required protection, and the importers of the metal, especially the Netherlands, who were already uneasy with the level of tariffs. Compromise with the British could thus only be obtained once the UK moderated its requests and sought only small-scale modifications to the *acquis*. Secondly, and still more crucially, the Six had among their number at least one country, France, which if not yet overtly opposed to British membership was already clearly unenthusiastic, and several other member states unwilling to precipitate an internal crisis by isolating the French. As a result unilateral concessions to the British of the type suggested by Luns in the course of the sixth ministerial meeting stood no chance whatsoever of being accepted unanimously. And without unanimity, the Six had decided, there could be no discussion with the British.[50]

An unnamed member of the Dutch delegation explained matters concisely to the British press:

> Because Britain is anxious to become a member of the Community as soon as possible it is for them to make far more radical proposals than they put forward. We, the Six, can hardly make proposals at this stage because all our decisions must be unanimous and there are one or two members who are not entirely enthusiastic about British membership.[51]

By mid-May when this comment was made, however, the message had already got through.[52] Abandoning the earlier hope that the creation of a crisis atmosphere would alone be sufficient to end the obstinacy of the Six, the British accepted that they would have to take the initiative.[53] The first sign that this was being done came in late April with the submission of a new position paper on the continuation of the British agricultural annual reviews under the CAP, but a still

[50] See Chapter 2.   [51] *Guardian* 14.5.1962.

[52] The clearest FO acceptance of this reality is in PRO. FO371 164784; M641/190, COMLEE(62)71, Barclay minute, 15.5.1962. British actions suggest that the lesson had in fact been learnt rather earlier.

[53] For the idea of trying to create a sense of crisis see PRO. FO371 164781; M641/121G, FO Review of Negotiating Strategy and Objectives, 12.4.1962.

more important advance was made on the eve of the sixth ministerial meeting when the British stance on both manufactured products from the developed Commonwealth and temperate zone foodstuffs was substantially altered.[54] It is on the practical progress made possible by these British concessions which the next section can concentrate.

The first successes

The most significant British change of position was over manufactured products from Australia, Canada and New Zealand. Instead of asking that these products retain their free entry into the British market, the United Kingdom accepted that the CET would have to be phased in gradually. In addition, the British declared themselves ready to see the tariff fully applied by 1970, when the Community's own transition period was due to come to an end. All that now divided the two sides on this issue was the exact speed at which the CET should come into force (and in particular the date at which the first tranche of the tariff should be applied), the number of products to which the tariff *décalage* should apply and the British insistence that a series of regular meetings be held between the Community and the three former Dominions to review the impact of the changes.[55]

To the consternation of all of his colleagues and the Italian Presidency in particular, Couve de Murville chose to object strongly to this last British request during the sixth ministerial meeting. Roberto Ducci, the chairman of the deputies' committee, briefed the ministers of the Six on the new British line on 11 May, in the obvious expectation that the ministers would rapidly agree upon a constructive counter-offer. The French, however, had other plans. Adopting a tactic which was to become very familiar over the following months, Couve de Murville insisted that the issue raised a fundamental point of principle. To agree to consult with the Commonwealth during the transitional period would set a dangerous precedent by implying that the date of 1970 by which the CET would have to apply fully was open to negotiation. Community generosity on this – an issue which Couve de Murville admitted was of little economic importance or complexity –

[54] *Agence Europe* 10.5.1962; CMA. 07.515. 19ème réunion des suppléants des ministres tenue les 9/10 mai; Aide-Mémoire à l'attention de M. le Président du Comité des Suppléants, 11.5.1962.
[55] CMA. 07.515. 19ème réunion des suppléants des ministres tenue les 9/10 mai; Aide-Mémoire à l'attention de M. le Président du Comité des Suppléants, 11.5.1962.

would undermine subsequent attempts by the Six to uphold the CET on other, more sensitive, imports.[56]

The attempt to link this fairly minor decision with later, more significant issues worked in the short term. Aware that with Couve de Murville taking this line agreement was impossible, Spaak suggested that discussions of this be postponed to a later meeting. Similarly, the Belgian Foreign Minister wisely dissuaded Heath from dwelling for too long on this issue when the British rejoined the discussions.[57] But the very stridency of Couve de Murville's tone revealed an unprecedented defensiveness on the part of the French. No longer able to dismiss the British position as unreasonable, the French representatives had to struggle harder to defend their own inflexible line. The new strident arguments of the French delegation should thus be seen as a somewhat desperate bid to conceal the new weakness of the French position, rather than a significant threat to future progress.

In the weeks that followed the sixth ministerial meeting, the fragility of the French line became progressively more apparent. Commonwealth manufactures were not discussed when the deputies met on 16–18 May, but the following week the Six put together a counter-proposal with surprising rapidity. Admittedly, the French did not lift their objection to a fixed consultation procedure with the Commonwealth. In their new offer the Six could do no more than point to the EEC's commitment both to reciprocal tariff reductions on industrial products and to the harmonious development of world trade, and argue that taken together these pledges amounted to a promise to consult with all major trading partners including the Commonwealth. Nevertheless, by allowing the gap between the two sides on the other two contentious issues – the timetable of tariff rises and the number of products to be included in this category – to be narrowed still further, the French increased their own isolation and vulnerability.[58]

The breakthrough was made at the seventh ministerial meeting on 29–30 May. Even before the meeting had officially opened, Couve de Murville softened his position; in the preparatory meeting of the Six

---

[56] ECHA. S/03057/62, Report No. 19 on the 6th ministerial meeting (11/12 May); BDT 145/88, No. 245.

[57] CMA. 07.51. Compte rendu de la 6ème session ministérielle entre les états membres des communautés et le Royaume-Uni, tenue les 11/12 mai 1962. RU/M/20/62.

[58] ECHA. S/03194/62, Report No. 21 on the 21st deputies' meeting (23/24/25 May); BDT 145/88, No. 245.

he continued to warn against anything which undermined the 1970 deadline or which committed the Six to a continuous negotiation with the Commonwealth, but he accepted that some form of consultation could take place.[59] This, coupled with the British decision to concede that the first 30 per cent of the CET should be applied to Commonwealth industrial products as soon as Britain entered the EEC, paved the way to the first agreement of the British membership negotiations.[60] It took a few hours – and, according to Heath, a successful Anglo-French lunch – for the final details to be sorted out.[61] Nevertheless, the French knew that they had been outmanoeuvred on this issue and that continued resistance would be of little use. They therefore abandoned their rearguard action with 'good grace'.[62]

Laying the foundations of the *vue d'ensemble*

This first success had a highly beneficial effect on the atmosphere of the negotiations. Over the next two months other agreements would follow, leading Hallstein to refer retrospectively to the summer of 1962 as 'the most fruitful phase' of the negotiations.[63] But in amongst such advances lay issues on which deadlock persisted, or on which progress proved halting and inadequate. The pages which follow thus cover a period in which a great deal was accomplished, but which was nevertheless marked by growing tension and urgency as the planned August marathon meeting approached.

One area in which much headway was made was the discussion of what customs regime to apply to British imports from India, Pakistan and Ceylon. This was an issue on which the Six were sensitive to Britain's insistence that the Indian sub-continent should not suffer commercially from Britain's decision to join the EEC and were inclined to be generous. In early May, for instance, Jean-François Deniau, the chief Commission negotiator at official level, acknowledged that the British case was 'philosophically' good.[64] As a result,

---

[59] ECHA. S/03376/62, Report No. 22 on the 7th ministerial meeting (28/29/30 May); BDT 145/88, No. 245.

[60] CMA. 07.51. Compte rendu de la 7ème session ministérielle entre les états membres de la CEE et le Royaume-Uni, tenue les 29/30 mai 1962. RU/M/24/62.

[61] PRO. FO371 164785; M641/209, CODEL 194, Heath to FO, 29.5.1962.

[62] *Ibid.*

[63] *Débats de l'Assemblée Parlementaire Européenne 1962–3*, vol. II, pp. 25–66.

[64] PRO. FO371 164783; M641/167, Delmar 69, Roll to FO, 4.5.1962.

debate on the issue was low-key, despite very active lobbying by both the Indian and Pakistani governments and the European textile industries. Ministers rarely intervened, preferring to entrust the matter almost entirely to the Committee of Deputies and a working group of experts. It was at this level that steady if unspectacular progress was made.

The first breakthrough was achieved in late May when the British accepted that at least some of the CET would have to apply to textiles imported from India and Pakistan.[65] This did not please the Indians – K. B. Lall, the Indian Ambassador to the Community, expressed immediate disappointment[66] – but it allowed the start of a constructive discussion about tariff levels rather than the vague debate about how the British market might be isolated, which had characterised previous discussions.[67] This was followed by the agreement in mid-June that the enlarged Community should declare itself ready to review its whole commercial policy towards the sub-continent and negotiate a comprehensive trade agreement with the region. There were also indications that the Six were ready to abolish their tariff on tea – another central element in the British package.[68] A week later further progress was made, with the acceptance by the Six of a mechanism which would allow remedial action to be taken should the gradual imposition of the CET on Indian textiles lead to a fall in sales.[69] There then followed a hiatus during which the Indian Minister of Finance toured Europe, pressing in vain for greater concessions. Nevertheless, as the tenth ministerial meeting approached, the elements of a final deal were all but in place.

There was rather more heat in discussions among the Six about which Commonwealth countries should be allowed to become Community associates. During the 11–12 May ministerial meeting, for instance, the Six had an animated debate among themselves both about the costs of accepting new associates – something which was of particular concern to the Germans and Belgians – and about the political problems posed by Nkrumah's Ghana. Couve de Murville had been the most promi-

---

[65] *Agence Europe* 25.5 and 2.6.1962.   [66] *Agence Europe* 1.6.1962.
[67] ECHA. S/02439/62, Report No. 16 on the 16th deputies' meeting (11/12 April); BDT 145/88, No. 245.
[68] *Agence Europe* 14.6.1962.
[69] ECHA. S/03895/62, Report No. 25 on the 24th deputies' meeting (20/21/22 June); BDT 145/88, No. 245.

nent in voicing this second anxiety.[70] In addition, the Six were worried about how to balance the need to reach some form of accommodation for the African and West Indian members of the Commonwealth with their separate commitment to conclude a new association convention with the African states already associated with the Community. The value of the new convention to the existing associates, at least as far as trade preference was concerned, would clearly depend upon how many former British colonies were included within the EEC's preferential zone.[71]

These problems, combined with the clear moral obligation of the Community to do something for the African and West Indian members of the Commonwealth, led some delegates to toy with emergency solutions. The Belgians, for example, tabled the Forthomme Plan – named after the most senior official in their delegation – which suggested creating, temporarily at least, a second EEC preferential zone in Africa reserved for Commonwealth members. In time the two zones could be merged.[72] By late June, however, the Six, encouraged by the progress of negotiations on the new association convention, had reverted to the original idea of simply adding Commonwealth members to the existing arrangement. This was made easier by the decision taken during a meeting of the EEC Council of Ministers on 20–21 June not to include in the new convention a clause giving current associates the right to veto new associates, a move which greatly lessened fears that hostility between former French and British colonies might undermine any agreement reached. A few difficulties remained, notably on the way in which independent countries such as Kenya could be invited to apply for association without destroying the EEC's right to take a final decision on each applicant.[73] There was also controversy about how long the offer of association should remain open.[74] As with the problems of the Indian

[70] ECHA. S/03057/62, Report No. 19 on the 6th ministerial meeting (11/12 May); BDT 145/88, No. 245.
[71] Deniau's description of the dilemma facing the EEC is in ECHA. S/01978/62, Report No. 14 on the 14th deputies' meeting (27/28/29 March); BDT 145/88, No. 245.
[72] PRO. CAB 134/1512; Common Market Negotiating Committee, 11th meeting, 19.6.1962.
[73] CMA. 07.51. Compte rendu de la 8ème session ministérielle entre les états membres des communautés européennes et le Royaume-Uni tenue les 28–30 juin 1962. RU/M/31/62. Draft minutes.
[74] ECHA. S/04067/62, Report No. 26 on the 8th ministerial meeting (28/29/30 June); BDT 145/88, No. 245.

sub-continent, however, the basic strength of the British case – accentuated in this instance by the lengths to which the Community had gone to accommodate the former French, Belgian and Dutch colonies – made it all but impossible for any of the Six to delay progress for long. Agreement, it was generally felt, could be reached at the vital tenth ministerial meeting, planned for the last week of July and the first few days of August.

Superficially at least the agreement reached on 20 July to imitate the British practice of conducting an annual review of farm incomes by carrying out a Community annual review was still more encouraging. So little advance had been made in the other discussions of British domestic agriculture that it was symbolically important that the ninth ministerial meeting, held in mid-July specifically to debate British agriculture, was able to close one part of the dossier. But it would be inaccurate to present the agreement as a major advance. The British suggestion of incorporating an annual review into the CAP had always been viewed favourably by the Six and had been constructively discussed among the deputies as early as April 1962.[75] That it had taken until mid-July 1962 to translate this basic consensus into an agreed text was thus a sobering reflection on the degree of mistrust on both sides. Also disturbing for the partisans of a rapid and successful conclusion of the British membership bid were the reasons for which a deal on the annual review was so long delayed.

Part of the problem was that neither the original British proposal nor subsequent revisions were compatible with the CAP or Community procedure. By placing the emphasis on national remedies to problems unearthed in each member state and by suggesting that the Community review be in essence a compilation of national reviews, the British were seen as endangering the European character of the CAP. Furthermore, the British insistence that the Commission be obliged to respond to the results of the annual review seemed a direct challenge to the concept of EEC institutional independence.[76] As Hallstein was to observe during the ninth ministerial meeting, even a watered-down version of the British proposal represented a threat to

[75] *The Times* 14.10.1961; ECHA. S/02691/62, Report No. 17 on the 17th deputies' meeting (26/27April 1962); BDT 145/88, No. 245.

[76] CMA. 07.151. Réunions du comité des suppléants tenues le 11 avril 1962. Note à l'attention de M. le Président du Comité des Suppléants: Sommaire des conclusions dégagés lors de la réunion préparatoire à 6 (26.4.1962).

'the very foundation of the Commission's existence'.[77] The Six had thus had to recast the basic British idea into a more *communautaire* form – a process which inevitably used up valuable time. In the final document, the task of putting together the annual review fell to the Commission, the decision about whether to react to any problem rested with the Commission initially and then the Council, and any remedial measures needed would be taken at Community and not at member-state level.[78]

Alongside a feeling that the British still had to be taught many of the norms of Community behaviour, went a still more worrying scepticism about the need of British farmers for Community guarantees. This had been already apparent in April, but was to peak in most dramatic fashion during the final stages of the 20 July meeting.[79] At issue was the British suggestion that EEC farmers should not simply be guaranteed a 'fair standard of living' – a phrase taken from the Treaty of Rome and thus acceptable to the Six – but also have their incomes explicitly linked with the general trend of incomes within each member state.[80] This would mean that should the income of farmers in any particular member state show signs of growing less quickly than that of other workers in the same country, the Community would immediately consider remedial measures. For the Italians, in particular, this was anathema. Colombo reduced matters to a personal level, reminding his EEC colleagues that he was the MP for Lucania – one of Italy's poorest regions. As such he could neither allow the introduction of precise criteria for judging farm incomes nor accept that the CAP should safeguard the level of farm incomes in every part of the Community. The aim of the CAP had to be an improvement of overall farm incomes and this might well entail some adjustments in income between different regions. Sicco Mansholt, the Commissioner responsible for agriculture, put matters still more vividly. In Middlesex, Mansholt explained, farmers had a standard of living which was comparable to that of a local mechanic; in Lucania

---

[77] CMA. 07.51. 9ème session ministérielle entre les états membres des communautés européennes et le Royaume-Uni, tenue le 20 juillet 1962. RU/M/47/62. Draft minutes.

[78] *Ibid.*

[79] ECHA. S/02691/62, Report No. 17 on the 17th deputies' meeting (26/27 April 1962); BDT 145/88, No. 245.

[80] CMA. 07.51. 9ème session ministérielle entre les états membres des communautés européennes et le Royaume-Uni, tenue le 20 juillet 1962. RU/M/47/62. Draft minutes.

this would not be the case for years. This being so, any attempt to link farm incomes to the local average might lead to a situation in which more Community aid was given to the farmer in Middlesex than to his much poorer counterpart in Lucania. This would not be acceptable.

The anxieties of Colombo and Mansholt were temporarily stilled when Heath agreed to drop this particular request. Nevertheless, such clear signals that some among the Six questioned the needs of British farmers, were an ill omen for the numerous other aspects of British domestic agriculture which remained to be settled.

While important for Britain, for the Commonwealth and for the Community, none of the issues discussed above matched the significance of the negotiations over temperate zone agriculture. For it was by the success or failure of Britain's negotiating efforts over agricultural imports from the former Dominions that the government was likely to be judged, both in the eyes of British domestic opinion and by the most influential Commonwealth leaders. There was thus cause for concern about the slow rate of advance during the late spring and early summer on this most crucial of issues.

In May admittedly, it had initially seemed that rapid progress might be possible. At the 22–4 May meeting of the Committee of Deputies the European Commission had presented its ideas about a possible solution. Of particular importance was the way in which the Commission plan differentiated between a transitional phase, during which Commonwealth exporters could expect to retain some privileges in the UK market, and a final phase, after 1970, when no specific measures for the Commonwealth could exist. Instead, Britain's traditional food suppliers would have to place their faith in an EEC declaration of intent. This would refer to the Community's price policy for cereals, outline the EEC's hopes for world-wide commodity agreements and point to the existence within the Treaty of Rome of mechanisms which would allow the Community to negotiate and implement any such world-wide schemes.[81]

These proposals were translated into an official Community negotiating position with remarkable speed. Barely a week after the first discussion of the Commission's ideas, at the seventh ministerial session Colombo was able to set out the most detailed Community

---

[81] ECHA. S/03194/62, Report No. 21 on the 21st deputies' meeting (22/23/24 May), BDT 145/88, No. 245.

prise de position so far on temperate zone agriculture. The Italian Minister of Industry began by rejecting the 'comparable outlets' still sought by the British; such commitments would be incompatible with the CAP, discriminate against non-Commonwealth and non-Community agricultural producers, and lessen the prospects of a global commodity agreement. He then outlined the two-stage solution as envisaged by the Community. During the transition period some special treatment of those Commonwealth imports which had hitherto enjoyed a preference in the UK market would be possible. But any privileges granted to Commonwealth exporters would diminish over time, so as to ensure that by 1970 at the latest the position of the Commonwealth producers would be indistinguishable from that of any other third country producers. Colombo accepted that the Commonwealth and many other agricultural producers would continue to be interested in the EEC market after 1970. During this second period, however, their needs would have to be met by a combination of world-wide arrangements and 'a reasonable price policy' on the part of the Community. In addition, Colombo reminded the British that from the end of Stage II of the Community's development (planned for 1966) voting on agricultural and trade policy would no longer require unanimity – a clear attempt to reassure the British that they would be able to exert a greater influence over Community policy once inside the EEC and that the French would not on their own be able to obstruct a liberal policy towards third country exports.[82] As was evident from Heath's reply to this statement, this Community plan was inadequate to meet British needs. Nevertheless, the Lord Privy Seal was among the first to acknowledge that so clear a statement of EEC thinking on the temperate zone issue was a definite advance.[83]

In the two months that followed, however, the attempt to flesh out this new approach was bedevilled by divisions both among the Six and in London. Thus, the new position paper submitted by the Six at the eighth ministerial meeting in late June was a much less comprehensive document than had been hoped. As finally presented to the British, it explained in some detail the mechanism by which cereals that had previously enjoyed preferential treatment on the British market would be given a temporary advantage over imports from the

[82] CMA. 07.51. Compte rendu de la 7ème session ministérielle entre les états membres de la CEE et le Royaume-Uni, tenue les 29/30 mai 1962. RU/M/24/62.
[83] PRO. FO371 164785; M641/209, CODEL 194, Heath to FO, 29.5.1962.

United States, Argentina or any other third country. It also indicated which commodities the Six felt were suitable for world-wide agreements.[84] But internal divisions, and in particular the very inflexible stance adopted by the French, ensured that the joint document finally agreed upon among the Six was less clear and generous than the original Commission draft had been. Omitted, for instance, was the EEC pledge to consult with the Commonwealth countries affected should the volume of exports to the Community fall significantly once the CAP system of customs levies began operation.[85] Furthermore, disagreements within the Community thwarted attempts to flesh out the suggestion that the EEC should initiate talks on world-wide arrangements for the principal temperate zone commodities. When the ministers of the Six debated this issue on 27 June, Olivier Wormser, standing in for Couve de Murville, explained French hopes that a world-wide agreement would raise prices and redirect any surplus towards the Third World, while Müller-Armack, flanked by Jan de Pous, the Dutch Economics Minister, argued that the principal aim of any world arrangement should be to safeguard existing trade patterns – aims which were not merely very different from each other but also incompatible.[86] As a result, the only text that could be agreed upon by the Six was much too vague to satisfy the British.[87] Finally and still more seriously, the tactics adopted by both Wormser and Couve de Murville during the June ministerial meeting indicated that the French intended to play upon British unhappiness about the financial provisions of the CAP agreements. These specified that from 1970 onwards levy payments on agricultural imports would belong to the Community and not to the importing member state – a system which would clearly penalise a large importer of foodstuffs such as Britain.[88] In May, Sir Pierson Dixon had outlined British unhappiness with this procedure, but had implied that the British government was aware that the Six themselves were divided on this issue and was

[84] CMA. 07.51. Compte rendu de la 8ème session ministérielle entre les états membres des communautés européennes et le Royaume-Uni tenue les 28–30 juin 1962. RU/M/ 31/62. Draft minutes. Annex II.

[85] ECHA. S/04067/62, Report No. 26 on the 8th ministerial meeting (27/28/29/30 June); BDT 145/88, No. 245.

[86] ECHA. S/04067/62, Report No. 26 on the 8th ministerial meeting (27/28/29/30 June); BDT 145/88, No. 245.

[87] Heath complained bitterly of 'the apparent inability of the Six to elaborate in more than half-hearted terms on their proposals'. *Financial Times* 29.6.1962.

[88] For a fuller explanation see chapter 3.

content to leave a final decision until after the British had joined.[89] Any French attempt to draw attention to this non-committal position, however, would undermine British tactics and force a further controversial issue on to the already crowded agenda of the tenth ministerial meeting.[90] It also endangered the somewhat fragile truce on the financial regulation that held among the Six.

The most significant progress made was over the fall-back arrangements to be used should world arrangements fail to materialise, an issue which quickly became known as 'the bridge'. The Community's first reaction to British requests for a 'bridge' was negative: not only would a special reserve solution for the Commonwealth constitute a form of 'permanent discrimination' but it would also prove an obstacle to the conclusion of world-wide agreements. The countries of the Commonwealth would be much less cooperative in any world commodity negotiations if they were allowed to feel confident that in any event they would continue to enjoy access to the Community markets.[91] By June, however, these arguments had been dropped. Under intense pressure to alter some aspect of their position, the Six held an animated discussion of the bridge, in which the Germans and the Dutch in particular pressed for a more generous Community approach. There was some French resistance to this idea, but with the Commission and the Italians siding with those in favour of change even Wormser soon had to give way. By the end of the meeting, a text which was more or less acceptable to the British had been put together. The price paid for this advance was that the Six, at French insistence, reaffirmed that any transitional measures agreed to for Commonwealth imports should taper before 1970 – a principle to which British objections had been so strong that the Dutch in particular had been eager to secure a Community rethink.[92]

---

[89] CMA. 07.515. 20ème réunion du comité des suppléants dans le cadre de la conférence avec le Royaume-Uni, tenue les 17/18 mai 1962. RU/S/74/62. Text of a statement by Sir Pierson Dixon.

[90] The French Finance Ministry had expressed immediate dissatisfaction with Dixon's statement, describing it as contradictory and unacceptable. Wormser, Clappier and the other French representatives in Brussels were thus under strict instructions to raise the issue. MAE. Série DE–CE 1961–6, Bte. 519; Note de la 3ème Sous-Direction, Direction des Finances Extérieures, Ministère des Finances, 24.4.1962.

[91] CMA. 07.51. Compte rendu de la 7ème session ministérielle entre les états membres de la CEE et le Royaume-Uni, tenue les 29/30 mai 1962. RU/M/24/62.

[92] *Agence Europe* 30.5.1962.

On the eve of the final marathon ministerial meeting of the summer much still remained to be done. The British persisted in their hope of securing a full *vue d'ensemble* by September. Despite useful progress in the preceding months on a range of issues, however, the prospects of reaching this target were increasingly slim. Rapid and complete agreement on British domestic agriculture, for instance, or on the controversial zero-tariff items was virtually unattainable. What could still be realistically hoped for was the tying up of a preliminary package, which would include arrangements for the principal Asian and African Commonwealth members plus a deal on the temperate foodstuffs so vital to Canada, Australia and New Zealand. This would provide the British with something concrete to present to the Commonwealth Prime Ministers in September and would allow Macmillan's government to point to significant progress in the Brussels negotiations. The frenetic fortnight of negotiation, which all but reached this lesser target, is the subject of the following chapter.

Already, however, certain conclusions could be drawn from the events of May, June and early July. The first, and most encouraging, was that progress could be made on the technical problems raised by British membership. Even without a clear change in their political instructions, the French could be pressurised into retreat. This was particularly true of those issues on which the British, by abandoning an excessive opening bid in favour of a much more reasonable follow-up position, had placed the onus for future advance very clearly on the Six. Equally, however, the three months of substantive negotiation had confirmed that the French would show no spontaneous generosity. Any weaknesses in the British case or still more any incompatibilities between British desiderata and the Community *acquis* would be ruthlessly exploited and turned into an opportunity to place the British requests rather than French obstinacy in dock. Although unique in the consistency of their opposition to the British, the French had proved themselves masters at rallying support; it was a rare occasion indeed, in which the French could not rely on at least partial backing from the Commission, the Italians, the Luxemburgers, or even the Germans. Finally, the three months of progress had confirmed the importance of a skilful Presidency. There is insufficient space here to examine either the numerous plaudits won by Colombo's handling of the negotiations or, still more revealingly, the unsuccessful Anglo-Dutch attempt to ensure that the Luxemburgers did not hold the post over July and August.[93] Both, however, confirm that the strange dynamics of a negotiation between a Community of Six and a powerful would-be member required a skilful lead from a chairman who was respected and trusted by all seven governments. Whether Eugène Schaus, the Luxembourg Foreign Minister who had replaced Colombo in the chair for the ninth and tenth ministerial meetings, would have the authority and tact to push the member states and applicant towards agreement would be of crucial import-ance to British hopes.

[93] PRO. FO371 164785; M641/209, CODEL 194, Heath to FO, 29.5.1962; FO371 164787; M641/246, Tel. No. 732, Heath to the Hague, 23.6.1962 and Tel. No. 280, Noble to FO, 24.6.1962; M641/248, Tel. No. 20, Aldington to FO, 25.6.1962.

5   A race against the clock: the tenth ministerial meeting
July–August 1962

> Sir Eric Roll
> Delivered an address to stir the soul
> But the Deputies of the Six
> Said 'nix'

As the tenth ministerial meeting, planned for late July, approached, the British gave no sign of having abandoned their hopes of completing a *vue d'ensemble*. Indeed almost every contact with the Six was used to stress the importance of wide-ranging progress in late July and early August. On 25 July, for instance, a letter from Macmillan to Konrad Adenauer, the German Chancellor, centred upon the need for haste:

> My main concern is that we should all agree that time is of the essence, that we must bring the negotiation to a clear issue so that it is possible for my Government to see whether the elements exist for a settlement which we can commend to the Commonwealth and to our own people.[1]

The final decision for or against membership, Macmillan explained, could only be taken in the light of the Commonwealth Prime Ministers' conference, due to take place in mid-September. As a result, the key elements of Britain's membership terms had to be concluded during the final ministerial meeting before the Commonwealth leaders met: 'I am convinced that if no clarity can be obtained on these terms by August, we shall all be in serious trouble. A great opportunity will have been missed and I would not like to say how soon it would be possible to repair the damage.'[2] Heath was equally adamant

---

[1] PRO. FO371 164791; M641/325G, Macmillan to Adenauer, 25.7.1962.
[2] *Ibid.*

138

that substantial progress had to be made in late July and early August, moving energetically to deny rumours that the British would actually prefer to confront the Commonwealth Prime Ministers without being bound by even a preliminary agreement.[3] And like Macmillan, the Lord Privy Seal deliberately chose to stress the serious consequences of delay; on 26 July Heath told the Belgian Foreign Minister, Paul-Henri Spaak, that 'those who thought that the negotiations should be allowed to drag on now and be resumed with more energy in the autumn were grossly underestimating the effect which the absence of a clear *vue d'ensemble* would have on the Commonwealth Prime Ministers' meeting and on British opinion'.[4]

This urgency appeared to have been recognised among the Six. Eugène Schaus, the President of the Conference in July and August, stated that the Six would be ready to work late into several nights, if necessary, to complete the *vue d'ensemble* before the summer's end.[5] Spaak followed suit, agreeing with Heath that a quick advance was essential; his deputy, Henri Fayat, went still further, declaring to journalists that the British and continental negotiators were 'condemned to agree'.[6] Adenauer, while more cautious, wrote to Macmillan of his hope that the negotiations would proceed 'as rapidly as the numerous difficult questions which are still open allow' and his former protégé Walter Hallstein, now the President of the European Commission, stated publicly his belief that the target which the British had set could be attained.[7] Even in France, *Le Monde* recognised the importance of what it termed 'a European race against the clock'.[8] Recognition that agreement was important, did not, however, lead the Six to accept British requests that meetings continue deep into the

[3] PRO. FO371 164791; M641/321, COMLEE (62) 100, Record of a conversation between the Lord Privy Seal and Dr Mende, 19.7.1962; M641/322, COMLEE (62) 99, Record of the Lord Privy Seal's conversations in Luxembourg, 16–17.7.1962. The British believed that such rumours originated in Hallstein's entourage; in fact, as will be discussed in the next chapter, they are more likely to have been attributable to Adenauer.

[4] PRO. FO371 164791; M641/333, Delmar 121, Conversation between the Lord Privy Seal and Spaak, 26.7.1962.

[5] PRO. FO371 164791; M641/322, Record of the Lord Privy Seal's conversations in Luxembourg, 16–17.7.1962.

[6] PRO. FO371 164791; M641/333, Delmar 121, Record of a conversation between the Lord Privy Seal and Spaak, 26.7.1962; *Financial Times* 2.8.1962.

[7] PRO. FO371 164791; M641/325G, Adenauer to Macmillan, 3.8.1962; *Le Monde* 22–23.7.1962.

[8] 'Une course européenne contre la montre'. My translation. *Le Monde* 26.7.1962.

August holiday season.[9] In order to be ready for the Commonwealth Prime Ministers, the *vue d'ensemble* thus had to be completed during the tenth ministerial session, planned for 25–7 July, but widely expected to spill over into the first week of August.

The scale of the task which the British had set themselves and the Six was demonstrated by the breadth of the agenda for this crucial meeting. The central prize was a deal on Commonwealth agriculture – the core of any outline agreement to be put before the Commonwealth Prime Ministers – but, at the insistence of the British, ministers were also scheduled to discuss arrangements for African and West Indian Commonwealth countries, for the Indian sub-continent and for British farmers. In addition, an effort would be made to end the impasse over the CET levels to be set for aluminium, lead, zinc and many of the other so-called zero-tariff items. This was a dangerous but quite deliberate ploy. By seeking agreement on so many issues simultaneously, the British hoped not only to be able to present a near complete package to the Commonwealth in September; they also sought to maximise their gains at a time when the pressure on the Six would be at its highest. The risk of course was that by seeking too much the British would see the negotiations adjourn for the summer break without any of the most valuable agreements secured.

Initial success

The first tangible fruit of this British strategy was the virtual completion of the package of measures designed to protect Indian, Pakistani and Ceylonese exports to Britain. As noted in the previous chapter, imports from the Indian sub-continent had not been the object of great controversy among the Six. By mid-July, Schaus and Heath had identified the Indian dossier as one area in which a settlement could quickly be reached.[10] And so it proved. On 2 August, the Six agreed to lower the CET rate for tea to zero – a move which at a stroke removed the principal threat to the exports of Ceylon – and a day later, after an unsuccessful last-ditch effort by Heath to improve the transitional arrangements offered by the Six, both sides initialled a joint text covering most other aspects of trade between Europe and the Indian

---

[9] PRO. FO371 164785; M641/226, Barclay to France, 8.6.1962.
[10] PRO. FO371 164791; M641/322, Record of the Lord Privy Seal's conversations in Luxembourg, 16–17.7.1962.

sub-continent.[11] Only the tariff levels to be applied to an assortment of tropical products, plus those on a handful of special manufactured goods, remained to be decided.

At the heart of the agreed package lay a promise by the Six that the enlarged Community would seek to negotiate a comprehensive trade agreement with India, Pakistan and Ceylon by 1966. The details of such an agreement would naturally be subject to negotiation between the Community and the countries concerned, but the Six undertook in advance to conclude arrangements which would 'develop mutual trade' and maintain or, if possible, increase the level of foreign currency receipts of the three developing countries. In addition, the Six raised the possibility that the trade agreement would contain provisions for financial and technical assistance. The second main element of the agreement was the staggered introduction of the CET on British imports from the sub-continent. For textiles, the most important category of goods affected, the Six had at the Commission's suggestion added provisions designed to avoid too rapid a fall or rise of imports from the region. It was thus agreed that should the volume of textiles from India and Pakistan arriving in Britain drop significantly, the Commission would first seek Council approval for remedial measures and then, if the Council failed to act, authorise Britain to take action unilaterally to halt and reverse the reduction of imports. The counterpart to this guarantee was, however, the inclusion of a safeguard clause designed to protect the Six from 'market disturbance', a euphemism for a flood of cheap Indian imports entering the Community via Britain.[12]

Viewed in its entirety, the package did, as Heath had conceded, give India, Pakistan and Ceylon 'a firm and far-reaching guarantee'.[13] Admittedly, it did not meet Indian hopes of preserving, if not improving upon, the status quo. Indeed, the very idea of the CET being applied to any Indian exports caused great dismay in Delhi. The deal was as generous as was possible, however, given both the great symbolic importance which every one of the Six attached to the imposition of the common tariff to all British imports except those from Community member states or associates, and the intense

---

[11] CMA. 07.51. Compte rendu du 10ème session ministérielle entre les états membres de la Communauté et le Royaume-Uni, tenue à Bruxelles les 24–27 juillet et les 1–5 août. RU/M/45/62 (Part 2); Draft minutes of the 10th ministerial session. The text of the agreement is in Annex X.
[12] CMA. RU/M/45/62 (part 2), Annex X.   [13] CMA. RU/M/45/62 (part 2).

lobbying by the European textile industry. It confirmed, moreover, that the Six were prepared to show considerably more sympathy and understanding towards developing members of the Commonwealth, than towards Australia, Canada and New Zealand. Not only was the rate at which the CET was to be phased in for exports from the subcontinent much slower than the rate agreed for manufactured products from the developed Commonwealth, but the Six had also accepted a mechanism which would counter a significant fall in Indian sales to the UK. British and Commonwealth requests that a similar device be adopted for Australian, Canadian or New Zealand manufactures had been categorically refused in April. Finally, it should be noted that this agreement had only become possible once Hong Kong, which had originally been grouped together with India, Pakistan and Ceylon, had been hived off to a separate category. This ended any prospect of the suspicion with which the Six regarded Hong Kong being tempered by their evident goodwill towards the Indian sub-continent.

The second breakthrough of the tenth ministerial session concerned the association of a range of Commonwealth countries and territories to the EEC. Here too ministers were able to build upon a substantial degree of consensus; indeed, by 2 August when the issue was discussed, the principal substantive questions which remained were connected to a small number of 'problem' countries and territories. These included Aden, which was problematical because of its large oil refineries, the so-called High Commission Territories (small British dependencies land-locked by, and sharing a customs union with, the Republic of South Africa) and two European colonies, Gibraltar and Malta. Once it had been decided to postpone discussion of these territories to the autumn, a joint text covering the less problematical members of the Commonwealth was quickly completed.[14]

For the majority of Britain's dependencies, the settlement reached was extremely straightforward: as soon as Britain entered the EEC, most of her dependencies would become associate members under Part IV of the Treaty of Rome – the set of arrangements originally designed to meet the needs of French colonies. The position of independent Commonwealth countries was somewhat more compli-

---

[14] CMA. RU/M/45/62 (part 2); the final details were sorted out in restricted session. No minutes were kept.

cated. The Six accepted that association constituted the appropriate solution in principle for the independent Commonwealth countries of Africa and the Caribbean. Formally, however, the Community member states stood by their refusal to give any applicant *a priori* guarantees that its request to associate with the Community would be accepted. To have done otherwise would have made a mockery of the Six's pledge to consult with existing associates before expanding the preferential zone. In practice, the Community's promise to 'give favourable consideration to independent countries having characteristics similar to those of present associates' meant that the rejection of any of Britain's former colonies was extremely unlikely. As a result, most of the African Commonwealth, plus the West Indies, could expect to benefit from the same combination of preferential trading arrangements and financial and technical assistance as the former French, Italian and Dutch colonies already associated with the EEC. Independent Commonwealth states in Africa and the West Indies would also have the right to participate in the new institutions planned under the association convention.

The only flaw in the arrangement was the lack of provision for Commonwealth countries in Africa which decided not to associate. As the British were all too aware Kwame Nkrumah, the Ghanaian Prime Minister, had become an outspoken critic of the association arrangements, describing them as neo-colonial. This not only made Ghanaian acceptance of the Brussels package unlikely but also threatened to dissuade several other African countries, including Kenya and Tanganyika, from applying for association.[15] There was thus every prospect of the British negotiators having to renegotiate special fall-back arrangements for a large part of former British Africa.

Discussions about two further topics, British domestic agriculture and the zero-tariff items, were distinctly less successful. On neither could the Six devise a common position, and, in its absence, negotiation with the British was impossible. Discussion of both subjects thus wasted valuable time. Such set-backs, however, would rapidly have been forgotten had the tenth ministerial session reached its central goal: an agreement covering British imports of foodstuffs from the temperate Commonwealth. It is to the lengthy, but ultimately unsuccessful, struggle to achieve this that this chapter must now turn.

[15] The problem was recognised as early as September 1961; PRO. CAB 134/1511; CMN(61)2, 4.9.1961; by June 1962, rejection of the deal by Ghana and others had become 'the main danger'. CAB 134/1512; CMN(62) 12th meeting, 26.6.1962.

The central prize

The British opened debate on this topic in dramatic style, announcing a major revision of their stance. Dropped after months of argument was the insistence that Commonwealth suppliers be granted 'comparable outlets'; in its stead Heath asked that the Six's own plan, set out most clearly by Colombo in June, should be modified and improved so as to guarantee Commonwealth exporters of food substantial access to the markets of the enlarged Community.[16] Examined carefully, this 'concession' proved less of a step towards the Six than it first appeared. As Heath admitted both to the British Cabinet and to the Six, the British aim remained constant – only the tactics had changed.[17] Nevertheless, by agreeing to negotiate on the basis of the Community's own text, the British succeeded in vastly increasing the pressure upon the Six to change their position.

The key British objectives were two alterations to the Colombo Plan. First, the British wanted the Six to agree that one of the central aims – if not the central aim – of the planned world-wide conferences on temperate foodstuffs should be to preserve the access of 'traditional suppliers' to European markets. Second, Heath asked for an improvement of the transitional arrangements applying to Commonwealth imports between British entry into the Community and the eventual conclusion of the world-wide agreements. In particular, the British hoped that the Six would drop their insistence that any privileges granted to Commonwealth exporters diminish over time. If, as the Six had suggested, Commonwealth suppliers were initially to benefit from the *abattement forfetaire* – a mechanism which was designed to give Community producers an advantage in other member state markets in the years before a common market for agricultural produce was fully established – the British felt that the Commonwealth should continue to benefit fully from this device until the end of the CAP transitional period in 1970. There could be no question of the Commonwealth's privilege being 'degressive'.[18]

On 25 July and again during the night of the 27 July, the Six were surprisingly solid in their rejection of this second British request. Only

[16] CMA. RU/M/45/62 (part 1), Annex II, Statement by the Lord Privy Seal.
[17] PRO. CAB 134/1512; CMN(62) 16th meeting, 23.7.1962; also CMA. RU/M/45/62 (part 1).
[18] CMA. RU/M/45/62 (part 1), Annex II.

Victor Marijnen, the Dutch Minister of Agriculture, argued that the transitional measures should remain unchanged until 1970; the other five ministers, plus Sicco Mansholt, the Commissioner responsible for agriculture, were adamant that any advantages given to the Common-wealth should gradually be phased out. Admittedly, several ministers, including Colombo, seemed ready to contemplate giving some ground over consultation with the Commonwealth – one of the lesser British demands. But those among the Six who felt that the Community had to soften its position if a deal on temperate foodstuffs was to be struck concentrated their attention on the core of the first British request – the issue of access.[19]

Several phrases containing the word 'access' had already been extensively discussed among the deputies. One in particular had won the support of all but the French delegation. But with the French refusing to lift their objection, the deputies had had no option other than to pass the matter on, unresolved, for ministerial discussion. At the more senior level, France was equally loath to move. Olivier Wormser, the Quai d'Orsay official who took Couve de Murville's place in the first half of the tenth ministerial meeting, stone-walled in determined fashion and managed to prevent any specific reference to access from creeping into the text. Such, however, was the pressure from the Five plus, crucially, the Commission, that the French had first to sue for time and then, following an adjournment, accept a joint Belgian and Italian compromise formula which replaced the word 'access' with 'outlets'.[20]

Two days later, the revised text having proved inadequate to meet British hopes, the French once more found themselves under sus-tained attack. This time the focus of discussion was an amendment to the Community's text tabled by the Commission which stated that the Community's price policy should seek to maintain a high level of agricultural trade between the EEC and third countries. A commit-ment of this type was totally unacceptable to Wormser: Community price policy should, the French maintained, be based on the twin

---

[19] In the absence of a Commission report on this meeting – the Commission did not meet during August, so there was nobody for Hallstein and Deniau to report to – the best public sources on the discussions among the Six are the innumerable press reports on the meeting. Of particular importance are: *Agence Europe* 25.7.–6.8.1962; *Financial Times* 26.7.–7.8.1962; *Le Monde* 26.7.–7.8.1962, 10.8.1962 and 11.8.1962; *Observer* 5.8.1962 and *Sunday Times* 5.8.1962.

[20] *Agence Europe* 26.7.1962.

objectives outlined in Articles 39 and 110 of the Treaty of Rome. These obliged the EEC to try to provide an adequate standard of living for European farmers and to work towards the harmonious development of world trade. Accepting the Commission's text would seriously compromise the necessary balance between these two important aims.[21]

These arguments were sufficient to fend off the first attack on the French position. Half an hour or so was spent on the merits and dangers of the Baumgartner or Pisani Plan – a French scheme designed to resolve the world glut of cereals by increasing the world price and redirecting the surplus production towards the starving of the Third World and an issue on which the divisions among the Six were much more complex than a simple five-to-one split. But as this debate petered out, Fayat once more focused attention on the proposed Commission amendment. This time Wormser's reaction was considerably more aggressive; the British requests, he declared, were no more than a reiteration of the UK starting bid. As such they were unacceptable and should immediately be withdrawn.[22]

French anger transformed the meeting. From Rolf Lahr, the State Secretary representing Germany, it provoked an impassioned outburst which first rejected any move which would humiliate the British and then criticised the spirit with which the Six had approached these negotiations. Britain and the Community member states were not, he reminded his colleagues, engaged in trade negotiation, in which each party could legitimately seek the maximum possible gain. Instead, the Brussels negotiations were intended to open the doors of the Community to a new member state. This meant that all the participants had a strong incentive to show goodwill towards the applicant. Similarly, de Pous, Fayat, Hallstein and Cattani all protested that the French position was too extreme. But significantly both the Commission and the Italian representatives stressed their agreement with much of what Wormser had said; their only complaint was about the final conclusion which he had drawn. This allowed Wormser a way out. Within an hour, the anger had all but disappeared from the discussion and the French official had ceased to demand a total rejection of the British requests. Instead, debate revolved around Wormser's own suggestion that the 'high level' of agricultural trade mentioned in the Commission's amendment be replaced by a 'satis-

---

[21] *Agence Europe* 27.7.1962.   [22] *Agence Europe* 28.7.1962.

factory level' – a proposal which, in the small hours of the morning, was finally accepted.[23]

The revised text was not enough to please the British. Ministers from virtually every member state, aware that the French were unlikely to allow a much better offer, implored Heath to accept the document as it stood. Hallstein claimed that the Six had made 'a real attempt to close the gap', Cattani pointed to the 'balanced structure' of the Six's offer while Spaak described the undertakings that the Six were ready to make on agricultural prices as 'a substantial promise'.[24] But these entreaties were to no avail. Complaining that the Six showed 'a reluctance to express in writing what had been said at the Conference table during the past two days', Heath made plain his dissatisfaction with the new offer.[25] It was thus amid an atmosphere of renewed crisis that the meeting was adjourned until 1 August.[26]

The crunch: part two of the tenth ministerial meeting

In the interval between the two halves of this vital ministerial meeting, there was intense discussion, both within each member state and, vitally, between the various Community delegations. Of particular importance were a series of secret meetings – reportedly instigated by Spaak – between the Benelux, German and Italian delegations at which the Five drew up a list of twelve further amendments to the EEC text on Commonwealth foodstuffs.[27] The changes included an additional reference to 'outlets' in the section outlining the scope of the proposed international conferences, a Community pledge not to seek autarchy in foodstuffs, and, perhaps most importantly, the suggestion that the transitional advantages given to Commonwealth exporters in the years following Britain's entry should only start to taper and decline from 1965. Given that the amended text also stated that the enlarged Community would do its utmost to ensure that world-wide commodity agreements were concluded by 1965 (or more geographically limited arrangements shortly thereafter), this amounted to a *de facto* promise that Commonwealth

---

[23] *Ibid.*   [24] CMA. RU/M/45/62 (part 1).   [25] *Ibid.*
[26] *The New York Times* of 28.7.1962 spoke of 'the first crisis in nine months of negotiation', while *The Times* of the same day described British circles as 'unusually pessimistic'.
[27] *Observer* 12.8.1962 and *Financial Times* 7.8.1962.

exports would enjoy the same treatment on the British market as Community produce for the whole of the period preceding the international commodity agreements. As long as the schedule envisaged by the Community for the world arrangements was adhered to, the concept of degressivity to which the British had so strongly objected would cease to be relevant.

When the Six met again on 1 August, the five member states which had devised the new changes sought to play down both the genesis and the significance of the modified text. The new proposals were tabled as 'Belgian' amendments – the product, it was claimed, of a few days of reflection. Fayat, moreover, assured his colleagues that the modifications did not affect the substance of the Community's position; they simply made the text easier to present to sceptical Commonwealth governments.[28] Neither the French nor the Commission – the two delegations not invited to the secret meeting – were taken in. Wormser and Hallstein joined forces to criticise 'Belgian' tactics, arguing that if the British disliked the latest EEC text it was up to them to put forward possible changes. Both were also sufficiently scathing about several of the individual amendments to threaten the cohesion of the Five. On several of the amendments Italian assent was withdrawn. Ironically, however, the blow which doomed the 'Belgian' amendments was delivered by Spaak himself. For it was only when the Belgian Foreign Minister lost his temper and accused Hallstein of being 'childish' that the meeting degenerated into a verbal brawl and was suspended. It was a fractious and disgruntled group of EEC ministers who met with Heath on the evening of 1 August to announce that the Community's position on temperate zone foodstuffs remained unaltered.[29]

With the Six paralysed by internal disagreements, movement could only come from London. Unfortunately, when the British did move, they overplayed their hand, thereby reducing some of the pressure on the French. On 3 August, the British proposed twenty-one new amendments: some of these were relatively innocuous textual changes, but others altered the entire philosophy of the Colombo Plan.

[28] The Belgians had tried to use bilateral contacts with the French to push the same line. On 31 July Fayat had told a French diplomat that the Six's position on temperate agriculture was 'fondamentalement juste'; all that was needed was for it to be presented 'plus agréablement' to the British. MAE. Série DE–CE 1961–6, Bte. 524; Lacoste to Quai, 31.7.1962.

[29] *Agence Europe* 1.8.1962 and 2.8.1962.

It was suggested, for instance, that market-sharing arrangements should form part of the planned world agreements, great emphasis was placed on the need to protect the interests of 'traditional suppliers of temperate foodstuffs' and the transitional measures to be applied to Commonwealth exporters in the years up to 1970 were made substantially more generous.[30] Predictably, the French were furious. Couve de Murville, who a day earlier had replaced Wormser as the principal French representative, denounced at length both the British proposals and the very idea that a solution was urgently needed. The Six, he argued, had agreed to try and reach a *vue d'ensemble* by the end of the summer, not out of any obligation, but simply as an indication of their goodwill towards the British. In so doing, however, they had had no intention of creating a situation in which the exigencies of the timetable would force the Community into accepting an unsatisfactory text. What was needed was not any agreement at the right time, but the right agreement, whenever it was ready. The British amendments, the French Foreign Minister proceeded, highlighted the huge remaining gap between the two sides – a gap which could not be bridged hurriedly without endangering both the CAP and the whole Community. For this reason, discussions with the British should be adjourned until the autumn.[31]

Confronted with the real possibility of an immediate breakdown, the reactions of France's partners were revealingly different. Lahr questioned the French contention that no agreement could be reached. Significantly, however, the German State Secretary was forced to concede that the British were still asking for the impossible and overall his attack on the French was cautious. Spaak, likewise, admitted that many of the British suggestions were unacceptable. The Belgian minister was, however, much less restrained in his criticism of the French, vehemently attacking a situation in which a minority dictated the policy of the Community. De Pous struck a similar tone to Spaak. Colombo by contrast adopted a conciliatory approach, designed not to isolate the French, but instead to reassure them that there was no danger of their being stampeded into an unsatisfactory agreement. Indeed, the main part of the Italian minister's speech concerned not the danger of irreparable disagreement between the Six

---

[30] CMA. RU/T/33/62; reprinted as an annex to RU/M/45/62 (part 2).

[31] *Agence Europe, Daily Telegraph, Guardian, Financial Times* 4.8.1962. See also Harkort's report to the *Auswärtiges Amt* about this meeting. BAK. BKA. B–136. Bd. 2561, Beitritt Großbritanniens zur EWG, FS 929 Harkort to AA, 4.8.1962.

and the British but of that among the Six. The temperate zone discussions ran the risk of highlighting serious divergences among the member states about the way in which the CAP had been negotiated and the way in which it was to be implemented. If this was allowed to happen, it would lead not merely to a delay in the membership negotiations, but also, much more seriously, to an internal Community crisis. Colombo went on to express his clear dissatisfaction with the British amendments – not just their individual shortcomings, but the continuing British desire to alter radically the whole shape of the Community's proposals – and, in an obvious bid to reassure the French, mentioned the need to clarify, once and for all, the British attitude towards the financial regulation. This approach, echoed moments later by Hallstein, who also pleaded for Community solidarity, enabled the French to abandon their earlier brinkmanship. At 8.00 p.m. on the penultimate day of the ministerial meeting, a systematic examination of the British amendments could begin.

In the early afternoon of 4 August, after discussions which had lasted until 2.00 a.m. and which had been resumed the following morning, the Six finally emerged with a new common position.[32] This new document, which signalled acceptance of a few of Britain's lesser amendments, but which left the substance of the EEC's position unaltered, represented a defeat for Lahr and de Pous – the two ministers who had most consistently argued for significant concessions to be made – and a victory not only for Couve de Murville, but also for Hallstein, Mansholt and Colombo. Fayat and Spaak, while prepared to make some movement towards the British, had also been critical of the German and Dutch approach. During the meeting, however, there had been clear signs that France apart, all member states plus the Commission were close to agreeing firstly that the promise of consultation with the Commonwealth already made about wheat could be extended to cover all cereals and secondly that a declaration should be made promising special treatment for New Zealand, the most vulnerable of the old Dominions. These tendencies were not yet reflected in the official EEC document. More disturbingly, the meeting had also made clear that neither the Italians nor the French were yet satisfied that the British had fully accepted the 14 January agreement on the financing of the CAP.[33]

The last seventeen hours of continuous discussions were frenetic –

[32] CMA. RU/M/45/62 (part 2), Annex VII.   [33] *Agence Europe* 4.8.1962.

so taxing indeed that Schaus collapsed from exhaustion and had to be replaced in the chair by Colombo.[34] In the final rush to complete an agreement both sides made important concessions. Heath accepted that transitional arrangements would have to be phased out, although a decision on the exact speed of their disappearance was postponed until the autumn. And the Six agreed to extend their promise of consultation with the Commonwealth to all cereals, rather than just those which had enjoyed a preference on the British market. In addition, the Six seemingly made a major gesture towards New Zealand, by agreeing that some special arrangement ought to be devised to address the abnormally high dependence of New Zealand's economy on agricultural exports to the United Kingdom.[35] Doubt, however, was subsequently cast on the validity of this pledge when the French claimed not to have given their consent to this statement.[36] But the prized goal of a completed *vue d'ensemble* was not attained: shortly before dawn on 5 August, after the longest continuous ministerial meeting in Community history, Colombo was obliged to postpone all further discussion to early October.[37] Macmillan would have to confront Commonwealth leaders in September without having secured a definitive arrangement for the agricultural exports so vital for Australia, Canada and New Zealand.

Virtually every minister involved in the discussions tried to stress that there had been no breakdown. Colombo claimed that a major part of the issues had been settled, Spaak denied talk of an impasse and Heath spoke of 'broad agreement' on many areas of Commonwealth concern.[38] Nevertheless, both immediate newspaper reaction and subsequent analysis have pointed to the failure to finalise the temperate zone foodstuffs deal as at best a disappointment, at worst a disaster.[39] Indeed, Sir Pierson Dixon, the leader of the British

---

[34] *New York Herald Tribune* 6.8.1962.
[35] CMA. RU/M/45/62 (part 2).
[36] Nora Beloff, *The General Says No* (London: Penguin, 1963), p. 130.
[37] *Guardian, The Times* and *New York Times* 6.8.1962; *Financial Times* and *Le Monde* 7.8.1962; *Observer* 12.8.1962.
[38] *New York Herald Tribune, New York Times* and *Guardian* 6.8.1962.
[39] According to the *Guardian* 6.8.1962: 'The Brussels negotiations have neither succeeded nor failed. They have stumbled . . .'; Beloff, *The General*, pp. 128–31 and Miriam Camps, *Britain and the European Community 1955–1963* (Oxford University Press, 1964), pp. 409–13 also see the meeting as somewhat disappointing.

negotiating team, wrote of 4–5 August: 'That was really the end of the Brussels negotiations.'[40]

According to Dixon, responsibility for the inconclusive end of the tenth ministerial session lay clearly with the French. In the early hours of 5 August, at a time at which only three minor points of disagreement separated the two sides, the French prevented a deal being struck with a blatant piece of sabotage. This took the form of demanding that the British sign, at 3.45 a.m., a text committing themselves to an interpretation of the financial regulation which would have been deeply inimical to Britain's interests. Once Heath refused, Couve de Murville placed a reserve on the entire temperate zone text, thus in effect making agreement impossible. This, Dixon claims, was a fatal blow. The talks never again achieved sufficient momentum, and with de Gaulle's domestic position vastly strengthened by the UNR's electoral triumph in November, the veto became inevitable.[41]

On close inspection, however, Dixon's claims become rather hard to accept. For a start, the financial regulation issue, brought up by the French at 3.45 a.m., was not a new point. Ever since April, the French had been stressing the vital importance of settling this as part of the temperate zone package and in the final ministerial meeting both Couve de Murville and Wormser had referred to the financial regulation with almost monotonous regularity. It is thus impossible to accept that the British were totally unprepared to confront the issue, even at so late an hour.[42] Secondly, Couve de Murville's request that Heath sign the new text on the financial regulation, while undoubtedly a source of discomfort to the British, need not be seen as a deliberate manoeuvre designed to prevent the *vue d'ensemble* being reached. Instead, the linking of a temperate foodstuffs agreement with the acceptance of an interpretation of the financial regulation which was very favourable to food exporters at the expense of food importers should be interpreted as an attempt to settle definitively a point still at issue among the Six, before the balance of the Community was altered

[40] Piers Dixon, *Double Diploma: The Life of Sir Pierson Dixon, Don and Diplomat* (London: Hutchinson, 1968), p. 292.

[41] Dixon, *Double Diploma*, pp. 288–92.

[42] That the British were aware that a document on the financial regulation was being prepared is confirmed by the British delegation's post-mortem on the negotiations. PRO. FO371 171442; M1091/542G, Draft Report on the Brussels Negotiations, 26.2.1963. Dixon, by contrast, claims that 'the first hint' that the issue would be raised came only at 6 p.m. on 4 August. *Double Diploma*, p. 290.

by enlargement – an attempt, moreover, which very nearly worked.[43] In a hurried meeting of the Six, deep in the Brussels night, the French, Italians and the Commission actually secured unanimous consent to the controversial text, so eager were Germany, Belgium and Holland to complete a deal with the British. Had Heath not held out, the food exporters of the Community would thus have won a major triumph.[44] Thirdly, Dixon overlooks the fact that the French did not act alone. The document presented to Heath at 3.45 a.m. was actually drafted by Robert Marjolin, Vice-President of the Commission, and approved by Colombo; likewise, on the morning of 4 August, it was the Italian Minister of Industry who insisted that the Six debate the matter before meeting the British once more.[45] France certainly stood to gain considerably from an acceptance of the Colombo–Marjolin text. It was not, however, engaged in a unilateral attempt to destroy the nego-tiation and clear the way for the veto five months later.

The biggest omission from Dixon's account, however, concerns British motives.[46] In Cabinet discussions in late July, several ministers had pointed to the presentational advantages of not concluding a binding *vue d'ensemble*. Thus, in the Common Market Negotiating Committee (the Cabinet Committee chaired by 'Rab' Butler which drew up the basic shape of the British negotiating position) the minutes record: 'In further discussion it was suggested that the best course might be to seek to improve the Six's proposals to the maximum possible extent during the course of the Ministerial session . . . but not to reach a provisional agreement with them except in the unlikely event of their accepting fully satisfactory safeguards.'[47] A day later the full Cabinet had discussed tactics. Once more the merits

---

[43] Correspondence between Valéry Giscard d'Estaing, the French Minister of Finance, and Couve reveals that the French were extremely worried by the support which the Germans and Dutch had appeared to give to the British case on CAP financing. The Finance Ministry was thus adamant that the issue had to be settled before enlarge-ment. MAE. Série DE–CE 1961–6, Bte. 519; Giscard to Couve, 20.7.1962.

[44] Nigel Lawson, writing in the *Sunday Telegraph* 12.8.1962, makes this point most forcefully.

[45] CMA. The Colombo–Marjolin text is reprinted as Annex VIII to RU/M/45/62 (part 2).

[46] The French immediately claimed that it was at British and not French request that the negotiations were brought to an end. They thus reacted angrily when the British White Paper about the tenth ministerial session appeared to suggest otherwise. A senior French diplomat was dispatched to see Heath to complain. MAE. Série DE–CE 1961–6, Bte.5 17; Wormser to London, 8.8.1962 and Wapler to Quai, 9.8.1962.

[47] PRO. CAB 134/1512; CMN(62) 18th meeting, 30.7.1962.

of stopping short of agreement had been aired, and while several strong counter-arguments had been put forward – in particular the detrimental effects of continued uncertainty – it had been agreed that the Brussels negotiating team should have the power to seek an adjournment of the discussions if the likely outcome was deemed insufficient.[48] In view of this conclusion, it is difficult to read the following extract from Heath's report to the Prime Minister about the tenth ministerial meeting without at least some suspicion that the British rather than the French bear most responsibility for the inconclusive end of the final night of discussion:

> a document emerged which both he [Heath] and the Commonwealth Secretary considered to contain acceptable provisions for the interests of the Commonwealth countries concerned; in accordance with their instructions, however, they had not accepted it but had explained the need for further consultation with the Commonwealth in view of the fact that the whole basis of the negotiation had been changed; they said that in this light the United Kingdom Government could not be said to have accepted the document other than as a basis for discussion with the Commonwealth.[49]

Strained unity – the Six as negotiators

Whether considered a near success or a major failure, the tenth ministerial meeting was very revealing about all of the participants in the negotiations. Under conditions of extreme pressure, the various national delegations plus the representatives of the Commission allowed many of their real priorities to emerge. The interplay among the Six was also at its most intense, with all the usual suspicion, mistrust and animosity but also the sense of solidarity and the desire for unity magnified by the importance and urgency of the occasion. Much of the remainder of this chapter is therefore devoted to an examination of the way in which the seven Community delegations behaved both individually and collectively throughout the summer's negotiations and in particular in the course of the tenth ministerial meeting.

Luxembourg, the smallest of the Community member states, played an unobtrusive role throughout much of the negotiation. Broadly in

[48] PRO. CAB 128/36 part 2; CC(62)51, 31.7.1962.
[49] PRO. CAB 134/151; CMN(62)49, 8.8.1962; Record of a meeting at Admiralty House, 6.8.1962.

favour of enlargement, the Luxembourg delegation tended to side with its more outspoken Benelux partners. On occasions, however, an unwillingness to offend its powerful western neighbour pushed Schaus and his colleagues into a more intermediate position. Little of this would have mattered had Luxembourg not occupied the chair at both official and ministerial level for the crucial months of July and August. As President, Schaus was hardly more forceful than he had been as a mere national representative. In the latter capacity, however, tentativeness damaged no one; in the former, it made it easier for the larger states, and in particular France, to dominate discussions. This was unfortunate for the British, as their prospects of success depended greatly on French obstructiveness being kept in check. One of the important unanswered questions of the Brussels negotiations is thus whether a stronger chairman (Colombo would have been the most popular choice) would have been able to steer the final summer meeting towards a more complete success.[50]

Tentativeness was not a problem suffered by the Dutch delegation. In May, the Foreign Minister Joseph Luns had called upon the Six to make concessions in order to secure British entry; throughout the spring and summer, de Pous and Marijnen at ministerial level, and Baron van Ittersum among the deputies, tried to put this suggestion into practice. Thus in June, de Pous had been the first minister among the Six to question the idea of phasing out transitional arrangements for the Commonwealth; in July, Marijnen had urged the Six to carry out the changes to the CAP regulations for eggs which the British had requested; and in August, de Pous once more had advocated the acceptance of many of the British amendments to the text on temperate zone products.

These and other Dutch views were advanced in a direct and forthright manner which undeniably made de Pous and his colleagues the most vociferous of British allies, but not necessarily the most effective.[51] On occasions, indeed, Dutch unwillingness to accept the defeat of a suggested amendment which was opposed by several of

---

[50] Although not conclusive, the way in which Colombo defied the French over New Zealand in the final hours of the tenth meeting, publicly offering the British more than had been agreed with the French, suggests that the meeting might have evolved in a different way had the Italian taken over the chair at a much earlier stage.

[51] One member of the German delegation could not conceal his admiration for Dutch strength and wished that his government would match it. PRO. FO371 164791; M641/378, Statham to Gallagher, 11.8.1962.

the Six delegations and disliked by the Commission led not only to the loss of valuable time, but also to unnecessary and counterproductive animosity among the Six. A good example of this occurred on the morning of 4 August, when the Six tried to bring to a close over eight hours of intensive debate. As soon as Schaus, the chairman, had noted with clear relief that the Six had at last reached a new common position, de Pous made a lengthy intervention suggesting that one of the first British amendments rejected the previous evening be incorporated into the text. Colombo and Fayat reacted angrily, the Italian warning de Pous not to revive an issue settled at 9.30 p.m. the night before, but their irritation was not enough to prevent Lahr, in particular, from rallying to the side of the Dutch. Further time was lost, but, predictably, the position of the Six, when discussion at last moved on to a fresh topic, had not been altered at all. Tempers all round had deteriorated further.[52]

The Belgians, especially when represented by Fayat rather than Spaak, tended to be more subtle. Their basic enthusiasm for British membership matched that of the Dutch. Furthermore, the Belgian government, like the Dutch, made no secret of its desire to see the Community adopt a relatively liberal trade policy and a CAP which did not penalise Benelux and the Germans for importing much of their food from non-European suppliers. The importance of these goals, however, did not blind the Belgians to the necessity of devising membership terms for the British that were not only acceptable in London, but also in Paris, Rome and Bonn. As a result, the Belgians became both masters of compromise – in both quantity and quality of compromise solutions advanced, the Belgians were second only to the Italians – and the most accurate and reliable source of advice for the British, a source which regrettably was under-employed. When Heath met Fayat in Brussels in mid-June, for instance, he was given the most exact and concise explanation for the French stance on temperate foodstuffs by Muller, Fayat's deputy *chef de cabinet* and a member of the Belgian delegation: 'If it were now agreed to have quantitative arrangements for the UK market – and not even for the benefit of UK farmers, but rather for those of the Commonwealth – the German government would come under strong domestic pressure to require quantitative arrangements for the German market again. The French

---

[52] *Agence Europe* 5.8.1962.

were worried by this.'[53] Information of this sort was immeasurably more valuable to the British than the endless Dutch mutterings about French ill-will.[54] The Belgians were also fortunate to have in Pierre Forthomme one of the most effective of the deputies. On subjects ranging from the problems of the African Commonwealth to the temperate zone dossier, the head of the Belgian delegation at official level was a fertile source of ideas and suggestions.[55]

The strongest counterweight among the Six to Dutch and Belgian Anglophilia was the distinctly cool French attitude towards British membership. As de Gaulle and Macmillan's discussions at Rambouillet, Birch Grove and Champs had indicated, and as the French President's January 1963 press conference would emphatically confirm, this coolness sprang largely from deep scepticism about whether Britain was ready to join the Community and, perhaps still more vitally, the fear that enlargement might prevent the organisation of Europe from proceeding in the direction sought by the French. De Gaulle might wish for a 'Europe à l'Anglaise' in that he shared Britain's traditional hostility to supranational institutions, but if Europe was to attain the independence from the United States that de Gaulle wished for, it would have to be 'sans les Anglais'.

Admitting to such sentiments was, however, highly risky at a time when so many, inside as well as outside France, were so publicly committed to Community enlargement. On 31 July, just before Couve de Murville, Wormser and Pisani returned to the Brussels fray, the French Cabinet committee for European affairs had held a detailed discussion about the negotiations with Britain. In the course of this meeting, it had become quite clear that de Gaulle was uncomfortable with the tactics that the French had pursued hitherto. The President appeared worried that the unity of the Six might not hold, that this

---

[53] PRO. FO371 164787; M641/257, COMLEE(62)84, Record of a conversation between the Lord Privy Seal and Fayat in Brussels on 22 June.

[54] These had a long history, going back at least to a comment made by Luns in March 1961 when he predicted that de Gaulle would find some means of preventing British entry 'even if it is a misplaced comma'. *Financial Times* 17.3.1961; more recent examples can be found in PRO. FO371 164782; M641/156, Tel. No. 228, Noble to FO, 7.5.1962; FO371 164783; M641/162, COMLEE(62)68, Lord Privy Seal's conversation with the Netherlands Ambassador, 3.5.1962; FO371 164787; M641/241, Delmar 85, Barclay to FO, 13.6.1962; FO371 164791; M641/335, Tel. No. 310, Carey-Foster to FO, 30.7.1962.

[55] See e.g. Forthomme's note on 'Aspect Commonwealth du Problème Agricole'. CMA. -1.823.1. Le problème des céreales traité dans le cadre de la conférence avec le Royaume-Uni.

unity was being bought at the cost of excessive French concessions and, most alarmingly of all, that Britain might be able to thwart French plans by accepting the terms offered by the Six. As the General put it, 'if the British accept all our concessions we will be most put out'.[56] But de Gaulle's ministers had been unanimous in telling their leader that no alternative strategy was possible. Giscard d'Estaing, Wormser, Clappier and Ortoli had all affirmed the undesirability of a situation in which France would be blamed for the breakdown of the negotiation; Pisani went further, underlining that the whole CAP would be placed in jeopardy. And it was left to Georges Pompidou, the Prime Minister, to pursue this line of argument to its logical conclusion, by pointing out that France could not afford to put the whole Community structure at risk:

> If the Common Market broke up, we would be, Italy apart, the greatest losers. Equally, we have an interest in the British affair not succeeding. In order to enter, Britain would have to break its ties with the Commonwealth. It would therefore be undesirable for us to take the blame for the breakdown of the negotiations. It would be better to try and let [the negotiations] run into the ground. After a while, a better solution than Britain's membership of the Community could probably be found – for instance some type of association.[57]

The meeting thus ended with a reaffirmation of existing French tactics. France would do nothing to assist the British in their attempt to enter, but equally would not overtly oppose enlargement. Instead it would use its legitimate right as a member state to defend its interests and to protect the existing Community policies and arrangements in order to slow, divert and, if possible, block the Brussels negotiations.

Fortunately for French opponents of British membership, there were a wide variety of legitimate national interests the defence of which could be employed to obstruct Britain's path. During both the

---

[56] 'Si les Britanniques acceptaient nos concessions nous en serions bien contrariés.' My translation. MAE. Série DE–CE 1961–6, Bte. 517; Compte-Rendu du Conseil sur les Affaires Européennes qui s'est tenu le mardi 31 juillet 1962 sous la présidence du Général de Gaulle, 1.8.1962.

[57] 'Si le Marché Commun éclatait, nous serions, l'Italie mise à part, les plus gros perdants. Nous avons également intérêt à ce que l'affaire anglaise n'aboutisse pas. Or, pour entrer, la Grande-Bretagne devrait rompre avec le Commonwealth. Il n'est donc pas souhaitable que nous prenions la responsabilité de la rupture de la négociation. Il vaudrait mieux tâcher de la faire se perdre dans les sables. Dans quelque temps, une solution préférable à l'entrée de la Grande-Bretagne dans le Marché Commun pourra probablement être trouvée sous la forme, par example, d'une association.' My translation. *Ibid.*

negotiation of the Treaty of Rome and the subsequent development of the EEC, France had been the dominant member state. French aspirations, priorities and special needs underpinned much of the *acquis communautaire*. Furthermore, France's strategy to modernise its economy and to transform its relations with its African empire was inextricably bound up with Community policies. As de Gaulle himself admitted to Alain Peyrefitte in June 1962, so serious were the woes of French farmers that any developments within the Community which put at risk the CAP could leave France facing 'another Algerian crisis, but on home soil'.[58] This made it almost inevitable that in any negotiation which threatened to alter the shape of the Community France would be among the most energetic defenders of the status quo. The nature of British needs only accentuated this stance. All three of the special interest groups which Macmillan had pledged to protect – EFTA members, British farmers and above all the Commonwealth – had interests which ran almost diametrically opposite to those of the French. Thus, the liberal attitude towards agricultural imports necessary to allow the continuance of Commonwealth exports was almost impossible to reconcile with French aspirations for a CAP which placed the interests of European farmers above those of non-European producers. Likewise the inclusion of African Commonwealth members into the planned association convention threatened to diminish the value of a preferential system designed primarily for former French colonies. That France drove a very hard bargain in Brussels was therefore explicable without reference to de Gaulle's fundamental beliefs. Furthermore none of the Five could question France's right to defend its interests – particularly as such a defence was often indistinguishable from the defence of a treaty system and *acquis* which all of the Six had pledged themselves to uphold.

The effectiveness of the French was further increased by the calibre of their representatives. Among the deputies, Bernard Clappier and François-Xavier Ortoli both confirmed their reputations as rigorous and effective negotiators, well able to fight the French corner without totally alienating either the British, or, more importantly from a French point of view, their Community partners. When discussions moved up to ministerial level, France was even better represented.

---

[58] 'Une autre affaire d'Algérie sur notre propre sol'. My translation. Alain Peyrefitte, *C'était de Gaulle* (Paris: Fayard, 1995), p. 302.

Olivier Wormser, although only a senior official, demonstrated an extraordinary ability to hold a difficult French negotiating position while under intense pressure from numerous more senior member state representatives.[59] He also showed himself to be an expert at the counter-attack, often using to good effect his great experience of previous international and Community negotiations. Towards the end of the heated discussions among the Six about the 'Belgian' amendments, for instance, Wormser deflected criticism of French obstinacy with a lengthy denunciation of British policy towards the Community during the 1950s. It was this, Wormser claimed, which explained the Commonwealth's reluctance to place its trust in the goodwill of the EEC. Couve de Murville was even more effective.[60] A full Foreign Minister from a major country, participating in a negotiation which most countries had entrusted to a less senior figure, Couve de Murville outranked most of his interlocutors. And yet he barely needed this advantage. The French Foreign Minister excelled in the dissection of arguments and was thus able to point out the weaknesses in both the British case and the Dutch, German or Belgian calls for concessions. He also made good use of the narrow margin of manoeuvre which his instructions allowed, linking minor French concessions to greater gains elsewhere. In the tenth ministerial meeting, for example, he successfully extracted a promise from his partners not to allow an alteration of the CET rate for coffee – an issue of importance to French West Africa – in exchange for agreeing to a zero tariff for tea – a commodity of little interest to the French. Finally, like Wormser, he made maximum use of his partners' inconsistencies. Germany's awkward attempt to balance its desire for high agricultural prices with its aspiration to provide a generous deal for the Commonwealth was a frequent target for Couve de Murville's jibes.

For all their skill and negotiating prowess, however, none of the French representatives could hold out indefinitely when deserted by all of their Community partners. To do so would be to risk the type of breakdown in the negotiations which the 31 July Cabinet committee

---

[59] Marjolin is one of many to pay tribute to Wormser's formidable negotiating skills. *Le travail d'une vie. Mémoires 1911–1986* (Paris: Robert Laffond, 1986), p. 311.

[60] Marjolin is even more fulsome in his praise of Couve de Murville, despite having held very different views on many 'European' issues. Marjolin, *Le travail*, p. 311. Still more remarkable was the praise which the French Foreign Minister received from Spaak. *Combats inachevés, de l'espoir aux déceptions* (Paris: Fayard, 1969), pp. 365–6.

had dreaded, and lead to a situation in which French interests in the Community, and possibly the very existence of the Community itself, would be endangered. It might also precipitate a domestic political crisis in France, since Pompidou's government still relied on Parliamentary support from a variety of MRP and centrist MPs whose views about European integration in general and enlargement in particular differed markedly from those of de Gaulle. The ability of the French to dictate the terms of British membership was thus highly dependent on the stance adopted by the three remaining delegations: the Germans, the Italians and the Commission. It is therefore useful to examine the behaviour and tactics of all three of these 'intermediate' delegations.

All the German officials and ministers directly involved with the Brussels negotiations were strongly in favour of British membership. Dr Günther Harkort, who combined the role of deputy with that of German permanent representative to the Community, was described by one British official as 'almost invariably the most useful of the Deputies'.[61] Similarly Rolf Lahr, Germany's principal spokesman at ministerial level, was seen as 'helpful'.[62] In this they reflected the almost unanimous support for British membership among both the German political elite and the wider German public. But the very fact that Lahr, a State Secretary, together with Professor Müller-Armack, Lahr's opposite number in the Ministry of Economic Affairs, played such a prominent role in the Brussels negotiations goes some way to explaining Germany's inability to counter the French. For, with neither Ludwig Erhard, the Minister of Economics and Deputy Chancellor, nor Gerhard Schröder, the Foreign Minister, attending regularly, Germany rarely had a representative who could hold his own with Couve de Murville. Critics of German weakness, both within Germany and in Britain, frequently pointed this out – in mid-August 1962 Erich Mende, the leader of the FDP, wrote to Adenauer about Schröder's non-attendance[63] – but apart from a couple of token visits to Brussels in June and July (during which his lack of back-

[61] PRO. FO371 164784; M641/190, COMLEE(62)71, Barclay minute, 15.5.1962.
[62] *Ibid.* Rather more direct evidence of Lahr's pro-British sentiments is provided by his clash with Adenauer in the German Cabinet meeting of 8 August 1962. BAK. BKA. B–136. Bd. 2561, Beitritt Großbritanniens zur EWG, Unkorrigiertes Manuskript aus der Kabinettsitzung, 8.8.1962.
[63] BAK. BKA. B–136. Bd. 2561, Beitritt Großbritanniens zur EWG. Mende to Adenauer, 22.8.1962.

ground knowledge made him an ineffective participant) the Foreign Minister stayed away, as did Erhard.[64]

Part of the explanation for Schröder's absence from Brussels may lie in a second, rather more important weakness in the German stance: the position of the Chancellor. Konrad Adenauer's views about British membership will be discussed in more detail in the next chapter. In order to analyse German negotiating tactics, it is sufficient to point out first that Adenauer became increasingly hostile to Community enlargement as 1962 progressed, and second, that he did not do so, as the British Ambassador in Bonn alleged, merely as a result of French pressure. Instead, the Chancellor's dislike was rooted in the belief that a strong political Europe could only be built on the basis of a Franco-German understanding – something which British membership would disrupt.[65] Given the strength of pro-British feeling in Germany as a whole, and within the CDU in particular, Adenauer was unable to translate this personal antipathy into a whole-hearted German stance against enlargement. The priorities of the Chancellor were, however, accurately reflected by the instruction given to German negotiators in Brussels not to do anything which might 'muddy the waters with the French'.[66] The ability of Lahr and Müller-Armack to go beyond general expressions of goodwill towards Britain and place real pressure on the French was decisively undermined.[67]

The Italians could also be accused of not translating their rhetorical enthusiasm for British membership into practical political support. Time and time again the interventions of Roberto Ducci at deputy level and Colombo and Cattani among the ministers lent support to the French in their stand against large-scale concessions and dissuaded the Dutch and Belgians from going too far. It was unfair, however, to attribute this behaviour merely to weakness, as did a senior British diplomat in Rome, or to suggest that, as a junior

[64] PRO. FO371 164790; M641/318, Delmar 116, Gorell Barnes to FO, 19.7.1962 and M641/320; Delmar 120, Robinson minute, 23.7.1962.
[65] Hans-Peter Schwarz, *Adenauer: Der Staatsmann, 1952–1967* (Stuttgart: Deutsche Verlags-Anstalt, 1991), pp. 747–53 and 762–9.
[66] PRO. FO371 164791; M641/378, Statham to Gallagher, 11.8.1962.
[67] One Luxembourg negotiator was quoted as saying that German representatives 'could not look the French in the eyes'. PRO. FO371 164791; M641/380, Delmar 125, Robinson minute, 10.8.1962. Despite this, Adenauer still rebuked Lahr in Cabinet for adopting a negotiating stance too close to the Dutch and insufficiently close to the French. BAK. BKA. B–136. Bd. 2561, Beitritt Großbritanniens zur EWG, Unkorrigiertes Manuskript aus der Kabinettssitzung, 8.8.1962.

member of the German delegation put it, 'the Italians . . . would follow the large battalions'.[68] For there are at least four more respectable reasons for Italian tactics.

The first was that Italian and French interests all but coincided on many of the issues being discussed in Brussels. In contrast to Germany or the Benelux countries, Italy shared many of the French fears about too rapid a reduction in the Community's external tariffs – the two countries perceived the CET both as a vital symbol of European integration and as an important practical protection for vulnerable European industries. Similarly, on agriculture Italy had much more sympathy for the French aim of a policy designed primarily to cater for European farmers than for the German, Benelux or British vision of a liberal CAP serving the needs of northern European food importers. Italy, while still in 1962 a net importer of cereals, had just under a third of its working population employed in the agricultural sector and was thought likely, with technical progress, to become a major exporter of agricultural produce.[69]

Italy's second motivation was a political desire to avoid alienating the French. From 1960 onwards, the Italians had been ardent supporters of the inconclusive attempt to create a political union and still fostered hopes of being able to restart the process. Cattani indeed had succeeded Christian Fouchet as the chairman of the intergovernmental committee designed to work towards political union. In order to progress once more, however, it was vital to avoid antagonising Paris. Moreover, by mid-1962, the Italians were also keen to dissuade both Adenauer and de Gaulle from making any move towards greater bilateral Franco-German cooperation. A political union *à deux* would marginalise the Italians, relegating them to Europe's second division alongside Belgium, the Netherlands and Luxembourg. This was to be avoided at all costs.

Third and perhaps still more important, the Italians were deeply committed to the European Community. Enlargement was to be welcomed, but only if it could be attained without in any way undermining or weakening the Community treaties, structure or *acquis*. It was thus unsurprising that the Italian delegation frequently assumed

---

[68] PRO. FO371 164791; M641/375, Laskey to Reilly, 8.10.1962 and M641/378, Statham to Gallagher, 11.8.1962.

[69] In 1960 the figure was 30.78 per cent. John Marsh and Christopher Ritson, *Agricultural Policy and the Common Market* (London: Chatham House/PEP, 1971), table VI, p. 173.

negotiating positions close to those of the other great defenders of the status quo, the French. Furthermore, the Italians were determined to prevent divisions among the Six appearing, as these might precipitate a Community crisis. As a result, Colombo and Cattani both sought to avoid situations in which a five-to-one division developed, if necessary by siding or almost siding with the French. Delay, even deadlock in the British membership negotiations, was a price worth paying in order to avert a major internal Community row. This approach was subsequently criticised within Italy.[70] Indeed, G. Frederick Reinhardt, the US Ambassador to Italy, distinguished two 'schools of thought' about British membership, with one, composed of politicians like Prime Minister Amintore Fanfani and Budget Minister Ugo La Malfa, favouring more flexibility in order to facilitate British membership. At least until August 1962, however, a second group, centred on the Farnesina but also including Emilio Colombo, prevailed, ensuring that Italian policy in Brussels was more consistently *communautaire* than Anglophile.[71]

The fourth reason for Italy's rather cautious negotiating style was purely practical. Not without reason Colombo and Cattani felt that Italy could have most influence and the negotiations overall would be best served if they acted throughout as honest brokers among the Six, trusted by both the enthusiasts for British membership and by the French.[72] And in this role they were extremely successful. Long after the Italians had officially relinquished the conference Presidency, Colombo, in particular, continued to act as a *de facto* chairman among the Six, cooling tempers, putting together compromise formulas and rebuking those delegations that threatened to break ranks. One conference participant reportedly described the Italian minister's voice as having the soothing effect of a violin – and certainly several

---

[70] A description of the policy disagreements within the Rome government, allegedly inspired by Quaroni, the Italian Ambassador in London, appeared in *The Economist* 1.12.1962.

[71] Ambassador Reinhardt's categorisations are cited in Leopoldo Nuti, 'Italy, the British Application to the EEC, and the January Debacle' in Richard Griffiths and Stuart Ward (eds.), *Courting the Common Market: The First Attempt to Enlarge the European Community 1961–1963* (London: Lothian Foundation Press, 1996), p. 108.

[72] Italian tactics in Brussels in 1961–3 appear to have been very much in line with the long-standing Italian tradition of seeking to be *il peso determinante*, i.e. not a major power in its own right, but one which by playing an intermediary role between the major powers, could have a significant effect on the final balance of power. Sergio Romano, *Guida alla politica estera italiana* (Milan: Rizzoli, 1993), pp. 65–6.

of Colombo's interventions appear to have saved tense meetings among the Six from collapsing amid total acrimony.[73] The 3 August meeting among the Six is a case in point: without Colombo's appeal for EEC solidarity and the Italian's willingness to concede that much of Couve de Murville's anger was justified, it is hard to see how the French Foreign Minister could have been coaxed away from his insistence on adjournment and back to detailed, but ultimately fruitful, negotiation.

Mediation was also the forte of the last delegation which must be examined. Less than a year before, the Commission had been a scared and depressed body, fearing total marginalisation in the forthcoming membership negotiations because of a combined French and Dutch effort to exclude the Brussels institution from any significant role. By August 1962, however, all had changed. Over the preceding months, Commission papers had formed the core of virtually all the progress made; Commission expertise, moreover, was continually called upon to explain the intricacies of the *acquis* to the would-be members and to assess the compatibility of British proposals with existing legislation. Still more impressively, two Commissioners – Hallstein and Mansholt – and one senior Commission official – Jean-François Deniau – had emerged as key actors in the negotiations, with several others – Marjolin, Caron and Rochereau to name but three – playing useful supporting parts. Far from being marginalised, the Commission was very much at the centre of the negotiation.[74]

Despite, or perhaps because of this prominence, the Commission's role was not without its critics. Hallstein, in particular, attracted ire for his rather legalistic and seemingly inflexible approach to the problems of enlargement. In addition to the clash with Spaak mentioned above, the Commission President was also accused of having a 'somewhat "theological" attitude' by Eric Roll, the deputy head of the British delegation.[75] In general, however, the alliance between the Commission and the French – a partnership likened by one delegate to that between the Pope and the Holy Roman Emperor[76] – was seen as

[73] Cited in Beloff, *The General*, p. 124.
[74] For a more detailed discussion of the Commission's contribution see N. Piers Ludlow, 'Influence and Vulnerability: The Role of the EEC Commission in the Enlargement Negotiations' in Griffiths and Ward (eds.), *Courting the Common Market*, pp. 139–55.
[75] PRO. FO371 164789; M641/281, Delmar 96, Roll to FO, 30.6.1962.
[76] Cited in Beloff, *The General*, p. 123.

legitimate, given the Commission's recognised role as the guardian of the Treaties. Moreover, the constructive side of the Commission's activities – its ability to start discussions off by submitting outline solutions, its valuable compromise suggestions and, perhaps most important of all, its role in ensuring that the Six Community member states remained united – won more general approval. In light of his earlier tussle with the Commission President, Spaak was particularly generous about this last facet of the Commission's contribution: 'The Six always ended up reaching an agreement among themselves and by presenting a common front. Subjected to a hard test, the Community "held firm" thanks, in large part, to the flexible authority of Hallstein's Commission. That at least is something positive to enter on to the balance sheet of this exhausting meeting.'[77]

Spaak's comment introduces the final topic of this chapter, namely the success – just – of the Six in maintaining a united front. As Spaak implied, this had not been easy. With such widely different hopes and expectations among its various members, the Community had not found it easy to speak with one voice and there had been, in the course of the meeting, several occasions on which one or two delegations had threatened to break the common front. That this had not happened, however, was a testament not only to the Commission's role, but also to the recognition by all of the Six that to endanger the Community was neither in their interest nor that of the British.

The first challenge to EEC solidarity during this phase of the negotiations had taken place at the very start of the tenth ministerial meeting. On 24 July the Six had sought to present the British with their unchanged position on subsidies for egg farmers – a position which Heath greeted with dismay. This had been too much for Marijnen, who, to French horror, launched into a vigorous attack on the system of consumer subsidies that lay at the heart of the Community's proposal. Wormser tried to stem the flow, but such was the discontent among several of the delegations at the French hard-line on

---

[77] 'Les Six ont toujours fini par se mettre d'accord entre eux et par présenter un front commun. Soumise à rude épreuve, la Communauté a "tenu" grâce, pour une bonne part, à la souple autorité de la commission Hallstein. C'est là un résultat qu'il convient d'inscrire au bilan de cette réunion laborieuse.' My translation. *Le Monde* 7.8.1962.

this issue, that Lahr and Mansholt backed up Marijnen's line. A crisis was averted by dint of sending the topic back to the Committee of Deputies for further discussion, but an important warning shot had none the less been fired.[78] In face of total French obstinacy the unity of the Six would not hold. A week later there was a further danger signal when rumours spread to Brussels that the Dutch Cabinet had debated a proposal that the Netherlands' delegation break the Community front. In response the French government was alleged to have made 'a high level approach' to the Hague in an attempt to dissuade the Dutch from so drastic a course.[79] But the threat failed to materialise. Indeed, it was the Germans and not the Dutch who came closest to rebelling: on the morning of 4 August, Lahr briefly suggested that he might make public his reservations about the new common position. A combination of Schaus, Colombo and Fayat was sufficient however to convince the German minister not to speak out. And in the small hours of the next morning the Germans, Dutch and Belgians disowned the Colombo–Marjolin text on CAP financing. Significantly, however, this occurred only after the British had rejected the proposal; none of the rebels, moreover, advanced any alternative text of their own. Discussion of the whole issue was simply postponed until the next ministerial session.

As the ministers and officials left on their delayed summer holidays, they could legitimately feel that much had been accomplished. With arrangements devised for Commonwealth manufactured products, exports from the Indian sub-continent, and most of the African and West Indian Commonwealth, three of the eight chapter headings set out in the April deputies' report had been all but completed. In addition, success was within grasp in a fourth chapter heading – temperate foodstuffs – while in two others – British agriculture and zero tariffs – useful progress had been made. But the positive impact of these achievements was blunted by the controversy which surrounded the final hours of negotiation and by the vast number of issues which still remained to be resolved. If Britain was to complete her membership negotiations before the year's end, or even just to prevent them from dragging too far into 1963, it was vital not only that the Commonwealth Prime Ministers' conference went well, but also that the momentum built up by the negotiators over the summer

[78] CMA. RU/M/45/62 (part 1).
[79] PRO. FO371 164791; M641/380, Delmar 125, Robinson minute, 10.8.1962.

of 1962 could be quickly recaptured in the autumn. Further success would dull the memory of the tension of late July and early August. Delay, by contrast, would bring to the fore the underlying disagreements which the summer had revealed.

6 Agricultural impasse
September–December 1962

Oh Lord we pray on bended knees
Please make up our deficiencies
God bless our feeding-stuff compounders
And save us from these foreign bounders

We also pray that every night
The Lord will let us get quite tight
On perry, mead and parsnip wine
That are not made by foreign swine.

The British had little time to waste on a detailed post-mortem of the summer's negotiations. On 10 August 1962 the Prime Minister attended a meeting of the Common Market Negotiating Committee at which it was decided that the terms so far agreed, while not ideal, were defensible. The temperate zone package, in particular, 'offered a realistic basis for discussion with the Commonwealth Governments concerned'. Nothing was to be gained from pressing further on this issue.[1] During the two-month adjournment of the negotiations, attention could thus turn to three new priorities. First, it was necessary to present and defend the agreements so far reached to the assembled Commonwealth leaders; second, the enthusiasm of the Conservative Party would have to be refuelled at the party's annual conference in early October; and third, the Foreign Office would have to prepare for a determined effort to reach a final agreement by the year's end. No formal deadline was set, but it was recognised that if the negotiations were allowed to run too far into 1963, British hopes of entering the Community on 1 January 1964 would be seriously compromised.

Macmillan opened the Commonwealth Prime Ministers' conference

---

[1] PRO. CAB 134/1512; CMN(62) 19th meeting, 10.8.1962.

on 10 September with a lengthy and detailed explanation of why Britain had decided to apply to the European Community. Eschewing, for once, the caution and qualifications which had characterised some of his earlier speeches about Britain and the Community – most notably the July 1961 announcement of the British intention to apply – the Prime Minister delivered 'the most forthright and strongest statement of the Government's political and economic reasons for applying for membership that had yet been presented'.[2] He was followed by Heath, who set out in some detail the terms agreed in Brussels. But as quickly became apparent, the Commonwealth Prime Ministers had not come to Marlborough House simply to listen to a statement of British policy. From the impassioned speech by John Diefenbaker, the Canadian Prime Minister, onwards, the leaders of the former Dominions and of the newer states of Africa and Asia alike attacked both the British decision to apply to the EEC and the special safeguards negotiated in Brussels. The arrangements devised for temperate zone agriculture were dismissed as too vague and imprecise to act as any real guarantee against the enlarged Community pursuing inward-looking and protectionist policies; the package for India, Pakistan and Ceylon was described as inadequate; and the EEC promise of association was rejected by the majority of those Commonwealth states to which it was offered. Only Jamaica and Rhodesia – the latter being the African state the Community was least willing to welcome as an associate – announced their readiness to participate in the new association convention between the EEC and its African associates.[3]

Commonwealth criticism caused surprise and gloom in the British government. 'Rab' Butler, presiding over the 13 September Cabinet meeting in Macmillan's stead, conceded that the whole tone of the conference was 'more critical than expected' and in discussion it was noted that 'the prospects for an acceptable outcome of the meeting were not good'.[4] Over the next few days a total disaster was, in fact, averted. The Commonwealth leaders, having vented their anger in the opening phase of the conference, agreed to a final communiqué which, while stopping short of endorsing British membership, ac-

---

[2] Miriam Camps, *Britain and the European Community 1955–1963* (Oxford University Press, 1964), p. 436.
[3] For more detail see Camps, *Britain and the EC*, pp. 434–44 and Alistair Horne, *Macmillan 1957–1986* (London: Macmillan, 1989), pp. 355–7.
[4] PRO. CAB 128/36 part 2; CC(62)56, 13.9.1962.

knowledged that the final decision on whether to join the EEC was one which only Britain could make.[5] An outright Commonwealth veto was thus ruled out, as was the prospect of a second Commonwealth Prime Ministers' conference once the negotiations were complete. But, despite this useful damage limitation exercise, the Marlborough House meeting could not be classed as a success. The complaints so stridently voiced by Commonwealth leaders undermined the British government's ability to claim that the terms agreed constituted a major negotiating achievement. More seriously, the dissatisfaction of Commonwealth leaders with the provisional agreements meant that Heath and his officials would have to return to Brussels in search of more generous arrangements on most outstanding issues. None of the provisional settlements reached would actually have to be reopened – although the British were obliged to seek a few additional concessions for India and Pakistan – but any new deals struck would be assessed, by British public opinion as much as by the Commonwealth, in the light of Commonwealth discontent with the first part of the package. This additional pressure would not be limited to Commonwealth matters alone. In mid-August, Norman Brook, the Cabinet Secretary, had argued to the Prime Minister that:

> If the Commonwealth Meeting goes reasonably well, there would be less support for any attempt to prevent or delay our entry for the sake of our domestic agriculture, and an increasing tendency to accept the view that we might have to reach a decision on the general merits of joining the Community and then, as a member, make the best arrangements we can for our own farmers.[6]

Such an approach, if adopted, would have transformed Britain's prospects and made rapid agreement on the technical issues an attainable target. In the aftermath of a Commonwealth Prime Ministers' conference which had not gone 'reasonably well', however, a scaling down of Britain's domestic desiderata became all but impossible. Once the Brussels negotiations restarted, the British would again be obliged to fight for the best possible terms on British agriculture and all other items discussed, however time consuming this proved.

[5] *The Times* 20.9.1962; Peter Pooley claims that Macmillan's success in avoiding too critical a communiqué was partly due to the successful exploitation of Diefenbaker's deafness. Whenever key phrases of the text were discussed, the British Prime Minister dropped his voice, thereby cutting the Canadian Premier and most vociferous critic of the British application out of the discussion. Interview with the author, 18.12.1995.
[6] PRO. PREM 11 3635; Brook to Prime Minister, 21.8.1962.

Unless the Six unexpectedly gave way, a rapid and final surge forward in the negotiations culminating in success by Christmas was thus much less likely.

Some apparent compensation for the unexpectedly turbulent Commonwealth meeting was provided by the Conservative Party conference at Llandudno. The gathering of Conservative activists in early October 1962 proved a triumph for the pro-European majority: the few isolated speeches made against the British application were overshadowed by the massive support for a pro-European conference motion and by the clear endorsement of British membership by the Deputy Prime Minister, 'Rab' Butler.[7] This last was given particular significance by Butler's previous reputation as one of the Cabinet members least supportive of Britain's EEC application. It also confirmed that the government had temporarily abandoned its policy of avoiding overtly pro-EEC speeches for fear of worsening Britain's bargaining position in Brussels.[8] Neither this new determination to explain the benefits of British membership, nor the almost frenetically pro-European tone of the Llandudno conference, can be understood, however, without reference to two rather more worrying trends for the government. The first was the increasingly overt hostility of the Labour Party to British membership – expressed most clearly by Hugh Gaitskell's speech to the Labour Party conference in late September.[9] The second was the steady erosion of public support for British membership. In early September, even before the Commonwealth conference, analysis of NOP opinion polls by the *Observer* revealed that support for British membership had fallen from 47.1 per cent in April 1962 to 37.8 per cent in September, while over the same period opposition had risen from 25 per cent to 52.2 per cent.[10] Both of

---

[7] *The Times* 12.10.1962; David Dutton, 'Anticipating Maastricht: The Conservative Party and Britain's First Application to Join the European Community', *Contemporary Record*, 3:7 (1993), 533–4.

[8] The Cabinet had somewhat reluctantly decided to take this step on 20 September. CAB 128/36 part 2; CC(62)57, 20.9.1962; the start of efforts to 'sell' EEC membership are chronicled in Conservative Party Archives (Bodley). CRD2/42/8. Minutes of the Parliamentary Group on the Common Market, 22.10.1962 onwards.

[9] For a discussion of Labour's evolving attitude towards the British application see Robert J. Lieber, *British Politics and European Unity: Parties, Elites and Pressure Groups* (Berkeley: University of California Press, 1970), pp. 166–85.

[10] *Observer* 9.9.1962; Lieber, *British Politics*, pp. 226–37 and James Spence, 'Movements in the Public Mood: 1961–75' in Roger Jowell and Gerald Hoinville (eds.), *Britain into Europe: Public Opinion and the EEC 1961–1975* (London: Croom Helm, 1976), pp. 19–23 contain more detailed analyses of British public opinion.

these developments accentuated Macmillan's need for favourable terms to be secured in the next phase of negotiations and lessened the government's room for manoeuvre.

Bilateral discussions between the British and the Community member state governments were rather more encouraging for Macmillan and his government. In September and early October, Heath held a series of bilateral meetings with ministers from each of the Six.[11] Although Couve de Murville gave little away in his conversations with Heath, in general these encounters helped raise Foreign Office morale. They confirmed that substantial goodwill towards British membership remained among the Six and, more importantly, suggested that most of the Five were willing to translate this goodwill into a readiness to press ahead in Brussels as fast as possible. Talks with the Dutch also enabled the British and the most Anglophile member state to plot the tactics for the forthcoming meetings. With the Netherlands holding the Conference Presidency until the year's end, the scope for maximising pressure on the French and avoiding situations in which Couve de Murville could dominate discussions among the Six would, it was hoped, be greater than ever before. Luns, van Houten and the remainder of the Dutch delegation also appeared to be willing to press for an intensive timetable of meetings. In this way, the momentum which had characterised the discussions over the summer could quickly be recaptured in the autumn.

As the Dutch themselves acknowledged, rapid progress depended less on their own efforts, than on those of the Germans. During his visit to Chequers, 'Dr Luns stressed the importance of enlisting active German support in setting the procedure for the next phase of the negotiations. The Germans were the only other member of the Community whose views carried weight in Paris.'[12] The positive tone of Heath's discussions in Bonn in late September was therefore extremely promising. Gerhard Schröder, Ludwig Erhard and Rolf Lahr were all eager to stress their support for British membership and their shared desire for swift success in Brussels. More importantly

---

[11] PRO. FO371 164799 and 164800; M641/491, M641/492, M641/493, M641/494, M641/496, M641/498, M641/501, M641/508, M641/509, M641/533, M641/534, M641/537, M641/538 and M641/539; FO371 164838; M648/129.

[12] PRO. FO371 164799; M641/493, COMLEE(62)121, Record of a conversation with the Netherlands Foreign Minister at Chequers, 21.9.1962.

perhaps, Erhard signalled German readiness to be flexible on some of the specific issues under discussion. Admittedly, the Minister for Economics unintentionally confirmed his scant knowledge of the detailed Brussels discussions by suggesting that the way forward in the talks about agricultural matters was a quantitative arrangement between the British and the Commonwealth – a position that the Six had spent most of the spring and summer trying to persuade the British to abandon. But the evident willingness to be cooperative was an important boost to British hopes.[13]

The previous inability of the Germans to influence the French over British membership had never been attributed directly to Erhard, Schröder or Lahr, however; the German problem, if one existed, could be traced to the views of the Federal Chancellor himself.[14] Adenauer's concern about the British approach to the EEC appears to have predated the application. In May 1961, for instance, he had responded to American suggestions that Britain was on the verge of a major policy change with an outpouring of scepticism: 'No, Macmillan will never join any serious move towards European unity. Heath might wish to and several of the other ministers. Selwyn Lloyd I believe has been converted. But the Macmillan government will never make the necessary decision.' Ominously for the British he added that he had just discussed this matter with de Gaulle and had found himself in full agreement with the French leader.[15] Then, as it gradually became clear that Britain was likely to revise its European policy, the Chancellor's basic mistrust of British intentions led him to fear that the UK government was intent upon undermining the European Community. In June 1961, when informed that Macmillan had told the House of Commons that Britain could not just sign the Treaty of Rome on the dotted line, the Chancellor had been sufficiently alarmed to check with the German Embassy in London that both their translation and

---

[13] PRO. FO371 164800; M641/508, Record of a conversation between the Lord Privy Seal and Herr Schröder, Professor Erhard and Herr Schwarz in Bonn, 25.9.1962.

[14] For further information on Adenauer's attitude towards British membership see Hans-Peter Schwarz, *Adenauer: Der Staatsmann, 1952–1967* (Stuttgart: Deutsche Verlags-Anstalt, 1991), pp. 747–53 and 762–9; Sabine Lee, 'The Federal Republic and the Enlargement Negotiations' in Anne Deighton and Alan Milward (eds.), *Acceleration, Deepening and Enlarging: The European Economic Community, 1957–1963* (Brussels: Nomos/Giuffrè/LGDJ/Bruylant, 1997).

[15] *Foreign Relations of the United States, 1961–1963, West Europe and Canada* (Washington: US Government Printing Office, 1994), vol. XIII, p. 22.

Hansard's original reporting of the speech had been correct.[16] And in the weeks and months that followed, somebody in the *Bundeskanzleramt*, and quite possibly Adenauer himself, had gone through the dispatches about Britain's final preparations for talks with the Six systematically underlining all those passages which referred to Commonwealth opposition to British membership, to the likely conditions which Britain would attach to its membership bid and to British aspirations of being allowed to modify the *acquis*. A passage of a telegram from London which mentioned the British desire to have a voice in the internal Community discussions about future policy had, for example, been heavily underscored and flanked with two large exclamation marks, as had a suggestion that Britain might seek to renegotiate a substantial portion of the CET.[17]

In 1961, however, Adenauer was no more able than de Gaulle to voice his anxieties publicly. The prospect of British membership had been warmly welcomed by most opinion in Germany and to oppose it, or even just to express concern about the form of the application, was to invite immediate controversy. Furthermore, the general elections of September 1961, the subsequent rebuilding of the governing coalition and the ongoing East–West crisis over Berlin occupied most of the Chancellor's time and attention. It was thus only in the spring of 1962 that Adenauer began, cautiously at first, to act. In March, in an interview with *Le Monde*, the Chancellor spoke of the danger that too great an enlargement would pose to the workings of the Community institutions and of the incompatibility between EEC membership and the UK's existing Commonwealth ties; a month later, he was widely reported to have told a meeting of CDU politicians in Berlin that the entry of Britain, Denmark, Ireland and Norway might swamp the EEC.[18] Meanwhile Dr Prass, a member of the Chancellor's private office, had been commissioned to prepare an array of reports detailing the likely effects of British membership. While neutral in tone, these did mention the economic problems which enlargement might cause for the German coal and textile industries, the possible disadvantages German agriculture might face and the legal difficulties which some German officials felt Britain might experience in accepting and

[16] BAK. BKA. B–136. Bd. 2560. Dr. Osterheld to AA, 9.6.1961.
[17] BAK. BKA. B–136. Bd. 2650. FS737. Thierfelder to AA, 24.8.1961.
[18] *Le Monde* 10.3.1961; the Berlin leak, and the subsequent German denials, are extensively covered in PRO. FO371 164783; M641/170, M641/173, M641/175.

implementing the Treaty of Rome as it currently stood.[19] All of these arguments would later appear in Adenauer's armoury.[20] And in June, Adenauer wrote to his former protégé Hallstein expressing his belief that British membership might fundamentally affect the Community, suggesting that he and the Commission President should meet to discuss this matter, and enclosing a cutting from *The Times* which speculated that Macmillan might actually prefer to confront the September 1962 Commonwealth Prime Ministers' conference without a detailed *vue d'ensemble*. As was noted in chapter 5, the British were subsequently obliged to quash widespread rumours which had originated from this newspaper article and which had spread via Hallstein's office to many of those involved with the Brussels negotiations.

Adenauer's opposition to British membership became more forceful in the wake of the Chancellor's state visit to France in July 1962. In part this reflected the relief in finding that his personal misgivings about EEC enlargement were largely shared by the French President. Alone with de Gaulle, the Chancellor's sarcastic comment that 'one should not approve the British application with three cheers' was not only well received but matched by the General's equally frank denunciation of the British decision to apply.[21] But the visit also reinforced Adenauer's commitment to further Franco-German *rapprochement* – an aim which, as will be explained below, the German Chancellor feared would be endangered by British membership of the EEC. The pomp and ceremonial of the state visit – culminating in a symbolic service of reconciliation at Reims cathedral – underlined the extent to which de Gaulle was committed to ending tension between France and Germany, while the warmth and wide-ranging accord which marked the two leaders' discussions seemed to hold out the

---

[19] BAK. BKA. B–136. Bd. 2560. Prass memos for Adenauer, 18, 21, 23 and 24.5.1962. The belief that Britain would face serious legal difficulties in accepting the Treaty of Rome sprang from a legal opinion prepared on behalf of Dr Schäfer, the Minister of the Interior, and widely circulated within German government circles. IA4–14320A–6/62, Schäfer to AA, 24.1.1962.

[20] Most of these arguments cropped up in Adenauer's regular discussions with journalists, both German and foreign, which are published as his *Teegespräche 1961–1963* (Berlin: Siedler Verlag, 1992), esp. pp. 207–9, 223–30 and 238–43; the use made by the Chancellor of the anxieties of particular sections of German industry is described in Markus Schulte, 'Challenging the Common Market Project. German Industry, Britain and Europe 1956–63' in Deighton and Milward (eds.), *Acceleration, Deepening and Enlarging*.

[21] 'Man dürfe einen englischen Beitritt nicht mit dreimaligem Hurra beschließen.' My translation. Cited in Schwarz, *Adenauer*, p. 762.

prospect of Franco-German unity acting as a stepping stone to greater European unity.[22] Indeed, on 5 July, de Gaulle suggested to Adenauer that the best way to advance in the quest for European political union might be for France and Germany to proceed initially *à deux*.[23] The amicable tone of the de Gaulle/Adenauer encounters also stood in stark contrast to the rather strained relations between Macmillan and the German Chancellor.

On 25 July Erhard, Schröder, Heinz Starke, the Minister of Finance, and Werner Schwarz, the Minister for Agriculture, were invited to a private discussion of the British application at Adenauer's house.[24] No minutes were kept, but it would appear from the pro-enlargement letter which the four ministers wrote to the Chancellor on the same day, that they had either received or were anticipating a very negative opinion from Adenauer.[25] Two weeks later the Chancellor aired his views to the whole Cabinet. Responding to a rather upbeat report on the state of the Brussels negotiations from Lahr, the German leader first questioned the State Secretary's optimism and then raised a series of political and economic objections to Community enlargement. An enlarged EEC would, he argued, be less effective and more prone to socialist influence than the existing body: the workings of the Brussels institutions might be paralysed by the influx of numerous officials from the new member states, while Britain and several of the Scandinavian applicants might soon be governed by left-wing administrations totally out of sympathy with the goals of European integration. Somewhat unconvincingly, the Chancellor pointed to the presence in government of two Communist ministers in Iceland – a country which had not even applied to join the EEC – as evidence of this second danger. Furthermore, British membership would pose serious problems for German coal producers and farmers. But most fundamentally, enlargement might disrupt the construction of a solid Franco-German understanding. As Adenauer put it: 'The political question which we have to confront is not our relations with Britain, but rather those

---

[22] *Le Monde* 10.7.1962; Schwarz, *Adenauer*, pp. 757–61.

[23] Jacques Bariéty, 'De Gaulle, Adenauer et la genèse du traité de l'Elysée du 22 janvier 1963' and Hans-Peter Schwarz, 'Le président de Gaulle, le chancelier fédéral Adenauer et la genèse du traité de l'Elysée' in Institut Charles de Gaulle, *De Gaulle en son siècle* (Paris: Plon, 1992), vol.V, pp. 359 and 368.

[24] BAK. BKA. B–136, Bd. 2560, Globke to Erhard, Schröder, Starke and Schwarz, 19.7.1962.

[25] BAK. BKA. B–136, Bd. 2560, Schröder, Erhard, Schwarz and Dr Debatin to Adenauer, 25.7.1962.

between us and France.'[26] A continuation of the pro-British stance adopted by German representatives in Brussels would place an immediate strain on this vital cooperation, while in the longer run British participation within the EEC and an eventual political union would open up the horrific possibility of France and Britain acting together against the Federal Republic: 'If the two of them jointly agree behind our backs, it would be the worst thing that could happen to us.' The Chancellor claimed not to have reached any definite conclusion about whether or not Britain should be allowed to join, but the overall thrust of his arguments was clearly against enlargement.[27]

The immediate reaction of Adenauer's Cabinet colleagues is not recorded, but is unlikely to have been positive. The extent of CDU opposition to the Chancellor's views was confirmed, moreover, two weeks later when Adenauer was fiercely criticised after repeating many of the above arguments to a meeting of the CDU *Fraktion*.[28] This clash was widely covered by the German press and provoked a furious article by the influential journalist Georg Schröder, who claimed that as a result of discord between the Chancellor and his party over Community enlargement Adenauer could no longer claim to lead his party.[29] Schröder also suggested that the Chancellor travel from Bonn – a town where the economic interests of the Ruhr loomed large – to northern Germany where the economic necessity of closer ties with Britain and Scandinavia was much more apparent. This last point was reinforced in early September when Dr Nevermann, the *Bürgermeister* of Hamburg, wrote to Adenauer stressing the vital importance of enlargement to the economic well-being of the northern *Länder*.[30] But the strength of such internal opposition was outweighed by the spectacular blossoming of Franco-German relations. In September de Gaulle conducted a triumphal two-week tour of West Germany, accompanied by much state and popular enthusiasm for Franco-German *rapprochement*.[31] In Hamburg, addressing German military

---

[26] 'Die politische Frage ist für uns nicht das Verhältnis zwischen uns und England, sondern das Verhältnis zwischen uns und Frankreich.' My translation. BAK. BKA. B–136, Bd. 2561, Beitritt Großbritanniens zur EWG, Unkorrigiertes Manuskript aus der Kabinettsitzung, 8.8.1962.

[27] 'Wenn die beiden sich auf unserem Rücken einigen könnten, wäre das das Schlimmste, was überhaupt passieren könnte.' My translation. *Ibid.*

[28] *Die Welt* 22.8.1962.   [29] *Ibid.* 23.8.1962.

[30] BAK. BKA. B–136, Bd. 2561, Dr Nevermann to Adenauer, 5.9.1962.

[31] Gerhard Kiersch, 'De Gaulle et l'identité allemande' in Institut Charles de Gaulle, *De Gaulle*, vol. V, pp. 305–9; Schwarz, *Adenauer*, pp. 765–8.

officers, the General spoke of France and Germany putting behind them their 'absurd duel' and understanding the importance of working together: 'Now at last, the state of world affairs makes them appreciate that they are in all respects complementary, that, in combining what they are, what they have been, and what they are worth, they can form the foundation of a Europe whose prosperity, power and prestige would match that of any rival.'[32] Behind the rhetoric and pomp, moreover, both governments continued to examine the possibility of pursuing by means of a bilateral agreement the type of political union which the Six had so far failed to realise.[33] With such a goal attainable, Adenauer was unlikely to relent on the British application.

Certainly, the Chancellor had not significantly altered his position when, in early October, he received Heath at his holiday home on the banks of Lake Como in Italy. Once again, Adenauer used most of the arguments that he had put to the German Cabinet: German economic problems were pointed to, the vulnerability of German farmers high- lighted and the institutional implications of enlargement dwelt upon. The German leader also expressed concern about Britain's legal position within the Community. Referring to a speech by Lord Dilhorne, in which the Lord Chancellor had explained that Parliament would retain the right to renounce the Treaty of Rome, Adenauer felt that this power would be contrary to the rules and the spirit of the Community: the Treaty of Rome was for indefinite duration and contained no provisions for revocation. Summing up, the Chancellor noted: 'If one added to this difficulty, the organisational and other problems of the Community in dealing with eleven members, he could not help wondering whether British membership was in fact the best way for her to resolve her economic relationship with Europe.'[34] By October, the British government was thus confronted with the realisation that its bid to enter the European Community was opposed by the two most powerful statesmen in continental Europe. The need for a rapid breakthrough in Brussels grew ever greater.

[32] 'Voici, enfin, que le mouvement général du monde leur fait voir qu'ils se trouvent, à tous égards, complémentaires, et qu'en conjuguant ce qu'ils sont, ce qu'ils ont été, ce qu'ils valent, ils peuvent constituer la base d'une Europe dont la prosperité, la puissance, le prestige, égaleraient ceux de qui que ce soit.' *Le Monde* 8.9.1962.

[33] Jean Lacouture, *De Gaulle, vol. III: Le souverain 1959–1970* (Paris: Editions du Seuil, 1986), pp. 306–7.

[34] PRO. FO371 164803; M641/543G, Record of a conversation between the Lord Privy Seal and Chancellor Adenauer at Cadenabbia, 1.10.1962.

In September 1962, admittedly, it was difficult to assess the full significance of either Adenauer's qualms about British membership or of moves towards Franco-German political union. The German Chancellor was widely seen as too weak and too isolated to act in a decisive fashion – Erhard, for instance, assured the British that if the Chancellor sought to obstruct British membership 'he would be defeated and this would hasten the end of his political life'.[35] Likewise the Franco-German *rapprochement* need not necessarily prove damaging. Indeed, there were even indications that the process might act in Britain's favour, so worried were the four remaining Community member states. The Italians in particular reacted with dismay to a move which if successful would marginalise them within the Community; as argued in the previous chapter, the Italian government was determined to avert a political union *à deux*. This anxiety found vent in talk of a rival Rome–London axis with which to balance the emerging Paris–Bonn link – Ugo La Malfa, the Budget Minister, suggested such a course to the British Embassy in Rome in December[36] – but it also strengthened the hand of those like Fanfani and La Malfa in the Italian government who were willing to pay a high price in order to secure British membership.[37] Rapid enlargement became a still greater priority for the Rome government as, not only would close cooperation between the French and the Germans be less threatening in a Community of nine or ten than within the existing Six, but the very need for it might disappear. British membership, the Italians hoped, would remove the obstacles to a political union comprising all Community members. Jean-Marie Soutou, a senior French witness to the discussions between Fanfani and Pompidou in Turin on 15 September, was almost certainly correct in attributing the new vigour with which the Italian Prime Minister accused the French of 'unnecessary toughness' in the enlargement negotiations to the

---

[35] PRO. FO371 164800; M641/501, Note for the Record: Lord Privy Seal's meeting with Professor Erhard, Bonn, 25.9.1962.

[36] Leopoldo Nuti, 'Italy, the British Application to the EEC and the January Debacle' in Richard Griffiths and Stuart Ward (eds.), *Courting the Common Market: The First Attempt to Enlarge the European Community 1961–1963* (London: Lothian Foundation Press, 1996), p. 112; Antonio Varsori, 'The Art of Mediation: Italy and Britain's Attempt at Joining the Common Market (1961–63)' in Deighton and Milward (eds.), *Acceleration, Deepening and Enlarging*.

[37] See chapter 5 for a discussion of the two divergent currents of opinion within the Italian government.

effects of de Gaulle's visit to Germany.[38] Given the way in which the Italians had often sought to lessen French isolation within the Six during the spring and summer of 1962, any suggestion that the Italians were losing patience with the French was of great significance.

The negotiations resume

The first ministerial meeting of the autumn of 1962 (the eleventh of the negotiations), held in Brussels on 8–9 October, was a low-key affair. Heath made a statement about the Commonwealth Prime Ministers' conference but, as the British and Dutch had intended, ministers were not given any time to discuss the outcome.[39] French and Commission unhappiness about what was perceived as a British attempt to reopen the provisional agreement on India, Pakistan and Ceylon was thus confined to the preliminary meeting of the Six.[40] The only controversial subject dealt with *à sept* was the timetable of future meetings and on this a compromise was fairly rapidly agreed. Definite dates were set for three ministerial meetings before Christmas, a few days at the end of November were set aside for an optional fourth and the possibility of an extra meeting in late December was also acknowledged.[41] If the supplementary dates were used, British hopes of all but wrapping up the negotiations before the New Year were still viable.

It was only with the start of serious discussions about British domestic agriculture – first raised at ministerial level during the 25–7 October meeting – that the prospects of quick success began to dwindle. The fate of British farmers had, of course, been debated before; the British desire to incorporate their practice of an annual review of farm incomes into the CAP had been the subject of lengthy and ultimately successful talks in June and July and brief, if inconclusive, discussions had been held about cereal prices and agricultural subsidies. But with both the British and the Six inclined to give

---

[38] PRO. FO371 164796; M641/453G, Dixon to FO, Tel. No. 431, 19.9.1962.
[39] CMA. 07.51. 11ème session ministérielle entre les états membres de la CEE et le Royaume-Uni, tenue les 8/9 octobre 1962. RU/M/50/62, Draft minutes. For British/ Dutch planning of this opening meeting, see PRO. FO371 164799; M641/493, COMLEE(62)121, Record of a conversation with the Netherlands Foreign Minister at Chequers, 21.9.1962.
[40] ECHA. S/06314/62. Report No. 33 on the eleventh ministerial meeting (8 October); BDT 145/80, No. 245.
[41] CMA. 07.51. 11ème session ministérielle entre les états membres de la CEE et le Royaume-Uni, tenue les 8/9 octobre 1962. RU/M/50/62, Draft minutes.

priority to Commonwealth matters until the end of the summer and with a hope on the part of the Community member states that the British would be able to soften their stance as they grew more used to the workings of the EEC, the details of how the CAP should be introduced in the United Kingdom had not been given great time or attention prior to October 1962. This lack of discussion allowed serious divergences of opinion, amongst the Six as well as between the Six and the British, to lie all but unheeded until October 1962. It also meant that the full implications of British requests were not thought out until this late stage of the negotiations. Jean-François Deniau, the Commission's chief negotiator at deputy level, for instance, admitted that he had only really understood what the British wanted on agriculture in early October 1962.[42] When the focus of attention did belatedly settle on British domestic agriculture, both Britain and the Six were disagreeably surprised to find themselves separated by a division of opinion comparable to that which had characterised the early discussions of Commonwealth agriculture.

The 25–7 October ministerial meeting was an ill-tempered affair. In the morning of 25 October, the ministers of the Six held their first systematic discussion of British agriculture and agreed on a fairly hard-line opening position with unusual rapidity. During these internal Community talks, there were admittedly signs aplenty that some delegations would be prepared to soften their stance at a later stage. Mansholt, for instance, conceded that the Six might have to be flexible on the length of the transitional period granted to British agriculture.[43] The deputies' report on which their discussion was based, moreover, was riddled with references to differences of opinion among the Six.[44] Many of these internal divisions were known to the British. But such was the determination to start the debate with the British at once, that all dissenting views were temporarily dropped in favour of a clear and firm common position. It was this that was outlined by van Houten, the Dutch Deputy Foreign Minister and Chairman of the Conference, as discussions with the British began.[45]

[42] PRO. FO371 164803; M641/544, Delmar 150, Record of a conversation with M. Deniau, 9.10.1962.

[43] ECHA. S/06901/62. Report No. 36 on the twelfth ministerial meeting (25/26/27 October); BDT 145/80, No. 245.

[44] ECHA. BDT 239/1980. No. 6 Agriculture: généralités 1961–2. RU/S/INT/8 rev., 19.10.1962.

[45] CMA. 07.51. Compte rendu de la 12ème session ministérielle entre les états membres de la CEE et le Royaume-Uni tenue les 25–27 octobre 1962. RU/M/54/62.

This apparent hardening of the Community's position dismayed and angered the British. In his reply to the Chairman's statement, Heath 'expressed his astonishment' at the position of the Six and claimed that no account had been taken of the progress made over the preceding nine months.[46] This angry British reply transformed the situation. After a lengthy attempt to justify their position, the Six adjourned the discussions *à sept* and began a long, and at times passionate, argument among themselves. In the course of this, the consensus achieved in the morning vanished and many of the differences referred to in the deputies' report reappeared: the Germans, Dutch and Italians all felt that the Community should soften its stance (although they did not all agree on where the Six should give ground), the Commission questioned whether the time was yet ripe for concessions and the French called vigorously for the Six to defend their position. Only a skilful compromise proposal tabled by Charles Heger, the Belgian Minister of Agriculture, followed by a restricted meeting during which ministers met without advisers or officials, allowed progress to be made: an amended text was agreed and van Houten was able to invite the British to rejoin the discussions.[47] But the slight change tabled by the Six neither broke the deadlock nor improved spirits on either side. An agricultural impasse had been created, which, despite countless attempts at compromise tabled by the Belgians, Italians and the Commission, was to persist until January 1963.

A problem of trust

At the heart of this deadlock lay five closely interlinked issues. The first was the date at which the British would scrap deficiency payments, the government subsidies designed to allow British farmers to compete with low-cost imports. The second was the length of the transitional period granted to British farmers. On this, the key question was whether or not Britain would fully participate from the outset in the single market for agricultural products which was due to start on 1 January 1970. The third controversy surrounded the nature of any transitional arrangements permitted by the Community. These would be designed to smooth the introduction of the CAP into the

[46] *Ibid.*
[47] ECHA. S/06901/62. Report No. 36 on the twelfth ministerial meeting (27/28 October); BDT 145/80, No. 245.

United Kingdom, either by softening the impact of food price rises through the use of consumer subsidies, or by helping farmers by means of producer subsidies. The fourth disagreement concerned the level at which cereal prices within Britain should initially be set, while the fifth centred upon a series of modifications to the CAP regulations which the British had requested.[48]

The British case was simple. Farmers in the United Kingdom, Heath argued, had grown accustomed to a type of protection which was both very effective and very different from that employed by most continental countries and by the CAP. As a result, any replacement of the British system of agricultural support would have to be gradual. Rapid change would cause large-scale disruption and would be both economically and politically damaging. Deficiency payments should thus be phased out only slowly – they would dwindle anyway as British market prices rose towards European norms – and the transitional period should be prolonged beyond January 1970 where necessary. The price of cereals moreover should be permitted to rise only gradually. A sudden rise of the British market price to a level comparable to that found in the cheapest Community countries would harm consumers and promote over-production.[49]

The Six countered this case with three basic arguments. The first was that the difficulties which Britain would face in adapting to the CAP were not fundamentally different from those confronted by every member state: 'British agriculture and horticulture does not differ significantly from the Community average, and is indeed, in many respects, in a more favourable position.'[50] All member states were having to make sacrifices in order to move towards a common European policy; Britain could and should do the same. Second, the Six argued that it was vitally important that the single market in agricultural produce be established throughout the Community simultaneously. There could thus be no exceptions to the January 1970 deadline. And third, it was politically all but impossible to grant wealthy British farmers privileges, such as the right to enjoy guaran-

[48] ECHA. BDT 239/1980. No. 6 Agriculture: généralités 1961–2. RU/S/INT/8 rev., 19.10.1962.

[49] CMA. –1.823.1. Période de transition spéciale pour l'agriculture britannique. RU/M/52/62, Note by the Lord Privy Seal, 19.10.1962.

[50] 'L'agriculture et l'horticulture britanniques ne diffèrent pas essentiellement de celles de la moyenne des Etats membres et se trouvent même, à beaucoup d'égards, dans une situation plus favorable.' My translation. ECHA. BDT 239/1980. No. 6 Agriculture: généralités 1961–2. RU/S/INT/8 rev., 19.10.1962.

teed prices, which were not available to continental farmers. Any such imbalance would encourage farmers elsewhere in the Community to push for similar treatment and endanger the whole political bargain on which the CAP rested. A combination of these arguments led the Community to insist that the British accept fully the CAP timetable, rapidly align British market prices with those of the Community and scrap the deficiency payment system as soon as they entered the EEC. Transitional measures – consumer subsidies if possible, failing that producer subsidies – would be permitted, but these would have to taper and disappear completely before the end of 1969.

Beneath these various arguments lay two very different but equally important sub-texts. One was commercial and centred on the ease with which the agricultural exporting member states could sell their produce on the British market. If British prices were brought into line with those of the Community upon entry, deficiency payments were quickly abolished and consumer subsidies were used to cushion the impact of price rises, French and Dutch exporters would face few obstacles in penetrating the lucrative British market. If important aspects of the traditional British system remained in place, however, the British market would be partially shielded from EEC competition. A lengthy transitional period, in the course of which the British would be permitted to retain their traditionally low market prices and to enable their own farmers to compete at these low price levels by means of direct producer subsidies (or still better deficiency payments) would keep Britain beyond the reach of most French or Dutch producers for years, unless the French and Dutch governments were willing to provide substantial export subsidies.

The other sub-text was political and was grounded on a clear lack of mutual trust between the British and the Six in agricultural matters. On the British side, the absence of trust was at its clearest in the vehemently anti-CAP pronouncements of the National Farmers Union (NFU). Whether in newspaper articles, pamphlets, public pronouncements or private conversations with the Prime Minister, Harold Woolley, the President of the NFU, lost no opportunity to denounce the new European policy as an ineffective system which would fail totally to safeguard British farm revenues.[51] Similar scepticism about the CAP's effectiveness was echoed by many within the Ministry of

[51] PRO. PREM 11 3635; Record of a conversation between Macmillan, Soames and Woolley, 9.7.1962; *Daily Express* 23.7.1962; Lieber, *British Politics*, pp. 116–32.

Agriculture and, in the person of Christopher Soames, the Minister of Agriculture, penetrated into both the Common Market Negotiating Committee and the Cabinet.[52] This meant that the repeated statements by the Six urging the British to put their trust in the CAP, not simply as it was, but as it would develop once Britain had a strong voice within the Community, were countered by a strong body of British opinion which would only accept a CAP which had been substantially modified before being implemented within the United Kingdom. Unwilling to rely on either the CAP system or the goodwill of the Six, the British thus went on pressing for greater safeguards and concessions than the Six felt able to give.

The problem of trust on the Community side was still more complex. The central difficulty was that the Six, and the French in particular, were not totally convinced that Britain had rid itself of its traditional dislike of agricultural cooperation in Europe. There was thus a strong fear that once in the Community, but while still protected by transitional arrangements from the full impact of the CAP, Britain might seek to undermine the agricultural policy. By insisting that Britain dismantle its own system as soon as it joined, the French hoped to render this less likely. As Edgard Pisani, the French Minister of Agriculture, explained to his colleagues among the Six in early December, only the acceptance by Britain of a transitional regime very different from its previous system would represent proof that the UK would in due course adopt the full CAP.[53] But there was a further complication, in that the strongest partisans of the CAP in the Community, again primarily but not exclusively the French, were very aware that not all of their partners were whole-heartedly in favour of the new system. This meant, as one British minister explained to his colleagues in December 1962: 'The rest of the Six feared that if we acceded without firm conditions binding us to accept the policy in its present form, we and the Germans would combine – for our separate reasons – to render it inoperable.'[54] German official documents, moreover, make clear that such fears were not totally without foundation. A memo prepared by the German agricultural ministry in June 1962 avoided any talk about the sabotage of the CAP, but its references to the harmony of interests between Germany and Britain and to the

[52] PRO. CAB 134/1512; CMN(62) 11th, 16th, 19th, 23rd, 26th, 27th and 28th meetings.
[53] ECHA. S/08134/62. Report No. 42 on the ministerial meeting between the Six (3/4/5 December); BDT 145/80, No. 245.
[54] PRO. CAB 134/1512; CMN(62) 27th meeting, 5.12.1962.

likelihood of the two states being able to act together once Britain had joined, were enough to suggest that the French had legitimate grounds for concern.[55] British and German voting power was unlikely to be deployed in the interests of French, Dutch or Italian farmers. Alarmist French language about the destruction of the CAP – at the ministerial meeting in early December, Pisani likened the probable fate of the CAP within an enlarged Community to that of an artichoke being eaten one leaf at a time – was designed to play upon such fears and emphasise the danger of ill-timed concessions.

Deep divisions had, of course, been encountered before in the Brussels negotiations. The debate over Commonwealth agriculture had also thrown up a vast array of political and economic, commercial and philosophical questions; it too had been complicated by mutual suspicion and mistrust, not to mention important fractures running within the Community. The basic shape of an agreement, if not all the final details, had nonetheless been agreed. There was thus no intrinsic element of the domestic agricultural impasse which ruled out future progress. There were, however, a series of factors, connected largely with the wider context within which the agricultural discussions were held, which made this deadlock particularly hard to overcome.

The first problem was the absence of other issues on which progress could easily be made. In May and June 1962, the atmosphere of crisis which had begun to form was lightened by the clear advances made by negotiators on secondary but still symbolically important issues. The deal struck on manufactured imports from the old Dominions and the headway made on exports from the Indian sub-continent had been important in creating a belief that solutions could be found and an expectation of success. They had hence been vital preconditions of progress in the discussions of temperate zone agriculture. In the autumn of 1962, however, there were few 'soft' subjects on which quick and tangible results could be attained.

A few agreements were, admittedly, concluded. In the second of the two ministerial meetings in October, the Six acceded to the British

---

[55] BAK, BKA, Bestand B–136, Bd. 2560, Bundesministerium für Ernährung, Landwirtschaft und Forsten, VII A 3, Zwischenbericht über den Stand der Verhandlungen mit Großbritannien über den Beitritt zu den drei Europäischen Gemeinschaften, 25.6.1962.

requests that the negotiations leading to trade agreements with India and Pakistan start within three months of Britain joining the Community.[56] Just over a fortnight later, on 15 November, a package of measures designed for those Commonwealth countries in Africa which had opted against association was accepted by both sides.[57] And in December, the special arrangements for Malta, Malaysia and the High Commission Territories of Basutoland, Bechuanaland and Swaziland were settled. But none of these steps forward were of a type sufficient to compensate for the impasse elsewhere. The first was overshadowed by the unwillingness of the Six to suspend the CET on Indian and Pakistani exports until the planned trade agreement had been concluded – from an Asian point of view by far the more important of the two requests – and by the irritation of the French and the Commission in particular at having to modify an agreement already reached. Similarly, the negotiators could gain little pleasure from the success of their efforts to secure fall-back measures for Ghana, Nigeria, Kenya, Tanganyika and Uganda – the very fact that further discussion had been necessary reflected the failure of their preferred solution. Only the agreements on Malta, Malaysia and the three tiny African territories represented genuine progress and, even here, pride in the gains made was tempered by the realisation that a great deal of valuable ministerial time had been devoted to the sort of technical detail normally left to officials.

Elsewhere, near paralysis was the norm. Perhaps the most serious obstacle to progress was the ongoing row among the Community members about 'the financial regulation', the part of the 14 January 1962 agreement on the CAP which specified how the agricultural policy should be financed. This conflict, sparked off in the spring of 1962 by French anxieties about the British attitude towards the financial regulation, had by the autumn degenerated into an enormously complicated and time-consuming dispute about the whole financing of the Community. As Hallstein observed in November, moreover, 'it is not so much a question which pits the Six against the British, but rather a dispute among the Six which has to do with

---

[56] CMA. 07.51. Compte rendu de la 12ème session ministérielle entre les états membres de la CEE et le Royaume-Uni tenue les 25–27 octobre 1962. RU/M/54/62.

[57] CMA. 07.51. Compte rendu de la 13ème session ministérielle entre les états membres des communautés européennes et le Royaume-Uni, tenue les 15–17 novembre 1962. RU/M/58/62.

British membership'.[58] Despite the internal nature of the conflict, however, Dutch efforts to move the discussion of the financial regulation from the conference on British membership to the Council met with no success and the Six continued to devote a significant portion of ministerial discussion to this question. The British were thus condemned to wait patiently in the corridor for hours as the Six became progressively more deeply embroiled in an arcane but nevertheless crucial battle, the final outcome of which appeared no nearer in December than it had in October.

A similar situation thwarted progress on the 'zero-tariff items', the Commonwealth raw material exports which Britain hoped would enter the Community unimpeded by tariffs. Here too, the British requests had opened up old wounds within the Community and had created a situation in which the Six spent considerably more time talking to each other than to the British. Aluminium was especially problematic, as not only was the Community divided between, on the one hand, protectionist producers and would-be producers, and, on the other, liberal importers, but there was also a continuing argument between the Commission and the Dutch about the rules governing the tariff quota on aluminium that the Netherlands had been granted.[59] Given these divisions, it was a significant achievement to have agreed upon the offer of a 5 per cent tariff quota covering most British imports of aluminium put forward by van Houten in October; the British rejection of this proposal left only slim hopes of the Six being able to put forward an improved offer before the New Year.

The short-term prospects of a deal on the importation of processed foods – mainly tinned fruit, but also, to the delight of cartoonists and satirists, canned kangaroo meat – from Australia and Canada were not much better. British hopes of obtaining tariff-free or virtually tariff-free entry into the Community for a list of processed agricultural products ran directly contrary to the interests of several member states, notably the Italians. They also fell foul of two somewhat more complex attitudes within the Community. The first of these was a strong feeling that the wealthy former Dominions did not require

[58] 'Ce n'est pas tellement une question qui oppose les "Six" aux Britanniques, mais plutôt, un problème qui se pose entre les six pays membres, en fonction de l'adhésion britannique.' My translation. ECHA. S/08146/62, Report No. 39 on the thirteenth ministerial session (15/16/17 November); BDT 145/88, No. 245.

[59] ECHA. S/06901/62. Report No. 36 on the twelfth ministerial meeting (25/26/27 October); BDT 145/88, No. 245.

further generosity from the Six – after all, they had already been given unprecedented arrangements in the negotiations on temperate zone agricultural produce. It was this sentiment that prompted Colombo to comment while at Chequers in November 1962 that 'the problems of Canada, Australia and New Zealand were not on the same plane as those of the other, much more poorly developed Commonwealth countries in Africa and Asia . . . Australia and Canada were strong enough to be quite competitive.'[60] The second difficulty – and again a problem which was not exclusive to the processed goods dossier – was EEC anxiety about lowering protective tariffs unilaterally on the eve of the Kennedy Round GATT negotiations. The strength of this argument was admittedly lessened by the US offer to give the Community credit for any tariff cuts it made in the enlargement negotiations. France and Italy, however, persisted in playing the GATT card long after this US stance was made public.[61] A sudden improvement upon the package of tariff cuts on a few items and the staggered introduction of the CET on the remainder, rejected by the British on 16 November, was thus unlikely without a substantial British quid pro quo elsewhere.

A more fundamental reason why progress proved so elusive in the last quarter of 1962 was that the pressure rapidly to obtain results and to conclude the negotiations, felt so keenly by some of the delegations in Brussels, accentuated the differences of opinion among the Six. British bilateral diplomacy with the emphasis Heath and others placed on the need for rapid advance, combined with a growing awareness on the continent that, as will be discussed below, not all was going well for Macmillan and his government, created a sense of urgency on the part of the Dutch, Belgians, Germans and Italians. This in turn affected the manner in which these four member states negotiated in Brussels. But the impact of this heightened pressure was not necessarily positive. First, it led to a general deterioration in the atmosphere of the negotiation – between October and December 1962, the discussions both with the British and still more in private among the Six acquired elements of anger, mistrust and mutual recrimination largely absent from the previous phase of debate. Secondly, the increased loneliness of the French position seemed only to strengthen

---

[60] PRO. FO371 164808; M641/616, COMLEE(62)178, Record of a conversation between the Lord Privy Seal and Signor Colombo at Chequers, 25.11.1962.
[61] See e.g. ECHA. S/08146/62. Report No. 39 on the thirteenth ministerial session (15/16/17 November); BDT 145/80, No. 245.

French resolve, in the short term at least. In his memoirs, Couve de Murville looked back at this period of the negotiations as a time of almost total isolation:

> Thus, as in 1958–9 . . . the negotiation tended to become a battle between the French and the British, the latter being all too often represented by the five other Community member states, individually or collectively. It was still a negotiation between the Six and a seventh state, but this last was not the candidate but France who became seen more and more as the isolated trouble-maker.[62]

In fact, the French Foreign Minister exaggerates: the case being argued by France's partners was rarely identical to the British position, nor, even had it been, would it have been possible, under the rules of procedure adopted, for a situation to develop in which the French were outnumbered six to one. If the Six failed to agree among themselves, discussions with the British would not take place. Nevertheless, the quotation does provide an accurate reflection of the position which the French negotiators felt themselves to be in.[63] It is thus not surprising that French rhetoric and dogmatism mounted steadily as the last months of 1962 progressed. And with the French so defiant, the common Community position so vital for any advance to be made became an ever more elusive goal.

A further aggravating factor in these final months of serious negotiation was the inept chairmanship of the Dutch. At both official and ministerial level, the Dutch proved to be much too opinionated to build consensus and too obviously *parti pris* to inspire any form of confidence among the very member states that they, as chairmen, were duty bound to represent. The pattern was set almost at once: in early October, in one of the first deputies' meetings since the recess, Hoogwater, the Chairman of the Committee of Deputies, tabled a

---

[62] 'Ainsi, comme en 1958–9 . . . la négociation tendait à devenir une confrontation entre les seuls Français et les Britanniques, ceux-ci trop souvent représentés par les cinq autres membres de la Communauté individuellement ou collectivement. C'était bien toujours une discussion entre Six et une septième, mais celui-ci était la France, non le candidat, elle-même devenant de plus en plus le trouble-fête.' My translation. Maurice Couve de Murville, *Une politique étrangère, 1958–1969* (Paris: Plon, 1971), p. 405.

[63] That Couve was not alone in feeling besieged is confirmed by Deniau, who recalls that by late 1962 the French delegation felt as if they were in a 'noose', and by a French diplomat in Bonn, who complained to a German counterpart about the collusion between the British and some of the Five. Interview with the author and AAA, Bestand B150, Bestellnummer 2, Ref. 200 (IA2), Bd. 1236, Aufzeichnung von Stempels, 22.1.1963.

string of personal suggestions designed to break the deadlock on various zero-tariff items of which not one was accepted.[64] Subsequent failings were less spectacular, but the Presidency remained much less adept at suggesting viable compromises than the Belgians, the Italians or the Commission. Still more serious was the progressive degeneration of trust between the chair and some of the national representatives. By November, when the Six sought to assemble a package offer on processed agricultural products, both Cattani and Fayat felt obliged to lecture van Houten on how the position of the Six should be presented to the British. It was vital, they both emphasised, that the Conference President made it clear this time that the Six were fast approaching the limit of their concessions.[65] Furthermore, the Dutch Presidency contributed significantly to the attempt to isolate the French, a policy which, as argued above, was probably counterproductive and which was certainly inappropriate for a supposedly neutral chairman.

All of the reasons discussed above contributed significantly to the situation of near total deadlock reached by early December 1962. None, however, would have been sufficient to delay progress substantially had the British been willing to make a series of well-targeted concessions. An element of flexibility on agriculture, a willingness to recognise that actual zero tariffs (as opposed to tariff-free quotas) for aluminium, lead and zinc were unobtainable and a degree of realism in the discussion of processed agricultural goods would have transformed the situation and obliged the Six to make counter-offers. As it was, however, Pisani, Wormser and Couve de Murville were repeatedly able to claim, with some justification, that there was no point in the Six making a move before the British had done so. When, for example, the ministers of the Six held a special ministerial meeting in early December intended to loosen their internal paralysis, Couve de Murville dismissed calls for the French to show greater goodwill towards Britain's need by pointing to the absence of flexibility on the part of the applicant.[66] The whole strategy of seeking to pressurise the

---

[64] ECHA. S/06487/62. Report No. 34 on the thirty-second deputies' meeting (9/10/11 October); BDT 145/88, No. 245.
[65] ECHA. S/08146/62. Report No. 39 on the thirteenth ministerial session (15/16/17 November); BDT 145/88, No. 245.
[66] ECHA. S/08134/62. Report No. 42 on the ministerial meeting between the Six (3/4/5 December); BDT 145/80, No. 245.

French into making concessions was thus weakened by the refusal of the British to lessen their own demands slightly.

American assistance or procedural change?

Faced with a seemingly unbreakable deadlock which, if left unresolved, threatened to undermine the whole enlargement process, several European governments began to look towards Washington for assistance. Both Britain and Germany had earlier tried to dissuade the US from becoming too directly involved in the membership negotiations, fearing that any transatlantic interference would infuriate de Gaulle and so prove counterproductive.[67] But by late 1962, French policy was already so negative and the prospects for progress so gloomy, that the attractions of an intervention from Washington which, *deus ex machina*, would resolve the Brussels deadlock began to outweigh the risks involved. At least two approaches to the Americans were made. First, in November 1962 Schröder asked George Ball whether Kennedy could use his forthcoming meeting with the Chancellor to rid Adenauer of his ambivalence towards British membership.[68] This resulted in a strange and inconclusive conversation between the two leaders, in which Kennedy reiterated his belief that enlargement was vital for the stability of Europe and for the survival of Macmillan's government, and the Chancellor stated his agreement with all that the President had said and his full support for British membership, but then went on to outline a series of doubts about the desirability of enlargement and criticisms of British negotiating tactics which suggested that his views had in no way been altered by the President's remarks.[69] Then a month later, Heath suggested that Ball might try to 'soften Hallstein up to play a more constructive role'. The Commission President was duly invited to Washington and told at some length by Ball of 'the seriousness that [the US] attached to a quick conclusion of these negotiations'. He also reportedly welcomed the idea that the US might act as a channel of communication between

---

[67] Kennedy had offered to help in a July 1961 letter to Macmillan. But by the time the Prime Minister met the President in Bermuda, the Americans had understood that silence was more helpful on their part than pressure. PRO. PREM 11 3559, T436/61, Caccia to Macmillan, 28.7.1961; PREM 11 3782, Record of a meeting at Government House, Bermuda, 22.12.1961.

[68] *Foreign Relations of the United States*, p. 123.

[69] *Ibid.*, pp. 124–8.

the Commission and the British.[70] But given that Hallstein, like Adenauer, had already been well aware of the US stance on enlargement, it is doubtful that this intervention had any more effect than Kennedy's discussion with the German Chancellor. Certainly there is little evidence that either German or Commission negotiating tactics in Brussels underwent any major change as a result of US pressure.

Of rather greater impact was the more mundane idea of overcoming the Brussels impasse by means of procedural change. Calls for a change in the way that the negotiations were conducted peaked at the special ministerial meeting of the Six, held in early December and in itself a procedural innovation. The most vociferous partisans for change were, predictably, the Belgians and the Dutch, neither of whom had ever concealed their dissatisfaction with the negotiating method adopted. Fayat, Spaak and van Houten thus combined to appeal eloquently for new rules to be agreed upon for the final stages of the talks. In this they were supported by Lahr, who recognised the need for the discussions to be given a new impetus. Colombo and Couve de Murville, however, were not prepared to countenance either a situation in which the Six dropped their self-imposed commitment to unity or the suspension of most other Community activities until the negotiations with the British were concluded. But while Colombo's determination to preserve EEC cohesion was as clear as ever, the Italian minister's intervention revealed that he too was angered and worried by a negotiation which was paralysing the work and further development of the Community, but which was nevertheless characterised by an endless repetition of incompatible national positions and by the dearth of constructive advance. The answer, Colombo suggested, was not a total change in procedure, but rather a shift in focus, away from the general debate about the implementation of the CAP in Britain to a much more detailed product-by-product examination, in the course of which concessions on one item could be compensated for by advances on another.[71]

A week later the Dutch appeared to respond to Colombo's advice. Confronted once more with immobility in the discussion of British agriculture, van Houten suggested the formation of a Committee of Investigation to study the issues involved in greater detail. On the Committee would sit the ministers of agriculture of the Six and Britain

[70] *Ibid.*, pp. 138–9.
[71] ECHA. S/08134/62. Report No. 42 on the ministerial meeting between the Six (3/4/5 December); BDT 145/80, No. 245.

plus, in the chair, Sicco Mansholt. Together they would try to assess the likely impact of the Six's proposals on British farmers and identify solutions compatible with the Treaty of Rome, where difficulties appeared likely. The Committee's report should be completed in time for the ministerial meeting due to start on 14 January 1963.[72]

The formation of the Mansholt Committee offered a glimmer of light in the agricultural discussions. Heath spoke of the Committee's work in glowing terms on 18 December, arguing that by reducing the 'negotiation temperature' and obliging the ministers of the Six to examine the realities of British agriculture for the first time, it offered a genuine chance of progress.[73] In addition, those eager to foresee a successful end to the negotiations could pin some hopes on the beneficial effects of a final marathon session, planned for January, combined with mediating skills of the Belgian Presidency, due to replace the Dutch at the year's end. The atmosphere of gloom, noted by journalists covering the October ministerial session, however, had deepened considerably by December and clear optimism was hard to find. The possibility of failure, for long a taboo subject, was now mentioned openly. The negotiations could still succeed in early 1963; to do so, however, would require substantial movement both from the French and still more from the British. The final section of this chapter must therefore examine the domestic developments in these two key countries and the bilateral contacts between them.

The road to Rambouillet

The last third of 1962 was a period of contrasting fortunes for Macmillan and de Gaulle. For the British Prime Minister it was a time of mounting anxiety. The unpopularity of the Conservative government, indicated by opinion polls, was confirmed by a string of disastrous by-elections. These had started back in March 1962 with the celebrated Orpington by-election disaster, in which the Conservatives had lost a previously safe seat to the Liberals, but they continued into the second half of the year despite Macmillan's sweeping reshuffle of July 1962. The 'night of the long knives' and, in particular,

---

[72] CMA. 07.51. Compte rendu de la 14ème réunion ministérielle entre les états membres de la CEE et le Royaume-Uni, tenue les 10–11 décembre, 1962. RU/M/61/62.

[73] PRO. CAB 134/1512; CMN(62) 28th meeting, 18.12.1962; equally revealing was French disquiet at the procedural innovation: MAE. Série DE–CE 1961–6, Bte. 519; Note, 18.12.1962.

Selwyn Lloyd's ignominious departure from No. 11 Downing Street had thus done little to end the government's run of ill-fortune.[74] Furthermore, the loss of the South Dorset by-election was directly attributable to the European issue, as an independent Conservative, standing on an anti-European platform, split the Conservative vote.[75] Meanwhile, within the Conservative Party itself, misgivings about some aspects of the Brussels negotiations continued, despite the triumph of the pro-Europeans at Llandudno. Total opposition to British membership was confined to a dwindling minority, but anxiety about further British concessions, particularly on agriculture, was nevertheless acute.[76] Labour taunts about Heath being forced to 'negotiate on his knees' only made matters worse.[77]

For the French President, by contrast, a troubled late summer and early autumn had been followed by unexpected and dramatic success. De Gaulle's announcement in September that he intended to hold a referendum on the direct election of the French President had triggered a Parliamentary crisis. This had culminated on 5 October in the fall of the Pompidou government. The referendum itself, while successful, had, moreover, been won by a smaller margin than the General had hoped. On 28 October, 62 per cent of French voters had approved the election of a President by universal suffrage, rather than the 70 per cent which de Gaulle desired. But the November elections, necessitated by Pompidou's fall, were an emphatic triumph for de Gaulle's political allies. After the second round, the UNR gained 229 seats, an advance of sixty-four, but more importantly a figure which meant that the Gaullists, plus their allies within the *Association pour la V République*, would hold an absolute majority of National Assembly seats.[78] De Gaulle's domestic position was thus dramatically strengthened; the check on his European policy, represented by his need for MRP and centrist support, had totally disappeared.

The Rambouillet summit between the two leaders on 15 and 16

---

[74] Lieber, *British Politics*, p. 231.
[75] Harold Macmillan, *At the End of the Day* (London: Macmillan, 1973), p. 333; Lieber, *British Politics*, pp. 213–14.
[76] See e.g. PRO. PREM 11 3635; Hailsham to Butler, 21.9.1962; Lieber, *British Politics*, pp. 203–5; Dutton, 'Anticipating Maastricht', pp. 536–7.
[77] The French were well aware of Macmillan's mounting difficulties – something which can only have strengthened their resolve to hold firm in Brussels. Couve de Murville, *Une politique étrangère*, p. 407.
[78] *Le Monde* 27.11.1962; Serge Berstein, *La France de l'expansion, vol. I: La République gaullienne 1958–1969* (Paris: Editions du Seuil, 1989), pp. 114–18.

December was an unequal affair. Macmillan arrived in France in need of French flexibility but without much to offer in return; de Gaulle, by contrast, was able to take advantage of his new domestic freedom and express more openly his long-harboured scepticism about British membership. As a result there was no real bargaining or negotiation at Rambouillet, but rather an exchange of views in which neither leader significantly modified his basic position. Throughout the two-day meeting, Macmillan sought repeatedly to emphasise that Britain was ready to become more European – both Commonwealth and Conservative Party hesitations, the Prime Minister stressed, had been overcome – but also to make clear that unless this opportunity was seized to bring Britain into the Community, the possibility might never recur. Success in Brussels, Macmillan underlined, had to be attained within 'one or two months'. In reply, de Gaulle denied all urgency:

> Personally he had not found it at all surprising that the economic negotiations had not been very quick. Britain's entry would involve a complete change in the character and methods of the Common Market including the rules . . . Certainly Britain's entry was not excluded but it would be wrong to think that the difficulties of the negotiations came from the obstinacy or short-sightedness of Ministers or experts.[79]

On the Sunday morning, de Gaulle was even more blunt:

> It was not possible for Britain to enter [the Community] tomorrow and the General felt that the arrangements inside the Six might be too rigid for the United Kingdom. The Prime Minister had said that unless agreement was reached at once it would never be reached but President de Gaulle's view was that the United Kingdom and the Prime Minister had embarked upon a certain course which they would continue to follow. In the end agreement would be reached.[80]

Macmillan replied that he 'was astonished and deeply wounded' by this. He then proceeded to reiterate that Britain had overcome all the obstacles that had previously barred her from entering Europe. He also suggested that the European political union sought by de Gaulle would be much easier to attain once Britain was a member. And the Prime Minister even sought to appeal to French agricultural interests, suggesting that the British market would be barred to French produce

---

[79] PRO. PREM 11/4230, Record of a conversation at Rambouillet, 15.12.1962.
[80] PRO. PREM 11/4230, Record of a conversation at Rambouillet, 16.12.1962.

unless Britain was allowed to join.[81] But it was all to no avail. De Gaulle's comments continued to cast doubt upon Britain's commitment to Europe and to dwell upon the practical difficulties that British membership would bring. It was on the latter that the General chose to dwell in his final comment of the summit:

> In the Six as they existed France had some weight and could say no even against the Germans. France could stop policies with which she disagreed because in the Six she had a very strong position. Once the United Kingdom and the Scandinavians entered the organisation things would be different. In addition the rest of the world would no doubt demand special arrangements; at that point who in the Common Market would be strong enough to resist such pressures? The result would be a sort of world free trade area which might be desirable in itself, but would not be European.[82]

Britain, de Gaulle had decided, was not ready for Europe, nor was the Community ready for Britain.

By the time Macmillan left Rambouillet, there could be little doubt in his mind that the French would try to block British membership. How they would do so or even whether they could do so remained unclear. It was hence unfortunate that Macmillan's next international engagement after Rambouillet was a meeting with Kennedy in the Bahamas to discuss nuclear weapons. For, by convincing Kennedy to sell Britain Polaris nuclear missiles, in place of the cancelled Skybolt, Macmillan underscored the closeness of Britain's transatlantic contacts and provided the French President with a convenient and plausible pretext to veto British membership.[83] Britain, apologists for the General could point out, had successfully concluded a complex bilateral deal with the Americans in forty-eight hours, while sixteen months of negotiation with the Six had so far failed to produce agreement. This demonstrated clearly that the UK had not turned away from the United States and towards Europe, but rather that the

[81] *Ibid.*

[82] PRO. PREM 11/ 4230, Record of a conversation at Rambouillet, 16.12.1962.

[83] The fullest account of the Nassau meeting and the Skybolt controversy is in the so-called Neustadt Report. NSF 322, Staff Memorandum, 15.11.1963. Other accounts include Ian Clark, *Nuclear Diplomacy and the Special Relationship. Britain's Deterrent and America, 1957–1962* (Oxford: Clarendon Press, 1994), pp. 404–18; Constantine Pagedas, 'Troubled Partners: Anglo-American Diplomacy and the French Problem, 1960–1963', PhD thesis, King's College, London (1996), pp. 326–34; George Ball, *The Past Has Another Pattern* (New York: Norton, 1982), pp. 262–8; John Newhouse, *De Gaulle and the Anglo-Saxons* (London: André Deutsch, 1970), pp. 213–22; Horne, *Macmillan 1957–1986*, pp. 437–43.

Anglo-American relationship remained as special and exclusive as ever.[84] As Rambouillet had made clear, however, the Nassau accord was no more than a pretext. De Gaulle's opposition to British membership predated the Anglo-American nuclear deal and his ability to act upon this opposition owed much more to his strengthened domestic position and to the closeness of his ties with Adenauer, than to the intricacies of nuclear high-politics. With his mind made up, his domestic and international position stronger than it had ever been, and a pretext at hand, de Gaulle had now only to select the timing and manner of his veto.

[84] Pompidou made this very point at a press corps dinner in February 1963. Cited in Bernard Picot, 'La France et l'entrée de la Grande-Bretagne dans le Marché commun', PhD thesis, University of Lyon (1965), p. 317.

7 'The end of a chapter'
January 1963

Kojève
Disait au Général 'Je lève
Mon verre à la destruction totale
De la civilisation occidentale'[1]

A select group of senior French and British officials and politicians apart, few people were aware of how negative de Gaulle had been at Rambouillet. Neither the British nor the French drew attention to the way in which their leaders had so signally failed to agree; not even President Kennedy was informed of the doubt which had been cast over British membership. Despite this, it was widely felt that, for reasons largely unconnected to the issues discussed between Macmillan and de Gaulle, January 1963 would be the month in which the fate of the British application would be decided. Uncertainty over the outcome of the Brussels negotiations was harmful both to the British – Macmillan referred at Rambouillet to the way in which British businesses were delaying much-needed investment decisions until it became clear whether or not the British would join the EEC – and to the Community, and on both sides there was frustration with the time being taken.[2] In late November, Dixon had reported from Brussels that 'there is a deep and widespread feeling that the negotiations have been going for a very long time and that they should now be concluded rapidly'.[3] Several key negotiators, the head of the British delegation continued, had indicated that they could not much longer

---

[1] Alexandre Kojève was a senior French civil servant, believed by the British to be both very close to de Gaulle and exceedingly anti-British.
[2] PRO. PREM 11 4230; Record of a conversation at Rambouillet, 15.12.1962.
[3] PRO. FO371 164807; M641/604, Tel. No. 274 Savings, Dixon to FO, 22.11.1962.

be spared from their normal domestic or EEC duties. Similarly, a German Foreign Ministry report prepared in early January predicted that the ministerial meeting due to start on 14 January would be decisive.[4] And a dispatch from von Etzdorf, the German Ambassador in London, underlined the possible damage to Macmillan's government that could be wrought by further delay in Brussels.[5]

This sense of urgency had increased with the announcement that a marathon ministerial meeting was planned for January.[6] No formal deadline had been set – the French Foreign Minister had blocked the creation of an artificial time limit – but the widespread expectation that an attempt would be made at this meeting to put together a package deal carried with it the implication that the absence of a deal would constitute a serious setback.[7] As Joseph Luns commented, with characteristic bluntness, to the Parliament in the Hague, the negotiations had reached 'a dangerous stage . . . a further delay in making decisions might result in the complete failure of the talks'.[8] A television broadcast by Macmillan, in which the Prime Minister stressed that the negotiations could not be allowed to drag on for much longer, confirmed that the British too were losing patience.[9] Further indication of how much was at stake was provided by the flurry of bilateral diplomacy which preceded the ministerial meeting planned for 14 January. Before assembling in Brussels, Schröder and Lahr had talks in London, Fayat, Colombo and Piccioni travelled to Bonn and Heath visited first Brussels and then Paris. In all cases, the need rapidly to conclude the British membership negotiations was high on the agenda.[10]

In marked contrast to the gloom and despondency of mid-December 1962, the tone of most of these bilateral conversations reflected the desire to complete the application process quickly. As Heath noted to the Cabinet before departing for Paris: 'There had

---

[4] AAA. Bestand B-150, Bestellnummer 2, Ref. 200 (IA2), Bd. 1236, Aufzeichnung, 200–81.12/6/97/63, 11.1.1963.

[5] AAA. Bestand B-150, Bestellnummer 2, Ref. 200 (IA2), Bd. 1236, FS 37, von Etzdorf to AA, 12.1.1963.

[6] *Agence Europe* 5.12.1962.   [7] *Ibid.*

[8] PRO. FO371 171412; M1091/17, Tel. No. 4, Noble to FO, 10.1.1963.

[9] *The Times* 11.1.1963.

[10] See for instance an account of the Schröder/Piccioni discussions in Hans-Peter Schwarz (ed.), *Akten zur Auswärtigen Politik der Bundesrepublik Deutschland, 1963* (Munich: R. Oldenbourg Verlag, 1994), vol. I, pp. 79–81.

recently been a marked change in the atmosphere of the negotiations; and the member countries of the Community, with the exception of France, were again earnestly seeking to reach a settlement on terms acceptable to the United Kingdom.'[11] One indicator of this renewed determination to overcome the remaining difficulties was the change in personnel expected in Brussels. Schröder, Luns, Spaak and Piccioni, political heavy-weights who had often been notable absentees from the Brussels ministerial meetings, all announced their intention to attend the final marathon session. This suggested an awareness that, as André François-Poncet, a distinguished French diplomat and a partisan of British membership, put it: 'The technicians have had their say. It is now for the statesmen to weigh up dispassionately the pros and cons, and to decide whether higher political interest does not justify making compromises at the economic level.'[12] Even the French government, while remaining very firm on all matters of substance, seemed more positive than might have been expected after Rambouillet. Asked by Heath whether the French would block British membership even if the Brussels talks reached a successful conclusion, 'M. Couve replied with some emphasis that if the economic problems could be solved nothing could prevent our acceding to the EEC.'[13] Likewise, Pompidou told journalists covering his meeting with the Lord Privy Seal: 'There is no political desire on the part of France to keep Britain out of the Common Market.'[14]

On the verge of success?

The technicians of whom François-Poncet wrote had also edged closer to success. The Mansholt Committee had continued to meet over the Christmas and New Year period, and while its official report was to prove a dry and technical work, the opportunity the Committee provided for detailed discussion of the problems likely to be faced by

---

[11] PRO. CAB 128/37 part 1; CC(63) 3rd conclusions, 10.1.1963.
[12] 'Les techniciens ont parlé. C'est maintenant aux hommes d'Etat de peser avec sangfroid, le pour et le contre et d'examiner s'il ne convient pas de se prêter à des compromis d'ordre économique, dans un intérêt politique supérieur.' My translation. *Le Figaro* 11.1.1963.
[13] PRO. PREM 11 4523; Summary of a discussion after lunch at the British Embassy in Paris, 11.1.1963.
[14] *Guardian* 11.1.1963.

British farmers stimulated the appearance of several important ideas.[15] Three were of particular significance. The first, hinted at by Soames at the 10 January Cabinet meeting, would involve British acceptance of the 1 January 1970 deadline for the establishment of an agricultural common market. In exchange, the British hoped that the Six would be more reasonable about the transitional arrangements to be used for the six or so years between British entry and 1970.[16] Second, the Germans – previously the member state most insistent that the British rapidly bring their prices into line with those of the Community – indicated a willingness to allow the traditionally low British market price for wheat to remain outside the much higher range of Community prices (known as the *fourchette*) for several years, on condition that the final, harmonised price to be fixed by the EEC before 1970 was not prejudiced by this arrangement.[17] And third, the Dutch, Germans and Italians all seem to have been considering a compromise on transitional arrangements for cereals which would permit the British to retain producer subsidies for some years at least but which would buy off French opposition by providing British Treasury support for French farmers wishing to export grain to the United Kingdom.[18]

None of these ideas yet represented a way out of the agricultural quagmire. British assent to the first compromise was to arrive only after General de Gaulle's press conference had transformed the negotiations, while neither of the other two schemes had received the blessing of the French. Indeed, on the only occasion on which the prospect of British cereal prices remaining outside the EEC *fourchette* was broached among the Six, Mansholt was almost as sceptical as Pisani, querying the way in which such an arrangement would work institutionally. Would Britain, the Commissioner asked, be entitled to vote when the Community debated how quickly the *fourchette* from

[15] CMA. –1.823.1. Travaux de la Commission d'Investigation. Rapport à la Conférence, 14 janvier 1963. RU/CI/15/63 Final.

[16] PRO. CAB 128/37 part 1; CC(63) 3rd conclusions, 10.1.1963.

[17] PRO. FO371 171412; M1091/13, COMLEE(63)1, Record of a discussion between the Lord Privy Seal and Herr Schröder at Chequers, 7.1.1963.

[18] PRO. FO371 171452; M1093/5, COMLEE(63)4, Record of a meeting between British and Dutch officials to discuss agriculture in the Brussels negotiations, 4.1.1963. For Lahr's reference to the same idea, with which Schröder perhaps significantly disagreed, see footnote 17 above. The Italian proposal was made in the course of the sixteenth ministerial meeting.

which British prices were excluded should be narrowed?[19] There were also warning signs that too protectionist a compromise on British agriculture might undermine the assurances given to the Commonwealth as part of the arrangement for temperate foodstuffs. In a tense Cabinet discussion of cereal price levels, the Commonwealth Secretary Duncan Sandys argued:

> The essence of those assurances had been that the Community would pursue a price policy which would offer reasonable opportunities in its markets for exports of temperate agricultural products. It could not be maintained that at present price levels those opportunities would exist; and in default of some change in the Community's policy it might be necessary to reopen discussion on questions of major principle which were now regarded as having been settled.[20]

Furthermore, as the Common Market Negotiations Steering Committee acknowledged, there were clear political difficulties involved in any arrangement which would see British Treasury grants being paid directly to French farmers.[21] Nevertheless the appearance of fresh ideas on agriculture combined with new signs of flexibility on the part of the British and the Five suggested that the near total deadlock on British agriculture of October–December might be coming to an end. Similarly, there were hints of progress in the long-running dispute about the financing of the CAP. A German scheme, which would have added to the treaty of accession both the text of the controversial financial regulation and a statement committing the Community to the principle of equitable contributions, won the backing of Benelux and Italy on 16 January, and even the French conceded that the new approach had its merits.[22] Again the issue was not settled, but the direction of a final settlement appeared somewhat clearer. Finally, the British suggestion that all the remaining tariff questions, including agricultural processed goods, the zero-tariff requests and assorted other items left over from previous dossiers, be considered at once, cleared the way for the type of eleventh hour horse-trading that many had always felt would be necessary.[23]

The conference was thus delicately balanced between success and

[19] *Agence Europe* 15.1.1963.
[20] PRO. CAB 128/37 part 1; CC(63) 3rd conclusions, 10.1.1963.
[21] PRO. CAB 134/1544; CMN(SC) 2nd meeting, 8.1.1963.
[22] *Agence Europe* 17.1.1963.
[23] See e.g. PRO. FO371 164808; M641/616, Record of a conversation between the Lord Privy Seal and Signor Colombo at Chequers, 25.11.1962.

failure on 14 January 1963.[24] The optimists – and there were many – could point to the indications of progress described above, and to the very definite will to succeed that characterised most of the Brussels negotiators. They could also recall the many previous Community negotiations – not least those setting up the EEC itself – which had appeared to hover between triumph and disaster before finally being successfully resolved.[25] Those more sceptical, by contrast, could mount an equally plausible case grounded on the great complexity of the outstanding problems and the very limited room for manoeuvre which remained for Macmillan's government.[26] Skilful French stone-walling combined with the varied and at times contradictory economic interests of the five member states better disposed towards enlargement could well have confronted the British negotiators with the choice of either returning to London with terms which were unlikely to obtain Cabinet or Parliamentary approval or breaking off the negotiations unilaterally and postponing British membership until a later date.[27] It was into this highly uncertain situation that de Gaulle so dramatically intervened.

---

[24] It is totally inaccurate to claim, as does Dixon, that 'it was only on eggs and bacon that [Britain and the Six] were still arguing when de Gaulle suddenly brought the whole thing to an end'. Piers Dixon, *Double Diploma: The Life of Sir Pierson Dixon, Don and Diplomat* (London: Hutchinson, 1968), p. 299.

[25] The most resolute of optimists was the Lord Privy Seal himself. See especially his comments to the Cabinet in PRO. CAB 128/37, CC(63) 3rd conclusions, 10.1.1963. On the Community side, Mansholt – both immediately after the veto and much more recently – has insisted that an agricultural breakthrough was near at hand. *Agence Europe* 23.1.1963 and Mansholt's testimony to the EUI Kennedy and Europe Conference, October 1992. Much of the analysis produced by the German Foreign Ministry also emphasised the prospects of success. See e.g. AAA. Bestand B–150, Bestellnummer 2, Ref. 200 (IA2), Bd. 1236, Aufzeichnung, IA 200–81.12/6/239/63, 22.1.1963.

[26] The French, in their efforts to prove that success was not yet obtainable, placed great emphasis on the whole EFTA/neutrals dossier – something which had barely been discussed at all between the British and the Six. See Maurice Couve de Murville, *Une politique étrangère, 1958–1969* (Paris: Plon, 1971), p. 409.

[27] Pessimists were scattered throughout the delegations and beyond. Hoogwater, the former Dutch deputy, was one such (PRO. PREM 11 4523, CODEL 54, 15.1.1963) and Quaroni, the Italian Ambassador in London, another. Marjolin, in the Commission, also felt that Britain's bid to join the Six was likely to fail. Robert Marjolin, *Le travail d'une vie. Mémoires 1911–1986* (Paris: Robert Laffond, 1986), pp. 333–4. Jean-François Deniau and Emile Noël should also be classed among those who expected a breakdown. The former describes the talks as having been on a life-support machine since August 1962. Interviews with the author.

The Gaullist challenge

The French President's press conference held at the Elysée in the afternoon of 14 January 1963 spanned a wide variety of topics. General de Gaulle started by analysing the state of French domestic politics in the aftermath of the UNR's electoral victory and ended by setting out his views on Franco-German reconciliation and on disarmament. In between, however, his comments on British membership of the EEC and his rejection of the American offer of Polaris missiles set out a defiant challenge not merely to British foreign policy but also to the hopes and plans of most other Western European countries and of the United States. In his report to the Prime Minister on French policy during the negotiations, Dixon noted that de Gaulle intended his press conferences to be 'great milestones in history'; that of January 1963 measured up to this aim.[28]

The main thrust of the section dealing with British membership was that the United Kingdom was too different from her continental neighbours to be incorporated into the Community without destroying the cohesion of the grouping.[29] The original Six, de Gaulle explained, were a cohesive group, sharing not only a common culture and a common land mass, but also compatible industrial and agricultural systems, comparable trade patterns and similar social structures. Furthermore, 'they are bound together by the fact that none of them is linked to the outside by any bilateral political or military agreement'.[30] This had allowed them, not without difficulty, to agree on the Treaty of Rome and to start work on a Community which was as yet incomplete. Of particular importance to the French was the completion of an agricultural policy which would provide adequate outlets for all French production.[31]

Britain, by contrast, had initially declined to join the Community. Indeed, de Gaulle alleged that the British had applied 'pressure on the Six to prevent the Common Market agreement from being properly implemented'.[32] The belated UK decision to apply for membership –

[28] PRO. FO371 171449; M1092/129, Dixon to Home, 18.2.1963.
[29] Charles de Gaulle, *Discours et messages* (Paris: Plon, 1970), vol. IV, pp. 66–71.
[30] 'Ils sont solidaires par le fait qu'aucun d'entre eux n'est lié au-dehors par aucun accord politique ou militaire particulier.' My translation. *Ibid.*, p. 67.
[31] *Ibid.*, p. 68.
[32] 'Quelques pressions sur les Six pour empêcher que ne commence réellement l'application du Marché commun'. My translation. *Ibid.*, p. 68.

and to apply moreover 'on her own terms'[33] – confronted the Six with several crucial problems.

> England is, indeed, insular and maritime, linked by her trade, her markets and her food supplies to diverse and often far-flung countries. She works primarily in industry and commerce, and hardly at all in agriculture. She has, in all her patterns of work, habits and traditions which are highly distinctive and original.
>
> In short, the nature, the structure, the economic situation, that characterise England, differ profoundly from the Continent.
>
> How then could England, as she lives, as she produces, as she trades, be incorporated into the Common Market as it was conceived and as it works?[34]

To illustrate this point, de Gaulle contrasted the British agricultural system with the CAP.

The problems posed by British membership were accentuated by the fact that the United Kingdom would not enter alone, but would be accompanied by several of her EFTA partners.

> It must be realised that the entry of Britain first, and then of all those other states, will completely alter the set of arrangements, deals, compensations and rules that have been agreed among the Six, because all of these states, like England, have very distinctive features. Thus it will be another Common Market that will have to be built. But that which will be built among the eleven, and then among the thirteen, and later perhaps among eighteen, will bear little resemblance to that which the Six constructed.
>
> Besides, a Community which grew in this fashion would soon confront the problem of her economic relations with a whole crowd of other states, notably the United States.
>
> It is likely that the cohesion of all the member states, so numerous and so diverse, would not long resist this challenge and that, in the end, there would appear a huge Atlantic Community dependent on,

---

[33] 'Suivant ses propres conditions'. My translation. *Ibid.*, p. 68.

[34] 'L'Angleterre, en effet, est insulaire, maritime, liée par ses échanges, ses marchés, son ravitaillement, aux pays les plus divers et souvent les plus lointains. Elle exerce une activité essentiellement industrielle et commerciale et très peu agricole. Elle a, dans tout son travail, des habitudes et des traditions très marquées, très originales.

'Bref, la nature, la structure, la conjoncture, qui sont propres à l'Angleterre, diffèrent profondément de celles des Continentaux.

'Comment faire pour que l'Angleterre, telle qu'elle vit, telle qu'elle produit, telle qu'elle échange, soit incorporée au Marché commun tel qu'il a été conçu et tel qu'il fonctionne?' My translation. *Ibid.*

and led by, America which would soon absorb the European Community.

This is a prospect which may very well appeal to some, but it is not at all what France has wanted and is seeking, namely a truly European construction.[35]

One day, General de Gaulle predicted, Britain might well change herself sufficiently to join the Community 'without conditions, without reservations, and in preference to any other arrangement'; when that happened France would place no obstacle in front of British membership. But, to judge from the 'long, ever so long Brussels negotiations', that day did not yet appear to have arrived.[36] Franco-British relations should not suffer from a British recognition that Community membership was, for the moment at least, premature – the General paid tribute both to Britain's role in both World Wars and to Macmillan's courage and vision in realising that Britain's long-term future lay with Europe. Furthermore he suggested that trade between Britain and the Six might be safeguarded by some form of association agreement.[37] But, if de Gaulle did not reject British membership outright, his implication was clear: Britain was not yet ready to join the Community.

The underlying motives of de Gaulle's remarks had little to do with the detailed questions of trade, agriculture and institutional

---

[35] 'Il faut convenir que l'entrée de la Grande Bretagne d'abord, et puis celles de ces Etats-là, changera complètement l'ensemble des ajustements, des ententes, des compensations, des règles, qui ont été établies entre les Six, parce que tous ces Etats, comme l'Angleterre, ont de très importantes particularités. Alors c'est un autre Marché commun dont on devrait envisager la construction. Mais celui qu'on bâtirait à onze et puis à treize et puis peut-être à dix-huit, ne ressemblerait guère à celui qu'ont bâti les Six.

'D'ailleurs, cette Communauté s'accroissant de cette façon verrait se poser à elle tous les problèmes de ses relations économiques avec une foule d'autres Etats, et d'abord avec les Etats-Unis.

'Il est à prévoir que la cohésion de tous ses membres, qui seraient très nombreux, très divers, n'y résisterait pas longtemps et, qu'en définitive, il apparaîtrait une Communauté atlantique colossale sous dépendance et direction américaines et qui aurait tôt fait d'absorber la Communauté européenne.

'C'est une hypothèse qui peut parfaitement se justifier aux yeux de certains, mais ce n'est pas du tout ce qui a voulu faire et ce qui fait la France et qui est une construction proprement européenne.' My translation. *Ibid.*, p. 69.

[36] 'Sans restriction et sans réserve, et de préférence à quoi que ce soit' and 'longues, si longues conversations de Bruxelles'. My translations. *Ibid.*, p. 69.

[37] *Ibid.*, pp. 69–71.

arrangements under discussion in Brussels.[38] The French President's unhappiness with the idea of British membership seems rather to have been grounded in the belief that EEC enlargement would undermine French leadership within the Community and augment American influence over the EEC. An enlarged Community including Britain would be more solidly Atlanticist and much less receptive to Gaullist ideas about an independent Europe willing, at times and on certain issues, to distance itself from the American line. It would not, as the General had put it, be 'a truly European construction'. The centrality of the Franco-German pairing might also be lessened, with alternative axes and groupings suddenly possible. France would, moreover, suffer economically from British membership. In addition to the problems for agriculture and French Africa described in chapter 5, enlargement also raised the prospect of the dominant supplier clause in the American Trade Expansion Act being used to all but eliminate the Common External Tariff – a protective barrier which the French regarded as vital to both their economic well-being and to the survival of an acceptable common market. This too would thus hasten the replacement of a European Europe with 'a huge Atlantic Community, dependent on, and led by America'. De Gaulle's central aim of using Europe as a means to increase the power of France to act autonomously on the world stage would be seriously damaged by British membership of the European Communities and by its inevitable sequel, namely British involvement in any future construction of a European political union.[39]

None of this French anxiety was new. De Gaulle's fear that British

---

[38] De Gaulle's motives have been extensively explored. In addition to de La Serre, 'De Gaulle' and Christopher Johnson, 'De Gaulle face aux demandes d'adhésion de la Grande-Bretagne à la CEE', both in Institut Charles de Gaulle, *De Gaulle en son siècle* (Paris: Plon, 1992), vol. V, pp. 192–218 and Sir Pierson Dixon's post-mortem to the negotiations (FO371 171449; M1092/129, Dixon to Home, 18.2.1963), see Jean Lacouture, *De Gaulle* (Paris: Editions du Seuil, 1986), vol. III, pp. 313 ff.; Edmond Jouve, *Le Général de Gaulle et la construction de l'Europe (1945–1966)* (Paris: Librairie Générale de Droit et de Jurisprudence, R. Pichon and R. Durand-Auzias, 1967), pp. 174–89; Roger Massip, *De Gaulle et l'Europe* (Paris: Flammarion, 1963), pp. 117–21; John Newhouse, *De Gaulle and the Anglo-Saxons* (London: André Deutsch, 1970), pp. 227–42; Nora Beloff, *The General Says No* (London: Penguin, 1963), pp. 148 ff.; Alain Peyrefitte, *C'était de Gaulle* (Paris: Fayard, 1995), pp. 363–85.

[39] Jouve, *Le Général*, pp. 718–25; Jean-Marc Boegner, 'Les principes de la politique européenne du général de Gaulle' and Wilfried Loth, 'Pour une nouvelle lecture de la politique étrangère du général de Gaulle' in Institut Charles de Gaulle, *De Gaulle*, vol. V, pp. 66–71 and 144–54.

membership would transform the Community, and in so doing thwart his hopes of using the ties between the Six for his own ends, predates the British application; as a result, the General's line of argument to Macmillan about British participation in the process of European unification was remarkably constant between the Rambouillet meeting of January 1961 and that of December 1962. The timing of the press conference is thus not explicable by any change in de Gaulle's fundamental view. Instead it reflected the fact that by January 1963 de Gaulle had lost faith in the previous French strategy and had for the first time since July 1961 the domestic strength, the international leverage and the pretext to adopt an alternative approach and end a membership bid to which he had always been opposed.

French tactics in Brussels until the end of 1962 had been based upon the belief that Britain's determination to join the Community was fragile and that a failure to secure adequate commercial and agricultural safeguards would result in the withdrawal of the membership application. Couve de Murville and many French officials appear to have believed that this strategy could still work.[40] But as de Gaulle was no doubt aware, the risks involved were growing, for as the political impatience with the impasse in the membership discussions increased so too did the danger that either the British or the Five might make a bid for a quick settlement in Brussels which the French would be hard pressed to resist.[41] Any such development would not, of course, remove France's ultimate power to block British membership; unanimous agreement amongst the Six was necessary before any new country could be admitted to the EEC. But if the Brussels negotiations moved much closer to success, a French veto could not be disguised as anything other than political. There were thus clear advantages in acting sooner rather than later. More fundamentally, de Gaulle now had the strength to act. As explained in chapter 6, the November 1962 election victory had freed the General from many of the domestic constraints that had previously affected his European

---

[40] Couve de Murville remained convinced that France was within striking distance of forcing Britain to withdraw its application and was thus reportedly furious with de Gaulle. Conversation of the author with Maurice Vaïsse. See also the comment by one of Clappier's assistants in Institut Charles de Gaulle, *De Gaulle*, vol. V, p. 222.

[41] According to Dixon, de Gaulle was extremely contemptuous of the Quai d'Orsay. If true, this would help explain his lack of confidence that French negotiators in Brussels would be able to prevent British membership. PRO. FO371 171449; M1092/ 129, Dixon to Home, 18.2.1963.

policy while the ever closer relationship with Adenauer was likely to ensure that the central international linkage of Gaullist foreign policy would survive an ending of the British application. The importance of Adenauer to de Gaulle's calculations also bolstered the case for immediate action. The German Chancellor was too old and politically vulnerable to last indefinitely – it was thus unwise to postpone action which would be much safer for so long as Adenauer held power in Bonn. Furthermore, if the General acted before 20–22 January when the Chancellor was due to visit France and sign a Franco-German agreement to which Adenauer was known to attach great importance, any qualms which the German leader might have about de Gaulle's press conference would be tempered by the desire to avoid jeopardising Franco-German *rapprochement*. And finally, the Nassau agreement between Macmillan and Kennedy provided an ideal cover for de Gaulle's real motives. Both internal French and international criticism could be blunted by references to an Anglo-American encounter which did indeed appear to confirm that Britain had extremely close ties to a major non-European power.

De Gaulle's intervention was thus based on a range of issues much wider than those discussed in Brussels. Nevertheless, the text of de Gaulle's press conference, if not its fundamental cause, was remarkable for the number of references to the actual membership negotiations. There was admittedly a comment about non-European political and military links – a clear allusion to the special relationship in general and the Nassau agreement in particular. In addition, the contrast de Gaulle drew between 'insular' Britain and the 'continental' countries of the Community seemed to imply that the United Kingdom's island position was a serious bar to EEC membership. But the main piece of evidence de Gaulle cited to support his contention that Britain was not suitable for membership in the short term was the state of the Brussels negotiations. It was Britain's supposed inability fully to accept the CET, her refusal to scrap deficiency payments and apply the CAP, and her reluctance to abandon her economic ties with the Commonwealth and EFTA that, the General argued, revealed her continuing ambivalence towards Europe and rendered her unfit for Community membership.

As the British were quick to point out, many of de Gaulle's claims were not accurate. Embassies across Europe were instructed to make clear that the British government had agreed to apply the CET, had accepted that the CAP would have to function in the UK also and had shown itself ready to alter British commercial links with both Commonwealth and EFTA partners. The difficulty was, however, that de Gaulle was able to play upon the fact that the greater part of the talks in Brussels had, inevitably, concentrated not on those many aspects of the Community that the UK could accept but rather on the parts of the *acquis* which would cause difficulties even if only in the short term. The very length of the Brussels negotiations and the large number of issues discussed thus gave an element of plausibility to de Gaulle's claims.

By portraying his action as a logical response to an impasse, rather than a deliberately hostile move against the British, de Gaulle may well have hoped to gain support from many of those who had welcomed his 1958 decision to end the free trade area negotiations. On that occasion many 'Europeans' had greeted with relief a French move which brought to a close a series of negotiations which few any longer expected to succeed but none had wanted openly to pronounce a failure.[42] But in 1963 his claim to be acting according to 'realities' while others allowed themselves to be guided by their sentiments was not only less convincing than in 1958, but also somewhat hazardous.[43] In his press conference the General had strongly suggested that the negotiations would fail, but, as the minister in the British Embassy in Paris noted, 'he did not suggest that France would impose a political veto on our admission'. Instead, 'he spoke as though he was sure that it would not be necessary'.[44] This represented a major risk. For if Britain were able to resolve quickly the outstanding issues and to sign a provisional document establishing the terms of British membership, de Gaulle would be forced either to accept an enlargement of the Community which he had publicly argued was both impossible and undesirable or to issue a clear political veto which would expose the hollowness of the arguments advanced on 14 January. To quote Rumbold once more: 'The most striking feature of the press conference was that [de Gaulle] has exposed himself to a major defeat if contrary to his expectations the negotiations nevertheless succeed.'[45]

---

[42] Miriam Camps, *Britain and the European Community 1955–1963* (Oxford University Press, 1964), pp. 166–72.

[43] For a sceptical critique of the French case by the *Auswärtiges Amt* see Schwarz (ed.), *Akten*, pp. 97–102.

[44] PRO. PREM 11 4523, Tel. No. 52, Rumbold to FO, 14.1.1963.   [45] *Ibid.*

Reactions in Brussels

It was this possibility that the General might yet be shown to be wrong which determined the immediate reactions of the Five and of the British. Spaak, Schröder and Luns all issued statements denying that the negotiations had no prospect of success, the Commission announced its intention to continue the search for solutions compatible with the Treaty of Rome, while in Italy La Malfa commented angrily that the Five could not be treated like colonies by de Gaulle.[46] But in general, public outbursts were tempered by the hope, shared by the British negotiators as much as by those of the Five, that by pressing on and overcoming the remaining technical problems, the will of the General could be thwarted. Heath reported from Brussels that despite the uncertainty over whether the French delegation would receive instructions to withdraw from the negotiations, 'the other four major delegations are more buoyant and determined than ever before, with the light of battle shining in their eyes. It is quite clear that so far the Press conference has proved counter-productive.'[47]

The clearest illustration of the way in which de Gaulle's intervention spurred the Five and the British onward rather than inducing immediate despair came in the discussions of agriculture. When news of the press conference first reached Brussels, the Mansholt Committee, which was slightly behind schedule, had not yet completed its report. In their eagerness to push forward, however, the British and the Five combined to keep the Committee in session until 3.30 a.m. on 15 January, systematically working through the fifteen pages of amendments submitted by the French. This effort allowed Mansholt to present the final report to ministers the following afternoon. Spaak and Heath then produced a carefully stage-managed exchange in which the Belgian Foreign Minister promised a new effort by the Six to agree to reasonable transitional arrangements in return for British concessions on the length of the transitional period. The Lord Privy Seal had discussed this option beforehand with Soames, and was therefore able to accept conditionally. Spaak, Luns, Schröder and Colombo all acknowledged that this constituted a major advance;

---

[46] *Agence Europe* 15.1.1963; AAA, Bestand B–150, Bestellnummer 1, German delegation's statement to the press, 15.1.1963.
[47] PRO. PREM 11 4523, CODEL 23, Heath to Macmillan, 15.1.1963.

Pisani, by contrast, said nothing. The meeting adjourned and a discussion *à six* of the new position began.[48]

Pisani was much less silent once the British had left the room. Confronted by Luns, Lahr, Spaak and Colombo all determined to allow some progress on British agriculture, and able to rely only on sporadic backing from Mansholt on some of the technical issues, the French Minister of Agriculture was obliged to fight a dogged rearguard action. He made some telling points, but in the wake of both de Gaulle's press conference and Heath's concession on the length of the transitional phase, the time-worn French argument that it was for the British and not the Six to make most of the running and to prove their need for special treatment had lost much of its force. Spaak, in particular, greeted this claim with scorn, pointing out that in the wake of the General's press conference, technical haggling was no longer appropriate. The time for political decisions had arrived. As a result, the French minister could do little more than sue for time. When the Italian and Dutch agricultural experts tabled a text which incorporated the idea of British subsidies to French exporters, Pisani briefly denounced this scheme as constituting little more than a petty bribe to French farmers which would in any case be inadequate compensation but then asked for the meeting to be adjourned so that the French could study the new proposal. Defiant until the end – Pisani left the meeting quoting Vergil: 'Timeo Danaos et dona ferentes' – the French were very clearly on the defensive.[49]

Wormser and Couve de Murville – who had arrived late because of an emergency meeting of the French Cabinet – found themselves in much the same predicament the following day. There were occasional reminders that the unity of the Five could not be guaranteed – when aluminium was discussed it was the Dutch and not the French who found themselves in dock accused of selfish rigidity – but for most of 16 January the French were more isolated than ever before.[50] By the evening they had had enough. Couve de Murville requested that a special meeting of the Six be held to discuss whether the work of the conference could be allowed to continue and Fayat, the conference

[48] *Ibid.* See also CMA. 07.51. Compte-rendu de la 16ème session ministérielle entre les états membres des communautés européennes et le Royaume-Uni, tenue les 14–18 janvier 1963. RU/M/70/63.
[49] *Agence Europe* 17.1.1963; AAA. Bestand B–150, Bestellnummer 2, Ministerbüro, Bd. 8435, Harkort to AA, 18.1.1963.
[50] *Ibid.*

chairman, was obliged to agree.[51] The meeting was scheduled for 10.00 a.m. on 17 January.

In the interval the Five and the British tried hard to devise a formula which might prevent the French from withdrawing their delegation from the Brussels talks. Encouraged by a conversation with Couve de Murville, in which the French Foreign Minister admitted that he had instructions to end the negotiations but seemed unclear as to how to accomplish this, Spaak discussed tactics with Fayat, Schröder and Colombo. The four ministers agreed that the negotiations should be kept alive at all costs, and to this end decided to propose that a committee be established, under the chairmanship of Colombo, to prepare a report which would review the state of the negotiations and propose possible compromise solutions. This idea was then relayed to Heath who gave his assent on condition that, if a breakdown did prove inevitable, the blame should lie clearly with the French.[52] In addition, Lahr sought to tackle Couve de Murville directly. In a tête-à-tête discussion the German State Secretary vigorously rejected Couve's claim that the negotiations had already been heading towards failure, insisting that, by contrast, two-thirds of the ground had already been covered and that the remaining portion was attainable. Couve de Murville appeared unmoved.[53]

There followed a day of meetings which Luns, with hindsight, was to describe as a circus: 'for thirteen-and-a-half hours six foreign ministers, intermittently assisted by seven other ministers, had battled passionately with the French'. Spaak, Luns continued, had been particularly vociferous, warning the French that their actions had caused a crisis not just in the enlargement negotiations but more generally among the Six. The Italians too had been outspoken: 'Piccioni had at times literally been banging the table.' And Luns himself had spoken severely to Couve de Murville:

> throughout the negotiations it had been the French who had been insisting that there must be a joint Six view, even on such trivialities as kangaroo meat from Australia; now at the crisis of the negotiations de Gaulle, without a word of warning to the others, had gone off on a line of his own that was clearly contrary to the wishes of the Five; not even the Russians treated their satellites as badly as that.[54]

[51] *Ibid.*
[52] PRO. PREM 11 4523, CODEL 40, Heath to Macmillan, 17.1.1963.
[53] Schwarz (ed.), *Akten*, pp. 96–7.
[54] PRO. FO371 171448; M1092/104, Noble to Reilly, 22.1.1963.

But the anger of the Five achieved only limited success. Impassive throughout – Luns expressed astonishment tinged with admiration that the French Foreign Minister 'had never even raised his voice'[55] – Couve de Murville resisted all attempts to create an investigative committee with the power to propose solutions to the outstanding problems. Instead, he suggested that Colombo should be asked merely to list the unresolved issues – a task which the Italian minister rejected as demeaning.[56] Only on the morning of 18 January, when faced with Dutch and German threats to block both the new association convention and future progress on the CAP, did the French buckle slightly, agreeing to issue a communiqué which, while noting the French desire to suspend the negotiations, postponed a final decision on this matter to the next ministerial meeting planned for 28 January.[57] The Five, in other words, had won themselves ten days' breathing space.

Countermeasures

The fortnight between de Gaulle's press conference and the 28 January meeting was characterised by frenetic diplomacy.[58] The vast majority of ideas and proposals discussed with such urgency between the British, the Community and, significantly, the American government can, however, be examined as one of three types. The first and largest category is that formed by the various schemes designed to keep the negotiations alive and thus win valuable time during which international pressure on the French would mount. One such plan, the idea of entrusting a committee of experts chaired by Colombo with the task of preparing a report, was described above. This was soon followed by a similar scheme, which would have allocated the tasks of assessing the state of the negotiations and of suggesting possible routes for advance to the European Commission rather than to an intergovernmental group. In both cases, the report would ideally provide the basis for a resumption of the negotiations with a high prospect of rapid success. And even if this were not possible, an independent and thorough audit of the negotiations would clearly illustrate the inaccuracy of de Gaulle's claims. A

---

[55] *Ibid.*
[56] PRO. PREM 11 4523; CODEL 54, Heath to FO, 18.1.1963.   [57] *Ibid.*
[58] For a detailed account of British diplomatic efforts during the weeks which followed de Gaulle's press conference see Rolf Steineger, 'Great Britain's First EEC Failure in January 1963', *Diplomacy and Statecraft*, 7:2 (1996).

variation on this theme was the Benelux suggestion that the British should continue to negotiate with either the Five or, failing that, with the Dutch or Belgians alone, in order to produce a draft agreement. This then could be presented to the French as a *fait accompli*. Spaak admitted to Heath that there was no guarantee that the French would accept the draft: 'but it would be a striking demonstration not only that the Five wanted [Britain] in the Community on political and economic grounds, but that practical arrangements to this end had been worked out'.[59] An approach of this type would be complemented by an effort to provide de Gaulle with some means of honourable retreat. Thus Jean Monnet arranged that the editorial in *Le Monde* on 21 January should conclude: 'it is true that it will still be possible for the General, if the English decided to make the concessions necessary in order to open the gates of Europe, to explain that it was his intransigence that made it possible'.[60]

Alongside the various attempts to prevent a formal suspension of the negotiations, the Five also sought to coerce the French into retreat by threatening reprisals. The two principal targets for such talk were the new association convention between the EEC and its African associates, which had been agreed in December but was yet to be signed, and the CAP regulations for beef, dairy products and rice which were due to be discussed in early 1963. Mention was also made of the still unresolved dispute over CAP financing and of the commercial concessions France was expected to seek on behalf of newly independent Algeria. Predictably, the Dutch were the most extreme, deciding at Cabinet level that retaliatory measures should be pursued even when they risked harming Dutch economic interests, but Belgium and Italy also indicated a willingness to delay Community policies in order to put pressure on the French.[61] There were even signs that Germany might follow suit, Erhard commenting to Heath:

[59] PRO. PREM 11 4524; CODEL 90, Heath to Macmillan and Home, 28.1.1963. For other examples of thinking along these lines see PREM 11 4523; No. 72, Nicholls to FO, 23.1.1963 and PREM 11 4524; CODEL 107, Hainworth to FO, 31.1.1963.

[60] PRO. PREM 11 4523; Tel. Nos. 94 and 97, Dixon to FO, 22.1.1963.

[61] Wendy Asbeek Brusse, 'Alone within the Six: The Dutch Cabinet and the Problem of EEC Enlargement' in Richard Griffiths and Stuart Ward (eds.), *Courting the Common Market: The First Attempt to Enlarge the European Community 1961–1963* (London: Lothian Foundation Press, 1996), p. 134. For Belgian threats see PRO. PREM 11 4523; CODEL 54, Heath to FO, 18.1.1963 and for Italian PREM 11 4524; Record of a conversation at Palazzo Chigi, 2.2.1963.

> if the French refused [to allow the negotiations to continue] and the negotiations broke up it was difficult to see how the Community could carry on except possibly for those provisions which were automatic. The Germans had made sacrifices in agriculture and on Association, particularly the Overseas Development Fund; and he did not see how they could possibly be asked to go on making the sort of sacrifice that would be involved in further developments, for instance on agriculture.[62]

The French were thus made well aware that a refusal to back down on British membership might seriously handicap their future prospects of success within the Community.

Still more radical was the third strand of thought. This included proposals which would, if not break up the Community as constituted, at least create a rival political grouping centred on London. The most forthright exponent of a move of this type was Sir Pierson Dixon, the British Ambassador in Paris and leader of the British negotiating team at official level. In a top secret telegram addressed to Heath and the Foreign Secretary on 23 January, Dixon suggested that in the aftermath of a final breakdown in Brussels, the Five plus Britain's fellow applicants should be invited to a conference in London 'in order to lay the foundations of a political union'.

> The proposals which we would make at such a conference could, so far as political union was concerned, be based on the version of the Fouchet proposals which was most favoured by the Five, plus perhaps something further in the direction of greater power for the European Parliament ... So far as defence was concerned the proposals could be related to the Nassau agreement and to the foundation of a European element in a multi-national and multi-lateral nuclear force to which we could contribute most if not all of our own nuclear armoury.[63]

The great merit of this scheme, Dixon argued, was that it would frustrate de Gaulle's European ambitions and reinforce the Atlantic Alliance without obliging the Five to abandon the Community –

---

[62] PRO. PREM 11 4524; CODEL 90, Heath to Macmillan and Home, 28.1.1963. The German Foreign Ministry advised against such retaliation, however. Wolfgang Hölscher, 'Krisenmanagement in Sachen EWG. Das Scheitern des Beitritts Großbritanniens und die deutsch–französischen Beziehungen' in Rainer A. Blasius (ed.), *Von Adenauer zu Erhard. Studien zur Auswärtigen Politik der Bundesrepublik Deutschland 1963* (Munich: R. Oldenbourg Verlag, 1994), p. 19.

[63] PRO. PREM 11 4523; Tel. No. 111, Dixon to Heath and Home, 23.1.1963.

something which Dixon thought to be possible but unlikely.[64] And it was not only the British who were tempted by ideas of this type. Luns, the Dutch Foreign Minister, told Heath on 28 January of the need for 'some kind of political demonstration to show up de Gaulle' and suggested that this might be done by holding a conference with the Five in London. This would demonstrate Britain's continuing interest in Europe and the fact that the Five were with the British. The conference could even discuss political union on Fouchet lines.[65] Spaak's *chef de cabinet* indicated that the Belgian Foreign Minister not only agreed but went further, foreseeing defence cooperation on non-nuclear matters and, if the British would agree, 'cooperation in nuclear arrangements in order to find means of producing a European element, of course within the framework of NATO'.[66]

A German rescue?

The radical nature of such ideas is very revealing about the depth of anger and resentment caused by de Gaulle's intervention. In the short term, however, the British, Dutch, Belgians and Italians all acknowledged that the best hope of forcing de Gaulle to change course lay through German pressure.[67] Not only was Adenauer known to be the only statesman within the Community for whom de Gaulle had respect, but Germany was also central to de Gaulle's long-term plans. The Gaullist vision of a Europe strong and independent enough to hold its own between the two superpowers was inconceivable without the active participation of France's largest and most powerful continental neighbour. Furthermore, it was widely felt that the German Chancellor's imminent visit to Paris and the planned signature of a Franco-German memorandum would give Adenauer both the opportunity and the leverage to persuade the French President to change course.

German reactions to de Gaulle's press conference had, moreover, been particularly strong. Both the Foreign Ministry and the Ministry of Economic Affairs had for instance put aside their usual disagreements

[64] *Ibid.*
[65] PRO. PREM 11 4524; CODEL 91, Heath to Macmillan and Home, 28.1.1963.
[66] PRO. PREM 11 4524; CODEL 97, Heath to Macmillan and Home, 28.1.1963.
[67] See e.g. PRO. PREM 11 4523; CODEL 92, Macmillan to Heath, 18.1.1963 and FO371 171448; M1092/113, Note of a conversation with Spaak, 29.1.1963.

about European policy and drafted remarkably similar papers about the negative consequences of a breakdown in Brussels.[68] The two departments foresaw disasters ahead for Britain and her EFTA partners, for Germany and the rest of the Community, for the US/ European relationship, and for the free world in general, should the French veto be allowed to stand. Amongst the adverse effects which were predicted were the fall of the Macmillan government and its replacement by a Labour administration which might adopt a quasi-neutralist line in East–West questions, a withdrawal of British troops from Germany, the ending of Franco-German reconciliation, the near paralysis of the Community, an escalating trade-war between the EEC and EFTA and the consequent loss of valuable German export markets among the Seven, the collapse of Kennedy's drive for freer world trade and a possible resurgence of American isolationism. The Ministry of Economics briefing document ended with an apocalyptic warning: 'If the old rift between the EEC and EFTA reappears and on top of this a new fracture between the Six and America is allowed to develop, the situation can produce only one winner: Khrushchev.'[69]

Civil service alarm was matched through most of Germany's ruling elite. President Lübke was reported to have told Adenauer that 'if he went to Paris and returned without asserting the will of the Parliament, that would mean "der grosse Krach", in other words the final explosion'.[70] The Foreign Affairs Committee of the *Bundestag*, meanwhile, quickly endorsed Schröder's statement criticising the French President; Erich Mende, head of the Free Democrats, promised Sir Christopher Steel, the British Ambassador in Bonn, that he would press for Adenauer's immediate removal if the Chancellor failed to speak firmly to de Gaulle; and Erich Ollenhauer, the SPD leader, wrote an open letter to Adenauer expressing the 'urgent wish . . . that you assert your influence particularly at this moment so that Great

---

[68] AAA. Bestand B–150, Bestellnummer 2: Bundeskanzleramt, B136/2561, Aufzeichnung, 18.1.1963; Abteilung 1(IA2), Bd. 144, Aufzeichnung Lahrs, 19.1.1963; Ref. 200 (IA2), Bd. 1236, Sprechzettel für Herrn Minister zur Kabinettsitzung am 25.1.1963, EA3–905 883, 22.1.1963.

[69] 'Wenn statt dessen der alte Riß zwischen EWG und EFTA neu entsteht und ein neuer Riß zwischen EWG-Europa und Amerika hinzukommt, kann es aus der ganzen Situation heraus nur einen einzigen Gewinner geben: Chruschtschow.' My translation. AAA. Bestand B–150, Bestellnummer 2, Ref. 200 (IA2), Bd. 1236, Sprechzettel für Herrn Minister zur Kabinettsitzung am 25.1.1963, EA3–905 883, 22.1.1963.

[70] PRO. PREM 11 4523; Tel. No. 67, Steel to FO, 18.1.1963.

Britain's entry to the EEC will not fail because of French opposition'.[71] These party views were combined in a joint statement made to the press on 18 January, in which the President of the *Bundestag* and the leaders of the three main political parties stated that: 'German policy must do everything possible to remove the obstacles in the way of British entry in the EEC.'[72] Similarly both *Länder*-level politicians and spokesmen for industry voiced their concern that German exports might be adversely affected by the failure of the enlargement process. Fritz Berg, the President of the Bundesverband der Deutschen Industrie, visited Adenauer on 16 January to express his hope that de Gaulle could be persuaded to change his mind, while on 23 January the mayor of Hamburg wrote to Schröder urging the German government to do all that was possible to safeguard the 800-year-old trade links between northern Germany and Scandinavia.[73]

There was also international pressure on the Germans. Four days after de Gaulle's press conference, Steel made a farewell visit to the Chancellor in the course of which he stressed that 'we [the British] relied upon him in Paris on Monday to save the situation'.[74] More importantly, perhaps, the Americans made their disapproval of de Gaulle's action clear and hinted that the failure of Britain's membership bid might precipitate a reassessment of American policy towards the whole of Western Europe. George Ball, in Bonn in order to persuade the Germans of the merits of the American Multilateral Force (MLF) proposals, outlined to Adenauer 'in lurid terms the dangerous repercussions which could arise from [the British] being rebuffed . . . the whole United States attitude to Europe would come under review'.[75] On 19 January, at Macmillan's direct request, Kennedy himself wrote to Adenauer, impressing on the German leader the need to use his influence with de Gaulle.[76] And on the same day a message to the Chancellor from the Secretary of State, Dean Rusk, spoke of Adenauer's 'historic duty' to prevent a 'downward trend of events' which might threaten both NATO and European

[71] PRO. PREM 11 4523; CODEL 41, Heath to Macmillan, 17.1.1963; Tel. No. 56, Steel to FO, 16.1.1963; Tel. No. 13 Savings, Steel to FO, 17.1.1963.
[72] PRO. PREM 11 4523; Tel. No. 68, Steel to FO, 18.1.1963.
[73] PRO. FO371 171445; M1092/51, Gallagher minute, 16.1.1963; AAA, Bestand B–150, Bestellnummer 2, Ref. 200 (IA2), Bd. 1236, Engelhard to Schröder, 23.1.1963.
[74] PRO. PREM 11 4523; Tel. No. 72, Steel to FO, 18.1.1963.
[75] PRO. PREM 11 4523; Tel. No.177, Ormsby-Gore to FO, 16.1.1963.
[76] PRO. PREM 11 4523; No. 793, Macmillan to Kennedy, 19.1.1963 and Record of a telephone conversation between Macmillan and Kennedy, 19.1.1963.

integration.[77] As he departed for the French capital, the Chancellor was very aware of the domestic and international expectations surrounding his visit.[78]

Adenauer quickly demonstrated his refusal to be coerced. Even before leaving for France, the Chancellor had won vital room for manoeuvre by dissuading the 16 January Cabinet meeting from making their approval of the Franco-German agreement conditional on the lifting of the French veto. This had been done largely by suggesting that the document to be signed in Paris take the form not of a memorandum but of a full treaty – requiring debate and ratification in the *Bundestag*. Once this was suggested Schröder rallied to the Chancellor's position.[79] And the Chancellor's defiance continued while he was in Paris. Relations between Britain and the continent were briefly discussed during the first meeting between Adenauer and de Gaulle, but rather than provoking a confrontation this instead produced agreement that Britain was still torn between Europe and the Commonwealth and, more fundamentally, was too attached to its special relationship with the United States. Both leaders agreed that the Nassau deal between Macmillan and Kennedy had been symptomatic of this latter problem.[80] Later in the same day Schröder was a little more forthright. But even the German Foreign Minister undermined his criticism of de Gaulle's press conference by acknowledging that while Franco-German *rapprochement* was 'a fundamental issue', the negotiations with Britain were just one problem among many.[81]

Much the same occurred in the second day of discussions between de Gaulle and Adenauer. True to the promises he had given to his domestic critics, the Chancellor raised the issue of British membership not once but twice. He advanced, moreover, an idea which he hoped might resolve the impasse: the European Commission could be asked to assess the state of the negotiations and make suggestions as to possible solutions for the outstanding issues. But the Chancellor did not pursue this point. Rather, Adenauer soon found himself in

[77] Schwarz (ed.), *Akten*, pp. 104–5.
[78] For a further description of the pressures being brought to bear on the Chancellor, see Hölscher, 'Krisenmanagement in Sachen EWG', p. 17 and Herbert Blankenhorn, *Verständnis und Verständigung. Blätter eines politischen Tagebuchs 1949 bis 1979* (Frankfurt: Propyläen, 1980), p. 437.
[79] Hans-Peter Schwarz, *Adenauer: Der Staatsmann, 1952–1967* (Stuttgart: Deutsche Verlags-Anstalt, 1991), p. 819.
[80] Schwarz (ed.), *Akten*, pp. 115–16.
[81] 'Eine Basisfrage'. My translation. *Ibid.* p. 129.

agreement with de Gaulle that EEC enlargement coupled with the American drive for free trade might lead to a disastrous situation in which the Community was deprived of a Common External Tariff. Discussion was thus allowed to move on to other matters without a major clash of views.[82] That the crisis in Brussels had not been allowed to mar Franco-German relations was emphatically demonstrated later that afternoon with the signature in the Elysée Palace of a treaty reaffirming the two countries' commitment to close bilateral cooperation and providing for regular and frequent official and ministerial meetings.[83] The Franco-German relationship had once again proved stronger than Germany's desire to see Britain more closely linked to the continent and, in a fashion extremely reminiscent of November 1958, the best single opportunity to salvage British hopes had vanished as a result.

The final meeting

The final act of the British membership negotiations was played out in Brussels on 28–9 January. On the evening of the first day and for much of the morning of the second, Schröder alone, and then all of the Five together, tried at length to persuade Couve de Murville to accept the idea of a Commission report as put forward by the Germans.[84] But the French Foreign Minister stood his ground, ready to contemplate a report, but only on three conditions. First the report should be broader than that envisaged by the Five, examining not merely the specific problems encountered during the negotiations with the British but also the wider problems thrown up by enlargement. Second, the report should not include any suggested solutions, as this would exceed the role of the Commission. Third, the normal business of the Community should continue uninterrupted during the period – and the French Foreign Minister implied that this would be a substantial period of time – in which the report was under preparation. These terms were totally unacceptable to the Five.[85] In

[82] *Ibid.* pp. 140–1 and 144–7.
[83] On the origins of the Elysée Treaty see Jacques Bariéty, 'De Gaulle, Adenauer et la genèse du traité de l'Elysée du 22 janvier 1963' and Hans-Peter Schwarz, 'Le Président de Gaulle, le chancelier fédéral Adenauer et la genèse du traité de l'Elysée' in Institut Charles de Gaulle, *De Gaulle*, vol. V, pp. 352–64 and 364–73.
[84] A fairly detailed record of discussions among the Six was leaked to the British: PRO. FO371 171419; M1091/146 and 147; Delegation minute No. 33, 29.1.1963.
[85] *Ibid.*

the early afternoon of 29 January, Fayat, the chairman of the conference, bowed to the inevitable. The meeting *à six* was adjourned and the British were invited to enter the chamber. After a brief statement by Fayat, in which the impasse between the French and the Five was explained, Spaak, Luns, Schröder, Colombo, Schaus, Hallstein, Couve de Murville and, last of all, Heath, made their final speeches to the conference.

The ministers of the Five did not hide their bitterness: Spaak spoke of his 'distress, anxiety and sadness', Luns and Schröder referred to their 'deep disappointment', and Colombo mentioned the Italians' 'sincere regret' at the outcome of the meeting. Likewise, they were unanimous in their conviction that a final agreement satisfactory to both Britain and the Six could, with time, have been reached. As Spaak commented: 'Today five delegations of the Six consider that these negotiations, although they have been long and sometimes difficult, have not reached an impasse, and that the wise policy would be to continue them in the spirit of cooperation and honesty.'[86] Several delegations also drew attention to the way in which French action betrayed the preamble of the Treaty of Rome which stated that the Community would remain open to any other European state wishing to join. But the tone of the interventions became more varied when the ministers of the Five looked to the future. Schröder appeared the most confident, appealing to the British to retain their desire to enter the Community, and saying that 'the day will come when we shall be able to solve this problem'. Spaak and Luns, by contrast, foresaw only difficulty ahead. The Belgian Foreign Minister, as so often, described matters in the most dramatic fashion:

> I think I can say that if the Treaty of Rome is not rent asunder as a result of what is taking place, the Community spirit will nonetheless be gravely and I fear mortally wounded for a long time.
>
> From the moment when, in a Community, one of the partners alone tries to compel all the others to take decisions which are of capital importance for the Community's life, the Community spirit no longer exists. It will be extremely difficult, I am convinced, to continue to develop the economic Europe. As for the political Europe of which we had dreamed as a necessary consequence of economic

---

[86] CMA. 07.51. Compte-rendu de la 17ème session ministérielle entre les états membres des communautés européennes et le Royaume-Uni, tenue les 28–29 janvier 1963. RU/M/73/63.

organisation, I do not know when it will be possible to speak of it again, because, unquestionably, confidence no longer exists.[87]

In similar fashion Colombo felt that the process of European integration had been seriously harmed. Unlike Spaak, however, the Italian minister ended on an optimistic note, restating that Italy 'wanted to continue in the belief and the hope that this [European] unification will be achieved'.[88]

Couve de Murville could do no more than restate the French position. The negotiations, he maintained, 'had been at a standstill since October': Britain could not accept 'the disciplines of the Treaty of Rome' and in particular those of the CAP. The French had therefore simply 'taken note of the facts as they forced themselves upon us, or would have forced themselves upon us sooner or later'. Couve de Murville then explained why he had been unable to agree with the Five on a mandate for a Commission report. He ended on a defiant note:

> I repeat that when Great Britain is in a position to accept all the provisions of the Treaty of Rome, nothing would be able to prevent her from entering the Common Market. But the burden of proof is on her, not on us. In other words, we are not saying: 'The United Kingdom must not enter the Common Market.' We are saying: 'Are the requirements fulfilled?'
>
> In reply to the criticisms voiced on all sides that we French want a little Europe, I will say again that we are not trying to keep Europe little or big, but we are trying to be sure that the Europe we are building is a European Europe. This, we believe, is the criterion according to which the problems ought to be judged.[89]

Heath made the last and longest speech. In it he stressed the sincerity and good faith with which the British had applied and reminded the Six of the warm and unanimous welcome they had given the opening statement by the British. The Lord Privy Seal then reviewed the sixteen months of negotiations, drawing attention to the numerous areas in which significant progress had been made and trying, one by one, to rebut French claims that Britain could not accept the principles of the Treaty of Rome. This accomplished, he noted: 'The plain fact is that the time had come when the negotiations were, for some, too near to success. It is clear to the world that they have been halted, not for any technical or economic reasons, but on purely

---

[87] *Ibid.*   [88] *Ibid.*   [89] *Ibid.*

political grounds and on the insistence of a single Government.'[90] The ending of the negotiations, Heath argued, was contrary not only to the Treaty of Rome, but also to previous statements by the French government. And he recalled specifically Couve de Murville's speech of 2 March 1961, in which the French Foreign Minister had publicly invited the British to apply for EEC membership. Finally, having generously thanked all those who had participated in the conference, the head of the British delegation concluded with a promise that Britain would not reverse its policy towards the Community:

> the events of the last few weeks have placed in jeopardy progress towards that true European unity which, I believe, many millions of people desire. But although, as has just been said, this is a sad moment for European unity, I should like straightaway to say one thing . . . We in Britain are not going to turn our backs on the mainland of Europe or on the countries of the Community. We are part of Europe; by geography, tradition, history, culture and civilisation. We shall continue to work with all our friends for the true unity and strength of this continent.[91]

The speeches complete, Fayat briefly thanked the British delegation for 'the spirit of cooperation' with which it had always negotiated, and then with 'great regret' declared the seventeenth ministerial meeting closed.[92] After sixteen months of detailed discussion, the Brussels negotiations on British membership were over. It was, as Macmillan was to comment to Piccioni a month and a half later, 'the end of a chapter but certainly not of the volume'.[93]

The epilogue

The crisis of January 1963 had four lasting effects. First and most obvious was the way in which de Gaulle had not only postponed Community enlargement, but had also avoided any significant change in the relations between Britain and the Six. As from 29 January 1963, the negotiations between the British and the Six were suspended indefinitely, and the issue of enlargement was removed from the Community agenda for the foreseeable future. Furthermore, neither the various plans for a British-led alternative European grouping, nor even the assorted palliatives designed to lessen British isolation and

[90] *Ibid.* [91] *Ibid.* [92] *Ibid.*
[93] PRO. PREM 11 4524; Record of a conversation at Admiralty House, 14.3.1963.

ensure that the Community and the United Kingdom did not drift further apart, led anywhere.

The former fell victim to both caution on the part of the Five and British ambivalence. Immediately after the formal end of the negotiations, the British and the Five met, under the chairmanship of Spaak, to discuss future action. With tempers running high and, according to one German participant, large quantities of whisky being consumed, there was a certain amount of wild rhetoric: Luns, for instance, suggested that the ending of the British membership bid would provoke 'an agonizing reappraisal' of Dutch foreign policy.[94] But even at this meeting, the caution of the Italians and Germans about any move which might antagonise the French was very apparent. Thus Schröder warned against over-hasty action while Piccioni felt that any future discussions between the Five and the British should take place in the WEU – a forum in which the French would also be present.[95] And the British too were increasingly apprehensive about the idea of discussing political union with the Five. A telegram from Macmillan and Home to the Lord Privy Seal sent just before the Five and the British started their discussion counselled great caution for three reasons. First, the Cabinet had decided that the prospects of a satisfactory economic settlement emerging from discussions held without the French were almost non-existent. Second, the Prime Minister and the Foreign Secretary were nervous about the implications of discussing defence matters with the Five. This could detract from NATO and 'would almost certainly mean pressure on us for increased commitments to the defence of Europe'. Any move of this type would also require American agreement.

> Thirdly, as regards the political future of Europe, we must bear in mind that the Five are all in varying degrees in favour of Federalism. While the risk in the long-term might have been one thing if we were to enjoy the economic benefits of membership of the Community, it would be quite another if we were to set out on such a course for political reasons alone.[96]

As a result, Macmillan and Home advised Heath to avoid setting the

---

[94] Alfred Müller-Armack, *Auf dem Weg nach Europa. Erinnerungen und Ausblicke* (Tübingen and Stuttgart: Rainer Wunderlich Verlag/C. E. Poeschel, 1971), pp. 139–40. For the Luns quote see next footnote.

[95] PRO. PREM 11 4524; CODEL 103, Heath to Macmillan and Home, 29.1.1963.

[96] PRO. PREM 11 4524; CODEL 224, Macmillan and Home to Heath, 29.1.1963.

date for any future meeting between the British and the Five. If one was necessary, the WEU might well prove the ideal forum.[97]

Plans to render less painful Britain's enforced exclusion from the Community also petered out. In the immediate aftermath of 29 January most of the Five seemed enthusiastic about some form of multilateral consultation machinery, which would give Britain, through the Five, a limited voice in Community decision-making.[98] But support for this idea soon faded as the Five realised that this would both raise significant institutional problems and make more difficult a normalisation of Community business. By mid-1963 it was clear that the British voice in Brussels could only be ensured by an enlarged UK Mission to the Community and by bilateral discussions with individual Community member states. In similar fashion, German and Belgian proposals for a limited free trade area linking Britain to the Community, while informally discussed with the British, failed to gather the momentum they needed to get off the ground.[99] There was thus no significant alteration in the relationship between Britain and the Community until 1967 when Britain once more applied for full membership.

The second lasting effect was the damage done to the reputations of two of the key political players in the crisis of January 1963 – Adenauer and Macmillan. An exact assessment of the impact which the events of early 1963 had on either leader is almost impossible – not least because both were in domestic political trouble before de Gaulle's press conference and both were to be assailed by further difficulties after January 1963. Nevertheless, it seems almost beyond dispute that the discontent which the German Chancellor had created by so clearly placing Franco-German relations above links between Britain and the Community was an important contributory element to the precipitous decline in Adenauer's influence. Admittedly, the Chancellor had already undertaken to resign by the end of 1963, and the crisis of January of that year cannot therefore be pointed to as a

---

[97] *Ibid.*

[98] See e.g. Schröder's musings to the Lord Privy Seal on 29 January. PRO. PREM 11 4524; CODEL 104, Heath to Macmillan and Home, 29.1.1963.

[99] Schröder floated the idea of some form of temporary economic arrangement to Heath on 29 January. PRO. PREM 11 4524, CODEL 104, Heath to Macmillan and Home, 29.1.1963. For the much more detailed Belgian plans see PREM 11 4524, No. 115, Home to Heath, 7.2.1963 and Treasury Note 'Belgian Proposal for a Customs Union between the UK and the Six', 8.2.1963. See also Hölscher, 'Krisenmanagement in Sachen EWG', pp. 40–4.

cause of his departure. It may well have contributed, however, to Adenauer's powerlessness in his last months in office, and in particular to his failure to prevent Ludwig Erhard from becoming his successor. Similarly, the destruction of so central an element in Macmillan's foreign policy only added to the woes of the Conservative government. The Prime Minister would, of course, have fared still worse had the negotiations ended unsuccessfully without de Gaulle's intervention – a unilateral British withdrawal from the Brussels discussions or a Parliamentary rejection of the terms secured would have been much more humiliating for the Premier. Nevertheless, the premature ending of Macmillan's last bold policy initiative further sapped the dynamism of both the Prime Minister himself and the government. Macmillan was to resign through ill health in the same month as Adenauer, and the Conservative's thirteen years in office ended with the Labour Party's victory in the general election of September 1964.[100] De Gaulle, by contrast, prospered, weathering with seeming ease the domestic storm caused by his 14 January press conference.[101]

Third among the lasting consequences of the January crisis was the damage done to the widespread hopes for greater political union in Europe. Such hopes had, admittedly, been in disarray since the breakdown of the Fouchet Plan discussions in April 1962. But the ambition to increase the political cohesion of the Community partners and to enable Europe to speak with a more coherent voice in world affairs had survived this set-back.[102] De Gaulle's behaviour in early 1963 snuffed out any prospect of renewed discussion. The alliance of convenience which had linked partisans of Gaullist intergovernmentalism and enthusiasts for a more supranational union became untenable and the prospects of political union *à six* seemed very poor. Also

[100] Macmillan's official biographer argues that 'for Macmillan it remained the gravest failure of all his policies . . . there was nothing to put in its place'. Alistair Horne, *Macmillan 1957–1986* (London: Macmillan, 1989), p. 450; see also pp. 454 ff.; David Dutton, 'Anticipating Maastricht: The Conservative Party and Britain's First Application to Join the European Community', *Contemporary Record*, 3:7(1993) 538–40.
[101] For an analysis of French domestic reactions to the veto including, significantly, the rather qualified and cautious criticism typical of many of de Gaulle's political opponents, see Bernard Picot, 'La France et l'entrée de la Grande-Bretagne dans le Marché commun' (PhD thesis, Lyon, 1965), pp. 342 ff.
[102] The Quai d'Orsay, for instance, told de Gaulle in September 1962 that the Fouchet scheme could be revived, provided that the idea of British membership was accepted. MAE. Série DE–CE 1961–6, Bte. 517; Soutou note, 1.9.1962.

adversely affected was Franco-German cooperation. In May 1963, the *Bundestag* took advantage of Adenauer's decision to make the agreement signed with France a full treaty requiring Parliamentary ratification by voting to add a preamble which reaffirmed Germany's commitment to the existing Communities and to NATO.[103] This did not end the utility of the document – the Elysée Treaty survived as a symbol of Franco-German reconciliation and the regular bilateral meetings for which it provided continued to enable the French and Germans to coordinate policy, especially on European matters. But the Treaty's function as a building block in a Gaullist Europe was all but totally undermined.

The fourth and most positive effect of the crisis was to underline the solidity of the Community. Despite the doom-laden rhetoric of Spaak during the final ministerial meeting of 29 January, the Community gradually appeared to edge back into normality. Admittedly, the stark divide between the Gaullist and the supranational vision of Europe which had been one of the sub-texts of the January crisis did not disappear. But it was in the interests of no one to allow this difference of view, however profound, to impede the functioning of the Community. Most of those involved in Community business were scarcely more willing to let the crisis over British membership paralyse the EEC institutions than they had been to allow the British negotiations themselves to delay the forward progress of integration. The various retaliatory measures thus faded away. In July 1963 the association convention – one of the Community policies delayed by the anger of the Five – was signed by the Six and the African Associates in the capital of the Cameroons, Yaoundé. Five months later, on 24 December 1963, the next tranche of CAP agreements was belatedly agreed. A year after the veto, peace appeared to have returned to the Community.

---

[103] For a detailed discussion of this episode see Oliver Bange, 'English, American and German Interests behind the Preamble to the Franco-German Treaty, 1963' in Gustav Schmidt (ed.), *Zwischen Bündnissicherung und privilegierter Partnerschaft: Die deutsch–britischen Beziehungen und die Vereinigten Staaten von Amerika, 1955–1963* (Bochum: Universitätsverlag Dr N. Brockmeyer, 1995), pp. 225–81.

Conclusions

January 1963 constituted a major European crisis. De Gaulle's press conference called into question not only the plans of the British government, but also those of most Western European governments and the Kennedy administration. The General's actions further confirmed that the fears that had surrounded de Gaulle's return to power in 1958 had not been without foundation. Newly free from the Algerian troubles and from many of the domestic political constraints which had characterised his first five years in power, the French President appeared to be in a position from which he could mount a major challenge to existing European and Atlantic arrangements. The deep anxiety – bordering occasionally on hysteria – that marked the reactions of the British, the Five and the Americans, was thus largely comprehensible. But while both fascinating and important, the events described in the preceding chapter have too often been allowed to colour and shape discussion about the entire 1961–3 attempted enlargement. As a result, de Gaulle has normally been portrayed as the central actor in the whole enlargement drama – with Macmillan, Adenauer and even Kennedy playing the other lead roles – and the Brussels negotiations themselves have been treated as a minor and rather tedious sub-plot which had little if any bearing on the final outcome.

This approach took its most extreme form in the report on the negotiations prepared by Sir Pierson Dixon and the staff of the British Embassy in Paris in the immediate aftermath of the French veto.[1] The British Ambassador argued that de Gaulle had always been against British membership, that his opposition was based on the fear that

---

[1] PRO. FO371 171449; M1092/129, Dixon to Home, 18.2.1963.

Britain would lessen, if not totally usurp, French leadership in the Community, and that, with the possible exception of a nuclear deal, the British government could never have done anything to overcome this negative French opinion.[2] As Dixon confessed in the final section: 'I am afraid that with the aid of hindsight I am driven reluctantly to the conclusion that because of General de Gaulle we scarcely had a chance of succeeding. There was never room for more than the Gaullist cock of the European roost.'[3]

Echoes of this view are evident in much of the subsequent literature. Few go quite as far as Dixon in maintaining that the British bid was doomed from the outset.[4] But many share his opinion that the fate of Britain's application was decided in Paris not Brussels and that the determining moments were the Birch Grove, Champs and Rambouillet summits between Macmillan and de Gaulle, rather than ministerial meetings in the Belgian capital.[5] In doing so, such authors push the murky questions about Anglo-French and Anglo-American nuclear diplomacy centre stage, and marginalise the largely commercial and Community agenda of the actual membership negotiations. The failure of the British attempt to join the EEC thus becomes either an episode in bilateral Anglo-French diplomacy or, alternatively, a study in the politics of the Western Alliance. The Community itself, the member states other than France, and the important questions which the prospect of enlargement had raised for the whole process of European integration are largely ignored.

This study has deliberately adopted a different approach. It has

---

[2] *Ibid.*   [3] *Ibid.*

[4] Although Wolfram Kaiser argues as much: 'To Join, or not to Join? the "Appeasement" Policy of Britain's First EEC Application' in Brian Brivati and Harriet Jones (eds.), *From Reconstruction to Integration. Britain and Europe since 1945* (Leicester University Press, 1993), pp. 144–54.

[5] Of other recent works, those which go furthest in this direction are: Françoise de La Serre, 'De Gaulle et la candidature britannique aux communautés européennes' in Institut Charles de Gaulle, *De Gaulle en son siècle* (Paris: Plon, 1992), vol. V, pp. 192–202 and Anne Deighton, 'La Grande-Bretagne et la Communauté économique européenne (1958–1963)', *Histoire, Economie et Société*, 1 (1994), 113–30; Wolfram Kaiser, 'The Bomb and Europe. Britain, France and the EEC Entry Negotiations (1961–1963)', *Journal of European Integration History*, 1:1 (1995) and Simona Toschi, 'Washington–London–Paris, an Untenable Triangle (1960–1963)', *Journal of European Integration History*, 1:2 (1995) focus on similar issues; among older titles: John Newhouse, *De Gaulle and the Anglo-Saxons* (London: André Deutsch, 1970) and Robert Kleiman, *Atlantic Crisis: American Diplomacy Confronts a Resurgent Europe* (London: Sidgwick & Jackson, 1965) do much the same.

sought to analyse the crisis of January 1963, it has covered the various bilateral encounters between Macmillan, de Gaulle and Adenauer, and it has also looked briefly at the debate about possible Anglo-French nuclear cooperation. The release of British, French and German documents relating to these issues has indeed allowed some new points to be made, particularly in connection with the evolution of the German Chancellor's views and the influence of the French Cabinet on de Gaulle's position. But this book's principal focus has been on the detailed negotiations conducted in Brussels by the six EEC member states and the British – in other words the very talks which, up until January 1963, most contemporary observers expected to be decisive. Such a redirection of the historical focus has at least four important merits.

The first is that a detailed examination of the Brussels negotiations reveals much about each of the EEC member states. The British application was a divisive and testing challenge to the Six. Although quite genuinely welcomed by most of the member states, the prospect of enlargement posed, earlier than might otherwise have been the case, a series of questions not only about the Community's relationship with the rest of Europe, but also the EEC's place in world, and in particular Atlantic, trade. It also challenged some of the internal bargains upon which European economic integration was based and obliged the Six to produce a series of unified positions on highly controversial agricultural and commercial issues. The heated debates among the Six which formed so central a part of the negotiations thus revealed much about the various national attitudes towards the Community in 1961–3 and about the roles that each of the member states had made their own within the European Community.

The most discontented members of the Community were the Dutch. As chapter 1 recalled, the Dutch government felt strongly that the Six were a narrower and less economically liberal grouping than would have been ideal. This dissatisfaction was initially tempered by the degree of liberalism which the EEC did promise, but by the early 1960s frustration had mounted once more. Both the Germans and the European Commission had been less effective champions of liberalism than the Dutch had hoped and many aspects of the Common Market appeared to owe more to Italian and French protectionism than to northern European openness. Alongside such economic frustrations, the Dutch were also assailed by mounting political doubts. The start of serious discussion about European political union was a particular source of concern, as not only would this risk being dominated by the nascent Franco-German axis, but it might also undermine the Atlanticist security framework to which the Dutch were strongly committed.

The prospect of British membership was extremely enticing for the Dutch. Once inside the Community, Britain seemed likely to curb French-inspired illiberalism, to provide a rival pole of attraction to Paris and to thwart any serious challenge to the Atlantic Alliance. Dutch negotiators were thus instructed to do all that they could to facilitate Britain's entry. Uniquely among Community delegations, the Dutch rarely lost sight of this long-term aim: de Pous, van Houten, Marijnen and the other Dutch negotiators were the most consistent advocates of Community generosity and often the most outspoken critics of the French. Unfortunately, as was pointed out in chapter 5, this did not necessarily make the Dutch most effective. Indeed, the Netherlands' hard-line position delayed agreement amongst the Six more often than it promoted concession. Matters grew still worse when the chairmanship of the conference fell to the Dutch in the autumn of 1962. Too extreme to promote compromise and too fiercely critical of Community laggards to win the trust of all Six delegations, both Hoogwater and van Houten proved ill-suited to guide the negotiations during one of their most awkward stages. The style of the Dutch Presidency confirmed, however, the Netherlands' status as the staunchest ally of the British within the Community.

The limits of Dutch flexibility and willingness to assist British entry, however, are almost more revealing than their general eagerness to help. For the Dutch were not prepared to pay any price in order to secure British membership. When the treatment of British farmers was discussed, for instance, Marijnen was quite clearly torn between the general injunction to assist the British and an understandable desire to safeguard a system which he had personally helped to negotiate and under which many of the farmers whom he represented stood to gain much. Furthermore, the Dutch were not willing to break ranks with their five partners. Despite their anger at French behaviour and their mounting annoyance with the seeming weakness of the other four member states, they did not, as threatened, disown the common stance of the Six. Nor did they abandon a negotiating procedure which, as chapter 2 made clear, they had correctly predicted would lead to delay. Dutch anger, as the aftermath to the veto would confirm, was ultimately powerless: the Netherlands needed the Community, and by extension it needed to continue close cooperation with France and Germany. While the Dutch could strive hard for an enlargement which would make the Community much more attractive, they could do nothing which imperilled a customs union which they, more than any other of the Six, had worked so hard to attain.

The Belgians were more ready to admit their political and economic need of the Community. It was significant that in late August 1961, the Belgian permanent representative to the EEC had initially declared his support for the most *communautaire* of procedural options, and only abandoned this position after a meeting of Benelux ministers opted for a joint Low Countries approach. Spaak, moreover, demonstrated his concern about the political implications of enlargement with a series of outspoken tirades against the EFTA neutrals, the association of which, he claimed, would constitute an obstacle to the political development of the Community. But the Belgians matched the Dutch in their belief that British membership would considerably improve the Community. They too anticipated greater economic liberalism, increased political stability and an end to all dangerous 'third force' dreams as the benefits of UK entry.

Around the Brussels negotiating table, these views translated into a slightly more moderate position than that of the Dutch, although the Belgians could be as vociferous as their Benelux partners when Spaak himself was present. The Belgian Foreign Minister had notoriously little patience for technical details, and tried repeatedly to remind his colleagues of the essentially political nature of their task. In so doing, Spaak was attempting to repeat his success during the Treaty of Rome negotiations in preventing technical hindrances from long delaying fundamental progress. But in 1961–3, unlike 1955–7, there was no unanimous political desire among the Six to succeed. Spaak's appeals, while passionate, thus tended to have little effect other than to distract attention away from the technical agenda which, however tedious, constituted the only route to success. In total contrast, Fayat, Spaak's deputy and a much more regular presence at the Brussels conference table, had skills much better suited to the British membership negotiations. A patient negotiator, who was less prone to bouts of temper than his superior, Fayat demonstrated a talent for devising the delicate compromises necessary to edge the Six and the British closer to agreement. When led by their Deputy Foreign Minister, the Belgians thus joined the Italians and the Commission as the principal mediators amongst the Six. In this capacity, Belgium was able to have an

influence over many of the agreements reached which was dispropor-
tionate to its economic size and political weight.

The Germans, by contrast, were less effective champions of British
membership than might have been expected. As noted in chapters 1
and 2, the Bonn government had both economic and political reasons
to support enlargement in general and British membership in particular. Economically, Germany stood to gain an important new
market as well as a useful ally in its efforts to steer the EEC's
commercial policies in a liberal direction. Politically, British membership would reinforce the Atlanticist majority to which Germany
belonged at the expense of French 'third force' ambitions. Furthermore, the Germans had seemed to be very flexible about Commonwealth and other problems when these had been discussed bilaterally
before Britain had applied. As a result, the British had been confident
that the Germans would be influential allies in Brussels.

British expectations only increased once the various Community
negotiators assembled in Brussels. Harkort, Müller-Armack and Lahr,
the principal German representatives, were all personally well disposed towards the British as was, indeed, the vast majority of German
opinion, whether at a diplomatic, political or business level. And
these views were reflected in the tone adopted by German spokesmen
as the negotiations started. But once serious bargaining began,
German weakness became apparent. To a certain extent this was
caused by specific economic problems. In the agricultural sector,
Germany's ability to frame viable compromises was greatly limited by
the political influence of its own, highly inefficient farmers; likewise,
its willingness to help Indian textile exporters was tempered by an
awareness of discontent amongst West German textile producers. But
a much more fundamental factor in Germany's inability to deliver the
assistance to Britain that its rhetoric implied was a political decision to
avoid serious confrontation with the French.

To a very large extent this German unwillingness to offend the
French was due to Adenauer. Support for a *rapprochement* between
France and Germany was a constant thread running through Adenauer's fourteen years in charge of German foreign policy. Moreover,
the Chancellor's emphasis on rebuilding ties between the two largest
Community member states had increased as Adenauer grew older
and less politically powerful. With time running out, the German
statesman's desire to make irreversible the process that he had started
grew ever stronger. The prospect first of European political union

through the Fouchet process and then, when that failed, political union *à deux* thus became so enticing that for Adenauer at least, nothing should be placed in its way. But it would be a simplification to place responsibility for Germany's cautious stance entirely with the Chancellor. For while Schröder, Carstens and other senior foreign policy officials did not share their ageing leader's dislike of British membership, they did resemble Adenauer in their support of closer ties to the French. As a result, they were prepared to accept that German policy in Brussels, while not actually placing obstacles in front of the British, should avoid trouble with the French. In practice this tended to result in German negotiators initially supporting the idea of movement towards the British stance, but abandoning this target as soon as the French made their determination to resist clear. It also greatly limited the capacity of the Germans to coerce the French into changing their view in January 1963.

The Italians were also surprisingly reticent in their support for the British. As had been the case with Germany, both Italian behaviour in the pre-negotiations and the rhetoric with which the British application had been greeted in Rome seemed to promise far-reaching cooperation and assistance once the negotiations began. And once more this had not proved to be the case. But the reasons for this discrepancy were rather different. The first was that, unlike Germany and the Benelux countries, Italy had little to gain economically from enlargement. Italy, while beginning to appreciate the merits of limited economic openness, had not yet rid itself of its traditional protectionist reflexes. The prospect of another liberal voter in Council of Ministers' meetings was thus no more appealing than the thought of another member state defending the interests of northern European as opposed to Mediterranean farmers. Second, the Italian political establishment, and Italy's representatives in Brussels in particular, were highly committed to European integration and anxious to avoid any situation in which either the *acquis communautaire* or the unity of the Six was threatened, even if doing so resulted in British membership being delayed. Integration *à six* was the keystone of Italian foreign policy and not even the highly desirable prospect of British membership was worthwhile if to accept it endangered in any way what had already been achieved. Furthermore, several key members of the Italian delegation in Brussels – Ducci and Cattani in particular – had been deeply involved in the Treaty of Rome negotiations and were thus loathe to see any of their handiwork undone. Likewise, Colombo's personal involvement in the creation of the *acquis*, first as Minister of Agriculture and subsequently as Minister for Industry, ensured that Italy's principal representative at a ministerial level was well aware of the effort which had gone into the creation of common policies and the fragility of the bargains upon which the outcome rested. And third, the Italians were anxious to avoid too sharp a confrontation with the French, as this would not only risk alienating de Gaulle and in so doing marginalise Italy in European decision-making, but it would also destroy the highly effective role which the Italian negotiators had been able to carve out as conciliators and mediators between the French and the other member states.

Yet even the Italians found it hard to tolerate French behaviour by late 1962. In Brussels there was a new note of impatience in the interventions of Colombo and the other Italian negotiators and a greater readiness to take some risks with the *acquis* in order to secure British membership. There were also signs that Fanfani was losing patience with the conciliatory line which the Italian negotiators had adopted towards the French. As Sergio Romano points out, the Italian Premier had strong incentives, both domestic and international, to distance himself from de Gaulle, as doing so curried favour with the Americans while simultaneously pleasing the Italian Socialists whom Fanfani was eager to woo.[6] But as was the case with the Dutch, the aftermath of de Gaulle's press conference underlined the strict limits of Italy's freedom to attack France. For while Fanfani and Piccioni were both publicly critical of the French action and even ready to contemplate retaliation, the Italians, as noted in chapter 7, were amongst the most cautious when the possibility of acting without France and with Britain was discussed. Integration *à six*, however imperfect, remained much better than no integration at all.

France was much less torn than its partners by the conflicting desires to accommodate Britain within the Community and to protect the EEC from being damaged in the process. Indeed, from the very outset of the British membership negotiations, General de Gaulle, his most senior ministers and a large body of opinion within the Quai d'Orsay were certain that British membership would be contrary to French interests, both economic and political, and should therefore be

[6] The linkage between Fanfani's foreign policy and *l'apertura a sinistra* are explored in Sergio Romano, *Guida alla politica estera italiana* (Milan: Rizzoli, 1993), pp. 102–4.

prevented if at all possible. Translating this clear hostility into decisive action was not an easy task, however.

An overt French challenge to Britain's application in 1961 or the first half of 1962 would have thrown the Community, the process of Franco-German reconciliation and the French political system into turmoil. In Brussels, both the implementation of the 14 January 1962 CAP deal and the negotiation of a new association convention with the mainly francophone Community associates in Africa and the Caribbean would have been called into question. Both of these policies were highly advantageous for France; anything that hindered their progress would have seriously compromised France's strategies for economic modernisation and disengagement from its former empire. In Bonn, Adenauer's ability to steer German foreign policy in the direction of ever closer cooperation with the French would have been placed in jeopardy. The emotional visit by the German Chancellor to France in July 1962, de Gaulle's triumphal tour of Germany in September 1962 and the Elysée Treaty of January 1963 would never have been possible. As such, three important elements in de Gaulle's strategy of harnessing Germany's economic potential and using this to increase France's stature in the world, as well as three milestones in the enduring process of Franco-German *rapprochement*, would have been lost. And finally in Paris, a naked challenge to British membership, deprived even of the fig leaves constituted by the negotiating impasse of late 1962 and the Anglo-American Nassau deal, and before the Gaullist electoral triumph of November 1962, would have put the coalition governments of Debré and Pompidou seriously at risk. A general election, fought at least in part on European issues where Gaullist foreign policy had yet to displace the pro-integration consensus of the Fourth Republic years, would have been the likely result. Pompidou's warning to the French Cabinet in July 1962 did not only apply in the case of total break-up of the European Community; even in a crisis that stopped short of the complete collapse that the French Prime Minister feared, France risked being 'the greatest loser'.

In recognition of such dangers, the French adopted a lower risk strategy. De Gaulle joined his fellow leaders in giving a formal welcome to the British application and France made no attempt to prevent the negotiations from beginning. But French negotiators in Brussels were instructed to set the price of British membership as high as possible. By so doing, their principal aim was to convince the British that full membership of the Community was not yet feasible.

But if this failed, and contrary to expectations the British were willing to accept Community membership even on terms which were disadvantageous for the Commonwealth, EFTA and the British Exchequer, the French would at least have the solace of having obtained enlargement very much on their terms.

French tactics thus centred on a resolute defence of the Treaty of Rome and of the *acquis communautaire*. Both bore the stamp of previous French influence within the Community and as such a defence of the status quo was often all but identical to a defence of French interests. But couching French objections in *communautaire* language had the added tactical advantage of making French obstructionism much more immune from criticism by the Five. After all, the Six had been unanimous in stating in November 1961 that the exceptions to the Treaty and the *acquis* should be kept to the barest minimum. French efforts to thwart the British were thus difficult to distinguish from genuine attempts to protect the Community – an aim which was shared by all of the Six.

Such tactics, combined with the skill of the French representatives at all levels of negotiation, were enough to ensure that, despite being the only member state to oppose British membership, France was rarely isolated among the Six until the autumn of 1962. As the second year of negotiations between Britain and the Six began, however, the very success of French tactics and the resultant protestations of the British began to push the Five into a bloc which, while still highly divided on many specifics, was increasingly unified in its reluctance to accept delay. The position of the French grew correspondingly more difficult. Notwithstanding claims from the Quai d'Orsay that French tactics could still attain their objective, there was thus a certain logic in de Gaulle's decision to jettison the previous French approach and, taking advantage of his new domestic and international strength, to impose French will in rather more emphatic fashion.

The final role which requires comment was that of the European Commission. For Hallstein and his colleagues, the enlargement negotiations constituted an ideal forum in which to demonstrate the utility and expertise of the Commission. It was an opportunity which they fully exploited. Throughout the Brussels discussions, Commission personnel – especially Hallstein, Mansholt and Deniau – were able to prove their capacity to act as guides to the intricacies of Community regulations, guardians of both the *acquis* and the Treaties and architects of invaluable compromise suggestions. All but one of the provisional agreements concluded between the British and the Six, for instance, were based upon Commission proposals. The Commission also played an important role in soothing dissent among the Community partners, particularly during the crucial ministerial meeting in late July and early August 1962. The Brussels institution could thus look back at its contribution to the enlargement negotiations with some pride.

Nevertheless, the enlargement negotiations also provided sharp reminders of the limits of Commission power. In the autumn of 1961 the Commission was marginalised in the procedural debate and was obliged to rely on others to justify its inclusion in the membership negotiations, while shortly over a year later during the discussions which followed de Gaulle's press conference Hallstein and his colleagues were again sidelined. Furthermore, Commission attempts to use the membership negotiations to pursue its own agenda – most notably Hallstein's attempt to turn the financial regulation dispute into a far-reaching discussion of Community finance – had met with little success.[7] There were thus sufficient disappointments to temper Commission pride about its overall effectiveness and in particular about its close cooperation with the French.

The second major advantage of looking more closely at the Brussels negotiations is that such a study can offer important insights into the stage of development reached by the European Community in the early 1960s. In particular, it can highlight the strange combination of collective pride in their achievements, widespread and far-reaching ambition about future development, and continual anxiety about the very survival of the EEC which characterised the Six. This unusual blend of optimism and uncertainty had a significant bearing on the fate of the first British application.

By 1962 the Six were well aware that they had already accomplished a great deal. The flood of applications for association or membership which they were continuing to receive only underlined the success of the EEC in resisting the challenge constituted by EFTA, while the substance of the negotiations with the British and the other applicants

---

[7] For a fuller discussion of this episode, see N. Piers Ludlow, 'Influence and Vulnerability: The role of the ECC Commission in the Enlargement Negotiations' in Richard Griffiths and Stuart Ward (eds.), *Courting the Common Market: The First Attempt to Enlarge the European Community 1961–1963* (London: Lothian Foundation Press, 1996), pp. 139–55.

highlighted the extent and the significance of the agreements previously reached among the Community member states. As the British were slowly and painfully discovering, the *acquis communautaire* was already highly complex and its acceptance would necessitate large-scale changes in the way in which aspirant members conducted their external trade and managed their domestic agriculture. Furthermore, as is highlighted by the above discussion of the Commission's contribution to the enlargement negotiations, the Six could look with some pride at the institutional system which they had devised. Perhaps most strikingly of all, the way in which the Six interacted while trying to devise common positions towards Britain's multiple and varied requests suggested that many of the habits and patterns of multilateral cooperation had already been learnt. Thus the tolerance with which the Five treated the seemingly endless series of French objections to Britain's demands, and their adherence to the doctrine of Community solidarity despite the increasingly obvious gap between the views of the French and those of their partners, signalled an acceptance by all of the Six that the EEC could only flourish if the difficulties and reservations of a member state, however extreme, were respected – even if doing so placed a check on the ambitions of the other members and led to great inflexibility vis-à-vis non-member states. The Six in other words had quickly learnt both the advantages and the constraints of working within a political and economic Community.

The success that the Community had so far encountered only strengthened the conviction of many among the Six that further-reaching cooperation could be developed. Opinions differed greatly as to the nature of such future progress – both the fields in which advance should be made and the choice of whether to extend the Community method of cooperation or to resort to a more intergovernmental model remained matters of dispute – but the notion that more cooperation was both possible and desirable was widely accepted. This led the Six to insist that Britain and her fellow applicants accept not simply the Community as it was when they applied but also as it might, with time, become. Such optimism also partially explains the Community's awkwardness when confronted with association requests from the EFTA neutrals. For Spaak and other 'European' enthusiasts, any form of linkage between the Community and states which stood aside from the East–West conflict might impair the Community's ability to develop an important political and defence role in that conflict. Furthermore the Six found it genuinely difficult to empathise with Britain's reluctance to trust the policies and institutions of the Community. One of the underlying features of both the negotiation about temperate zone agricultural products and that focusing on British domestic agriculture was the gulf between deep British cynicism and the very real (if perhaps naive) expectation on the part of most of the Six that the CAP arrangements, as they had been developed and as they would evolve, would be able to reconcile the needs of European farmers and the goal of freer world trade.

Alongside such confidence there was equally profound uncertainty. This was perhaps most obvious from the way in which the Six chose to negotiate. As noted in chapter 2, the Six had committed themselves to a negotiating procedure designed to protect their unity and safeguard the Community institutions and *acquis* even at the expense of speed and flexibility. This reflected a belief – widespread in Italy, Germany and the Commission but also detectable elsewhere – that any membership application, but in particular a conditional application, needed to be handled with caution. Otherwise, the very merits of the Community which had prompted the membership request might be undermined. But anxiety was also apparent in many of the substantive points raised by the Six. Throughout the negotiations, the British were repeatedly asked not simply to promise to adhere to Community policy but to demonstrate this commitment upon entry by taking a clear first step towards the EEC norm. Thus the Six insisted that a first tranche of the CET be applied immediately to all Commonwealth manufactured products and tried extremely hard to force the British to move decisively away from their own agricultural support system as soon as the United Kingdom became an EEC member. This quest for cast-iron guarantees reflected a mistrust of the United Kingdom, especially in the realm of agricultural policy. But it also bore witness to the wariness of each others' intentions that persisted amongst the Six and to the fear that any exemption from Community rules granted to the British would be rapidly followed by demands for similar treatment from within the original Community member states. Likewise, the way in which both the French and the Commission rallied support for hardline positions by suggesting that too much leniency would threaten either a particular common policy or in certain instances the very existence of the EEC, demonstrated that the Six were not at all complacent about the continuation of the integration process. Whether such fears were justified is, of course, a separate issue. But real or not, the apprehensions of the Six as much as their hopes made the task of the British negotiators considerably harder.

The fact that it is possible to make such general points about the Six also draws attention to the way in which the Community had, by 1961–3, already modified the relations between its member states. Even at this early stage of development, a close-knit group of diplomats and ministers had become the insiders of the Community system, well used both to cooperation with each other and to the peculiarities of diplomacy under Community rules. Such men, and important currents of opinion within the national governments which they represented, had a substantial stake in the system and were committed both to the protection of what they had already achieved and to ambitious future goals. They were also convinced that the process in which they were involved was changing forever the face of diplomacy in Western Europe. As a result the anger unleashed by de Gaulle's veto was not merely characterised by disappointment at the postponement of Community enlargement, but was also marked by the conviction that the General had broken all the conventions and habits of multilateral Community action and had returned to the unilateral diplomacy of an earlier era. Thus figures such as Hallstein or Marjolin who were not partisans of early Community enlargement shared much of the fury of those like Rolf Lahr who were. But ironically, both de Gaulle's behaviour itself and the frantic diplomacy that followed it only served to confirm that diplomacy in Europe had been profoundly altered by the process of European integration. For it was surely significant that even a strong leader of Western Europe's most powerful nation had hesitated long and hard before defying the will of his European partners, and still more notable that, despite their very real anger in the weeks that followed the 14 January press conference, the Five drew back from any action – against France or with Britain – which might have undermined the achievements of the preceding decade. January 1963 was the Community's first encounter with crisis, but while testing, it ultimately served to underline that a fundamental change had occurred in the relations between the Six.

The third reason why the Brussels negotiations deserve historical attention is that they had a decisive influence on the outcome of the British application. For it is the contention of this study that had the Brussels negotiations been handled differently by both the British and the Six a French veto might well have been averted; as it was, however, the slowness of progress in Brussels allowed the French President to block an application which he would otherwise have been obliged to accept. They were thus not, to resume the metaphor used above, the rather dreary technical side-show that Dixon and others implied. They were, by contrast, a central part of the plot, and one which if acted out differently, could have totally altered the dénouement.

Neither the importance nor the length of the Brussels negotiations was inevitable. Community enlargement was an issue of vital political significance. As such it might have been expected to be discussed and settled at the highest political level. Then, if a decision to accept the British as members had been taken, the technical and logistical problems posed by British membership could have been quickly and efficiently addressed. In 1961–2, however, this did not prove to be the case: both the balance of opinion among the Six and the nature of the British application combined to prevent a clear political decision. And it was this impasse which gave the Brussels negotiations much of their importance.

On the Community side, the French were primarily responsible for preventing a clear political decision in favour of British membership. As argued above, de Gaulle was consistent in his opposition to the entry of Britain into the Community. Until late 1962, however, Community, international and domestic constraints made it impossible for the General to express this view openly. Similarly, Adenauer's increasing hostility to Community enlargement could not be overtly stated without causing a major domestic crisis which might loosen the Chancellor's already tenuous hold on power. But what de Gaulle and to a lesser extent Adenauer were able to prevent was a political decision by the Six in favour of British membership. French hesitancy was enough to ensure that the mandate given to the Community's negotiators was politically neutral – the delegations were not instructed to find a solution acceptable to the British at any cost – and without any form of deadline. Likewise, the position of the French, combined with the instructions which Adenauer gave to his diplomats from the spring of 1962 onwards, was sufficiently strong to prevent the sort of general solutions for which Spaak pleaded in early May 1962. No political short-cut out of the technical maze was feasible without French and German consent.

The way in which the Community was unable to voice a clear

political choice for or against British membership mirrored the position of the British government. Indeed, de Gaulle's ability to tread this middle way between outright rejection of British membership and a resigned acceptance of the inevitable was entirely due to the highly conditional nature of the British bid. Had Macmillan been able to follow Monnet's advice and apply for membership unconditionally, working out the arrangements for the Commonwealth and EFTA from within the EEC, the Six would have been confronted, in 1961, with a clear political choice. In these circumstances, de Gaulle would almost certainly have been unable to oppose enlargement. But the British never felt able to pose the question in so stark a fashion. Like the French President, Macmillan was hampered by domestic and international opposition. There was considerable scepticism about the practical consequences of British membership in the Cabinet, the Conservative Party, public opinion and amongst Commonwealth leaders. In order to placate this dissent, the Prime Minister chose not to make an unequivocal decision in favour of British membership. Instead, the British government emphasised the importance of the precise membership terms which could be agreed between British negotiators and the Six, arguing that only once these were known would a final decision for or against membership be possible. 'The negotiations themselves were to be the test', as a senior member of the British delegation recalled.[8] The technical discussions were thus elevated from a routine negotiation which would seek ways of implementing a political decision that had already been taken, to the principal arena within which the success or failure of the enlargement process would be determined.

This did not mean, however, that the negotiations were condemned to failure from 1961 onwards. British caution may well have encouraged both the French President and the German Chancellor to hope that the technical obstacles would eventually prove too much for Macmillan's government and force the British to withdraw their application. French tactics in the negotiations indeed centred on the possibility that Britain would decide that the cost of membership would be too high. But neither the inability of the Community to decide immediately in favour of British membership nor the conditional nature of the British bid made a successful outcome impossible. It simply meant that the struggle over the future size and political

[8] Eric Roll, *Crowded Hours* (London: Faber & Faber, 1985), p. 107.

complexion of the EEC would be fought out not at a summit of European leaders openly expressing their views, but at ministerial meetings in Brussels which were ostensibly about Australian wheat, tea from Ceylon or British farm subsidies. If the Community member states which supported British membership were able to overcome French obstructionism over such matters and if the British and their Commonwealth entourage could have shown the necessary flexibility, Macmillan's gamble would have been vindicated; neither de Gaulle nor Adenauer would have been able to reject an agreement reached at the Brussels negotiating table. If, by contrast, neither side had proved ready to give sufficient ground and deadlock prevailed, de Gaulle and Adenauer would have won.

In this context, many of the national and Community characteristics analysed above became crucial. Skilful French obstructionism, Italian and German reluctance to attack the French and ineffective and time-wasting Dutch bluster ceased to be merely irritants which the British were obliged to endure before reaching their goal, but instead became factors which could jeopardise the whole application. Likewise, the general defensiveness of the Community, and particularly the Six's choice of procedure and the long delays that this inevitably produced, became serious obstacles in the United Kingdom's way. The desire to deepen European integration did make it harder to widen the membership of the EEC.

It was Britain's own tactics, however, that contributed most to the slow pace of the Brussels talks. First, the British erred in attaching so many conditions to their original application. Second, Macmillan's government failed to alter tactics once it became apparent just how inflexible the Six would be. Despite repeated pleas from those members of the British delegation who were in daily contact with the Six and who were acutely conscious of the Community's very limited room for manoeuvre, the British government refused to scale down the task which its negotiators had been set.[9] There was thus no reduction in the overall number of issues to be explored and only a slow and grudging acceptance that it was the British and not the Six who would have to make the most telling concessions. Similarly, the UK government refused either to accept general pledges from the Six or to place their trust in the Community institutions and rules:

[9] The delegation's post-mortem on the negotiations is very clear on this point. PRO. FO371 171442; M1091/542G, 26.2.1963.

detailed undertakings and precise arrangements continued to be sought. As a result, the British government was badly positioned to counter deadlock among the Six with a stream of new ideas, proposals and concessions. Instead, with the inflexibility of the Community being all but matched by British rigidity, the negotiations were allowed to languish while de Gaulle built up the domestic and international strength to intervene.

The slow rate of advance led many of those involved with the Brussels negotiations to pine for a quick, political solution that would end the impasse. In May 1962, for instance, the Secretary-General of the Dutch Ministry of Foreign Affairs, van Tuyll, was one of many to look with expectation towards the meeting between de Gaulle and Macmillan planned for early June. Often these hopes involved factors far removed from the subject-matter of the Brussels talks. In particular, great speculation surrounded the prospect of a nuclear deal between Britain and France in which British atomic know-how would be passed on to the French in exchange for the rapid and successful completion of the Brussels negotiations. The attractions of such a bargain were obvious. Roberto Ducci, one of the senior Italian negotiators in Brussels, vividly recalls the way in which a meeting at Chequers between Heath and Colombo was transformed when the Lord Privy Seal broke off a prolonged discussion of processed agricultural goods and embarked upon an exposition about the prospects of future European defence cooperation. The effect, as Ducci recalls, was extraordinary:'We felt ourselves lifted from the muddy terrain in Brussels where for so many months we had gone round in circles up to an altitude where the air was light and exhilarating.'[10] Unfortunately, however, a nuclear deal remained an alluring but unrealistic prospect. Despite intensive discussion within the British government, it proved impossible to construct an offer to the French which overcame three fundamental problems: first, the opposition of the Americans to any further nuclear proliferation; second, the lack of credibility of any British offer made without US consent; and third, French ambivalence, if not actual hostility, towards any bargain which would diminish the independence of the French *force de frappe*. To the dismay of Ducci and many others, the only route which led towards the successful conclu-

---

[10] 'Ci sentivamo trasportati dal terreno appiccicoso in cui da tanti mesi ci aggiravamo a Bruxelles a un altura ove l'aria era leggera e esilarante.' My translation. Roberto Ducci, *I capintesta* (Milan: Rusconi, 1982), pp. 288–9.

sion of the British application lay through the 'muddy terrain' and continual frustrations of the Brussels negotiations.

Any assessment of the British membership bid should thus focus less on the nuclear high-politics that so fascinate several authors and concentrate more on the technical discussions. For it was in Brussels, not in Paris, that de Gaulle's hopes of blocking British membership could have been frustrated. That they were not, highlights the hazards of a negotiation in which detailed discussions were allowed to start despite the lack of either a political agreement on their ultimate objective or a fixed timetable; draws attention to the rigidity of the Community when negotiating about issues which affected the heart of its *acquis*; and, above all, underlines the inability of the British to respond to technical impasse with the necessary flexibility. All three factors combined to ensure that progress in the negotiations was neither fast nor smooth, and that the Six and Britain were still too far from agreement in January 1963 to defy de Gaulle.

The fourth advantage of studying the Brussels negotiations of 1961–3 more closely is that they highlight several important features of the enlargement process itself. Given that the need to accommodate new member states has been, and seems likely to continue to be, a recurrent feature of the Community's development, such features have an importance which transcends the 1961–3 episode and may even persist into the 1990s.

The first such characteristic is the need for the applicant state to accept, in its entirety, the *acquis communautaire*. The failure to grasp this was one of Britain's great mistakes in 1961–3. Misled by the warmth of the rhetorical welcome which their approach had received and by the eagerness to help which several member states had shown in bilateral discussions, acutely conscious of the demands and expectations of their own Commonwealth and EFTA entourages, and perhaps somewhat arrogant in their belief that their membership represented a prize for which the EEC would be willing to pay almost any price, the British were extremely slow to understand that the onus of adaptation lay squarely with the applicant and not with the Community. The Community would not, and could not, reconsider or renegotiate its rules at the behest of a would-be member. Temporary exemptions from, and a few minor adaptations to, the EEC's rules were possible, as were quite extensive transitional arrangements; wide-scale change to the Treaty or to the Community's existing policies was not. Instead the British were asked to put their trust in the ability of the Community's institutions and mechanisms to adapt to the needs of the new member state, once that state had taken its place within the Community. In other words, the applicant had to accept that its bargaining position during the application process was not, as the British initially hoped, exceptionally strong, but rather was much weaker than it would become once membership had been achieved and the new entrant enjoyed the full rights and privileges of a member state. The procedural arrangements used in 1961–3 graphically illustrated this reality. As an applicant Britain was forced to wait patiently while the Six struggled to reach a common position in discussions from which the UK representatives were excluded, and was then confronted with the choice of either accepting what the Six proposed, or of rejecting it and waiting again for the Six laboriously to reach a new common position. As a member, by contrast, the British would have been involved in the discussions among the Six from the outset, would have been able to express their views at every point of the process, and would have been beneficiaries of that same remarkable tolerance for the individual difficulties of a member state which the Five displayed towards France for most of the membership negotiations. British qualms about the CAP for instance, many of which have been borne out by subsequent experience, would have been better addressed from the inside of the Community, than from the outside.

The unwillingness or inability of the Community to renegotiate its *acquis* during enlargement negotiations only accentuates the importance of a second 'lesson' that can be drawn from the 1961–3 episode, namely the importance of a strong political decision in favour of Community membership in the applicant state. The absence of such a decision was to prove a major handicap for the British. Anxious to demonstrate that it was not irrevocably committed to EEC membership, and fearful that too much eagerness to join would be a cue for the Six to raise the price of entry, Macmillan's government postponed both a definitive decision to go in and the start of a determined effort to build a domestic consensus in favour of membership. Senior ministers hostile to, or ambivalent about, EEC membership were allowed to remain in the Cabinet (and in the case of Butler was actually given responsibility for the key committee determining the British negotiating position) and the publicity campaign designed to win over the public to the merits of membership did not get underway until the autumn of 1962. As a result, when the deadlocked negotiations required British flexibility, the government did not have a reservoir of political support or public enthusiasm to fall back on, nor had it so conclusively demonstrated the long-term merits of membership that short-term concessions appeared worthwhile. Instead it was confronted with mounting public and political unease at the number of demands made by the Six, and was forced to stand firm in Brussels in the vain hope that the nerve of the Community member states would crack, allowing Britain to enter without further sacrifices.[11] The process of adapting to the rules of an existing Community is likely to be a painful one; it can only sensibly be undertaken by a government which has decided that membership is a desirable or necessary aim and is prepared to win the country round to the same viewpoint.

A third aspect of the enlargement process which is underlined by this study is that it is extremely difficult for any member state to block the entry into the Community of another European and democratic state. This may appear a perverse conclusion, since 1961–3 is primarily remembered as the enlargement attempt that failed precisely because of the veto imposed by a single member state. But, as this book has sought to make clear, even a leader of de Gaulle's stature, and a country as central to European integration as France, was only able to thwart the enlargement process due to the hesitations of his partners and the rigidity and ambivalence of the principal applicant. Furthermore, not even de Gaulle could prevent the crisis that followed his intervention from temporarily paralysing the Community and postponing the achievement of cherished French aims for nearly a year. The ability of any member state to run this risk in a Community which is now much more complex and the paralysis of which would pose a still greater risk to any member state than was the case in 1963 is all but non-existent. As a result, any state willing to show sufficient flexibility to overcome the technical obstacles – genuine or otherwise – placed in its path and prepared to make a clear political decision in favour of European integration should be able to thwart minority opposition to its membership.

Enlargement should have been possible in the early 1960s. The balance of opinion among the Six was clearly in favour, while both the

---

[11] These ideas are explored in greater detail in N. Piers Ludlow, 'A Mismanaged Application: Britain and the EEC (1961–3)' in Anne Deighton and Alan Milward (eds.), *Acceleration, Deepening and Enlarging: The European Economic Community, 1958–1963* (Brussels: Nomos/Giuffrè/LGDJ/Bruylant, 1997).

advantages of entry and the penalties of exclusion seemed sufficient to propel Britain into the Community. But in the event a lack of decisiveness on both sides allowed the opportunity to be missed. Britain's approach to the EEC was overly cautious, its desire to enter often much less apparent than its residual attachment to the Commonwealth, to EFTA and to its national agricultural policy. Many of the Six meanwhile were equally torn, unable easily to reconcile their support for enlargement with their commitment both to the Community as it existed and to close cooperation with the French. These conflicting loyalties resulted in a painfully slow advance in Brussels. And they ensured that when, at length, a determined move was made by the French President, both the British and their numerous allies within the Community found themselves powerless to resist.

Appendix 1
The key texts

Harold Macmillan's statement to the House of Commons, on 31 July 1961, announcing Britain's decision to request the opening of membership negotiations with the European Economic Community

'With permission, I wish to make a statement on the policy of Her Majesty's Government towards the European Economic Community.

The future relations between the European Economic Community and the United Kingdom, the Commonwealth and the rest of Europe are clearly matters of capital importance in the life of our country and, indeed, of all countries of the free world.

This is a political as well as an economic issue. Although the Treaty of Rome is concerned with economic matters it has an important political objective, namely, to promote unity and stability in Europe which is so essential a factor in the struggle for freedom and progress throughout the world. In this modern world the tendency towards larger groups of nations acting together in the common interest leads to greater unity and thus adds to our strength in the struggle for freedom.

I believe that it is both our duty and our interest to contribute towards that strength by securing the closest possible unity within Europe. At the same time, if a closer relationship between the United Kingdom and the countries of the European Economic Community were to disrupt the long-standing and historic ties between the United Kingdom and the other nations of the Commonwealth the loss would be greater than the gain. The Commonwealth is a great source of stability and strength both to Western Europe and to the world as a whole, and I am sure that its value is fully appreciated by the member Governments of the European Economic Community. I do not think that Britain's contribution to the Commonwealth will be reduced if Europe unites. On the contrary, I think that its value will be enhanced.

On the economic side, a community comprising, as members or in association, the countries of free Europe, could have a very rapidly expanding economy supplying, as it eventually would, a single market of approaching 300 million people. This rapidly expanding economy could, in turn, lead to an increased demand for products from other parts of the world and so help to expand world trade and improve the prospects of the less developed areas of the world.

No British Government could join the European Economic Community without prior negotiations with a view to meeting the needs of the Commonwealth countries, of our European Free Trade Association partners, and of British agriculture consistent with the broad principles and purpose which have inspired the concept of European unity and which are embodied in the Treaty of Rome.

As the House knows, Ministers have recently visited Commonwealth countries to discuss the problems which would arise if the British Government decided to negotiate for membership of the European Economic Community. We have explained to the Commonwealth Governments the broad political and economic considerations which we have to take into account. They, for their part, told us their views and, in some cases, their anxieties about their essential interests. We have assured Commonwealth Governments that we shall keep in close consultation with them throughout any negotiations which take place.

Secondly, there is the European Free Trade Association. We have a treaty and other obligations to our partners in this Association and my right honourable Friends have just returned from a meeting of the European Free Trade Association Ministerial Council, in Geneva, where all were agreed that they should work closely together throughout any negotiations. Finally, we are determined to continue to protect the standard of living of our agricultural community.

During the past nine months, we have had useful and frank discussions with the European Economic Community Governments. We have now reached the stage where we cannot make further progress without entering into formal negotiations. I believe that the great majority in the House and in the country will feel that they cannot fairly judge whether it is possible to join the European

Economic Community until there is a clearer picture before them of the conditions on which we could join and the extent to which these could meet our special needs.

Article 237 of the Treaty of Rome envisages that the conditions of admission of a new member and the changes in the Treaty necessitated thereby should be the subject of an agreement. Negotiations must, therefore, be held in order to establish the conditions on which we must join. In order to enter into these negotiations it is necessary, under the Treaty, to make a formal application to join the Community, although the ultimate decision whether to join or not must depend on the result of the negotiations.

Therefore, after long and earnest consideration, Her Majesty's Government have come to the conclusion that it would be right for Britain to make a formal application under Article 237 of the Treaty for negotiations with a view to joining the Community if satisfactory arrangements can be made to meet the special needs of the United Kingdom, of the Commonwealth and of the European Free Trade Association.

If, as I earnestly hope, our offer to enter into negotiations with the European Economic Community is accepted we shall spare no efforts to reach a satisfactory agreement. These negotiations must inevitably be of a detailed and technical character, covering a very large number of the most delicate and difficult matters. They may, therefore, be protracted and there can, of course, be no guarantee of success. When any negotiations are brought to a conclusion then it will be the duty of the Government to recommend to the House what course we should pursue.

No agreement will be entered into until it has been approved by the House after full consultation with other Commonwealth countries by whatever procedures they may generally agree.

Source: *Hansard Parliamentary Debates*, House of Commons 1960–1, vol. 645, cols. 928–31

Article 237 of the Treaty of Rome, under which Britain applied for membership

Any European State may apply to become a member of the Community. It shall address its application to the Council, which, after obtaining the opinion of the Commission, shall act by means of a unanimous vote.

Appendix 1

The conditions of admission and the amendments[1] to this Treaty necessitated thereby shall be the subject of an agreement between the Member States and the applicant State. Such agreement shall be submitted to all the contracting States for ratification in accordance with their respective constitutional rules.

Source: *Treaty Establishing the European Economic Community and connected documents* (Luxembourg: Publishing Services of the European Communities, 1958)

[1] The use of the word 'amendments' in this, the unofficial translation used by the British government as it prepared the UK's bid, became somewhat controversial. As the European Commission was to point out on the very eve of Macmillan's House of Commons statement, a more accurate translation from the French would have been 'adaptations'. This 'mistake' gave rise to fears that Britain would expect more scope for change than was in fact the case (see the *Observer* 30.7.1961).

Appendix 2
The key players

The ministers involved

Paul-Henri Spaak: Belgian Foreign Minister

Henri Fayat: Deputy Belgian Foreign Minister

Charles Heger: Belgian Minister of Agriculture

Maurice Couve de Murville: French Foreign Minister

Olivier Wormser: Directeur des affaires économiques et financielles at the French Ministry of Foreign Affairs

Edgar Pisani: French Minister of Agriculture

Heinrich von Brentano: German Foreign Minister until October 1961

Gerhard Schröder: replaced von Brentano as German Foreign Minister

Rolf Lahr: German Secretary of State at the Ministry of Foreign Affairs

Alfred Müller-Armack: German Secretary of State at the Ministry of Economic Affairs

Werner Schwartz: German Minister of Agriculture

Attilio Piccioni: Italian Foreign Minister

Emilio Colombo: Italian Minister for Industry and Commerce

Mariano Rumor: Italian Minister of Agriculture

Attilio Cattani: Secretary-General of the Italian Ministry of Foreign Affairs

Joseph Luns: Dutch Foreign Minister

Hans van Houten: Dutch Under-Secretary of State for Foreign Affairs

Jan de Pous: Dutch Minister for Economic Affairs

Victor Marijnen: Dutch Minister of Agriculture

Eugène Schaus: Luxembourg Deputy Prime Minister and Minister of Foreign Affairs

Walter Hallstein: President of the European Commission

Sicco Mansholt: Vice-President of the European Commission responsible for agriculture

Robert Marjolin: Vice-President of the European Commission responsible for economic union

Giuseppe Caron: Vice-President of the European Commission responsible for the internal market

Jean Rey: Member of the European Commission responsible for external relations

Edward Heath: Lord Privy Seal and leader of the British delegation to the Brussels negotiations

Christopher Soames: British Minister of Agriculture

Duncan Sandys: British Secretary of State for Commonwealth Relations

The principal officials involved

Pierre Forthomme: Belgian representative on the Committee of Deputies

Bernard Clappier: Joint French representative on the Committee until the spring of 1962. Thereafter sole French representative among the deputies.

François-Xavier Ortoli: alternated with Clappier until April 1962

Günther Harkort: Germany's representative on the Committee of Deputies. Also Germany's permanent representative to the EEC

Roberto Ducci: Italian representative on the Committee of Deputies

Albert Bourschette: Luxembourg's representative on the Committee of Deputies

Baron van Ittersum: first Dutch representative on the Committee of Deputies

J. de Ranitz: meant to replace van Ittersum from October 1962 but in fact only took over for the final stages of Dutch Presidency

J. H. W. Hoogwater: acted as Dutch representative to the Committee of Deputies in the interim between van Ittersum's departure and de Ranitz's arrival, i.e. for most of the Dutch Presidency

Jean-François Deniau: leader of the Commission's delegation at official level. Sat on the Committee of Deputies

Sir Pierson Dixon: leader of the British delegation at official level. Also British Ambassador to France

Sir Eric Roll: deputy leader of the British delegation at official level, and the UK's senior representative on the Committee of Deputies during Dixon's frequent absences

Conference chairmen

October–December 1961

Ministerial level: Ludwig Erhard/Rolf Lahr
Official level: Günther Harkort

January–March 1962

Ministerial level: Maurice Couve de Murville
Official level: Bernard Clappier/François-Xavier Ortoli

April–June 1962

Ministerial level: Emilio Colombo
Official level: Roberto Ducci

July–September 1962

Ministerial level: Eugène Schaus
Official level: Albert Bourschette

October–December 1962

Ministerial level: Josef Luns/Hans van Houten
Official level: J. H. W. Hoogwater/J. de Ranitz

January 1963

Ministerial level: Henri Fayat
Official level: Pierre Forthomme

Appendix 3
Interviews conducted

Sir Christopher Audland, 21.2.1994
Viscomte Etienne Davignon, 30.7.1993
Jean-François Deniau, 15.12.1995
Sir Michael Franklin, 1.7.1993
Max Kohnstamm, 15.12.1991
Roger Lavelle, 30.6.1993
Karl-Heinz Narjes, 18.5.1992
Emile Noël, 16.12.1995
François-Xavier Ortoli, 14.10.1992
Peter Pooley, 18.12.1995
Sir Patrick Reilly, 30.6.1993
Jean-Marie Soutou, 20.11.1991
Berndt von Staden, 30.6.1993

Bibliography

Unpublished sources

Archives of the EEC Council of Ministers

Council secretariat summaries of the procedural discussions among the Six of September/October 1961 plus extracts from the minutes of the COREPER and General Affairs Council debate about how the negotiations should be organised

A variety of national and Commission drafts for the member states' official reply to Heath's 10 October speech

A copy of the Commission's working document analysing Heath's opening speech

The official minutes of all the ministerial discussions between the British and the Six

Conference secretariat summaries of the conclusions of all the deputies' meetings

A wide variety of the reports compiled by the conference working groups, both *à six* and *à sept*.

Historical archives of the EEC Commission

General

The minutes of the Commission's weekly meetings in 1961–3

The Commission's report to the European Parliament on the state of the negotiations, written in February 1963

From the Secretary-General's files

The reports to the Commission prepared by Deniau on every deputies' meeting

The reports to the Commission prepared by Hallstein on all but one of the ministerial meetings

From the files of Sicco Mansholt's cabinet

Various documents relating to the procedural discussions held in COREPER in September–October 1961

From the files of DGVI

A Commission analysis of the problems posed by British and Commonwealth agriculture

A DGVI commentary on Heath's 10 October speech

Archives of the Auswärtiges Amt

Referat 200 files on Great Britain and the EEC, July 1960–May 1962 and on EFTA, January 1960–January 1961

Referat 304 files on Great Britain and the Commonwealth

Buro Staatssekretar files on Great Britain, January 1959–December 1962

Bestand B–150 microfiches on 1963

Bundesarchiv

Bundeskanzleramt files

Historical archives of the French Ministère des Affaires Etrangères

The files of the Direction des Affaires Politiques, Sous-Direction Europe

The files of the Service de Coopération Economique

Public Record Office

From the Prime Minister's files

PREM 11 files

From the Cabinet files

CAB 128; CAB 129; CAB 130; CAB 134 files

From the Foreign Office files

FO371 files

Conservative Party archive

Conservative Research Department files including the minutes of the Parliamentary Group on the Common Market

Published sources

Acheson, Dean, 'The Practice of Partnership', *Foreign Affairs*, 41:2 (January 1963)

Adenauer, Konrad, 'The German Problem, A World Problem', *International Affairs*, 41:1 (October 1962)

    Erinnerungen 1945–53, 1953–55, 1955–59 and *1959–63* (Stuttgart: Deutsche Verlags-Anstalt, 1965, 1966, 1967, 1968)

Teegespräche 1961–1963 (Berlin: Siedler Verlag, 1992)

Aldous, Richard and Lee, Sabine (eds.), *Harold Macmillan and Britain's World Role* (London: Macmillan, 1996)

Allen, H. C., 'The Anglo-American Relationship in the 1960s', *International Affairs*, 39:1 (January 1963)

Alphand, Hervé, *L'étonnement d'être. Journal 1939–1973* (Paris: Fayard, 1977)

Balfour, Nancy, 'President Kennedy's Plan for Expanding World Trade', *World Today*, 18:3 (March 1962)

Ball, George, *The Past Has Another Pattern* (New York: Norton, 1982)

Bariéty, Jacques, 'La perception de la puissance française par le chancelier Adenauer de 1958 à 1963', *Relations internationales*, 58 (summer 1989)

Bark, Dennis and Gress, David, *A History of West Germany* (Oxford University Press, 1989) vols. I and II

Barman, Thomas, 'Behind the Brussels Breakdown', *International Affairs*, 39:2 (1963)

Becker, Josef and Knipping, Franz (eds.), *Power in Europe? Britain, France, Italy and Germany in a Postwar World 1945–50* (Berlin: Walter de Gruyter, 1986)

Bell, Coral (ed.), *Europe Without Britain* (Melbourne, 1963)

Bell, Lionel, *The Throw that Failed: Britain's Original Application to Join the Common Market* (London: New European Publications, 1995)

Beloff, Max, 'Britain, Europe and the Atlantic Community', *International Organisation*, 17:3 (summer 1963)

The United States and European Unity (London: Faber & Faber, 1963)

Beloff, Nora, *The General Says No* (London: Penguin, 1963)

Benoit, Emile, *Europe at Sixes and Sevens: The Common Market, the Free Trade Association, and the United States* (New York: Columbia University Press, 1961)

Bernier, Serge, 'Aspects des relations politiques anglo-françaises 1947–1958' (PhD thesis, Ottawa, 1981)

Berstein, Serge, *La France de l'expansion. La République gaullienne 1958–1969* (Paris: Editions du Seuil, 1989) vol. I

Bidault, Georges, *D'une résistance à l'autre* (Paris: Les Presses du Siècle, 1965)

Bjøl, Erling, *La France devant l'Europe. La politique européenne de la IVème République* (Copenhagen: Munksgaard, 1966)

Blankenhorn, Herbert, *Verständnis und Verständigung. Blätter eines politischen Tagebuchs 1949 bis 1979* (Frankfurt: Propyläen, 1980)

Blasius, Rainer A., *Von Adenauer zu Erhard. Studien zur Auswärtigen Politik der Bundesrepublik Deutschland 1963* (Munich: R. Oldenbourg Verlag, 1994)

Bloes, Robert, *Le 'Plan Fouchet' et le problème de l'Europe politique* (Bruges: College of Europe, 1970)

Boegner, Jean-Marc, '1958, le général de Gaulle et l'acceptation du traité de Rome', *Espoir*, 87 (1992)

Bossuat, Gérard, *La France, l'aide américaine et la construction européenne, 1944–54* (Paris: Comité pour l'histoire économique et financière de la France, 1992)

Bibliography

Bossuat, Gérard (ed.), *D'Alger à Rome, 1943–1957, choix de documents* (Louvain-la-Neuve: CIACO, 1989)

Bourrinet, Jacques, *Le problème agricole dans l'intégration européenne* (Montpellier: Editions CUJAS, 1964)

Bouwman, Bernard, 'The British Dimension of Dutch Foreign Policy (1950–1963)' (D.Phil. thesis, Oxford, 1993)

Bowie, Robert, 'Strategy and the Atlantic Alliance', *International Organisation*, 17:3 (summer 1963)

von Brentano, Heinrich, *L'Allemagne, l'Europe et le monde* (Paris: Albin Michel, 1965)

Brivati, Brian and Jones, Harriet (eds.), *From Reconstruction to Integration. Britain and Europe since 1945* (Leicester University Press, 1993)

Burgess, Simon and Edwards, Geoffrey, 'The Six plus One: British Policy-Making and the Question of European Economic Integration, 1955', *International Affairs*, 64:3 (1988)

Burin des Roziers, Etienne, *Retour aux sources, 1962, l'année décisive* (Paris: Plon, 1986)

Burns, A. L., 'Australia, Britain and the Common Market: Some Australian Views', *World Today*, 18:4 (April 1962)

Butterwick, Michael and Neville Rolfe, Edmund, *Food, Farming and the Common Market* (London: Oxford University Press, 1968)

Campbell, John, *Edward Heath. A Biography* (London: Pimlico, 1994)

Camps, Miriam, *Britain and the European Community 1955–1963* (Oxford University Press, 1964)

European Unification in the Sixties. From the Veto to the Crisis (Oxford University Press, 1967)

Carrington, C. E., 'Between the Commonwealth and Europe', *International Affairs*, 38:4 (October 1962)

Casadio, Gian Paolo, *Una politica agricola per l'Europa* (Bologna: Istituto Affari Internazionali/Il Mulino, 1967)

Cerny, Philip, *The Politics of Grandeur: Ideological Aspects of de Gaulle's Foreign Policy* (Cambridge University Press, 1980)

Charlton, Michael, *The Price of Victory* (London: BBC, 1983)

Clark, Ian, *Nuclear Diplomacy and the Special Relationship. Britain's Deterrent and America, 1957–1962* (Oxford: Clarendon Press, 1994)

Cleveland, Harold van B., *The Atlantic Idea and its European Rivals* (New York: McGraw-Hill, 1966)

Coombes, David, *Politics and Bureaucracy in the European Community* (London: PEP, 1970)

Costa Bona, Enrico, 'L'Italia e l'integrazione europea: aspetti storici e diplomatici (1947–57)', *Il Politico*, 53 (1988)

Couve de Murville, Maurice, *Une politique étrangère, 1958–1969* (Paris: Plon, 1971)

Crossman, R. H. S., 'British Labour Looks At Europe', *Foreign Affairs*, 41 (1963)

Debré, Michel, *Trois républiques pour une France* (Paris: Albin Michel, 1988)

Deighton, Anne, 'La Grande-Bretagne et la Communauté économique europé-enne (1958–1963)', *Histoire, Economie et Société*, 13:1 (1994)

Deighton, Anne (ed.), *Building Postwar Europe: National Decision-Makers and European Institutions, 1948–1963* (London: Macmillan, 1995)

Deighton, Anne and Milward, Alan (eds.), *Acceleration, Deepening and Enlarg-ing: The European Economic Community, 1957–1963* (Brussels: Nomos/ Giuffrè/LGDJ/Bruylant, 1997)

Diebold, William, 'Economic Aspects of an Atlantic Community', *International Organisation*, 17:3 (summer 1963)

Dingemans, Ralph, 'Nederland en de Britse toenadering tot de Zes, 1955–1963' (Masters dissertation, University of Groningen, 1995)

Dixon, Piers, *Double Diploma: The Life of Sir Pierson Dixon, Don and Diplomat* (London: Hutchinson, 1968)

Dockrill, Michael and Young, John W. (eds.), *British Foreign Policy, 1945–56* (London: Macmillan, 1989)

Donnadieu de Vabres, Jacques, 'Souvenirs de négociations', *Journal du Marché Commun*, 100 (March 1967)

Ducci, Roberto, *I capintesta* (Milan: Rusconi, 1982)

Duchêne, François, *Jean Monnet. The First Statesman of Interdependence* (New York: Norton, 1994)

Dumoulin, Michel (ed.), *La Belgique et les débuts de la construction européenne: De la guerre aux traités de Rome* (Louvain-la-Neuve: CIACO, 1987)

Duroselle, J. B. and Serra, E., *Italia e Francia 1946–1954* (Milan: Istituto per gli studi di Politica Internazionale, Franco Angeli, 1988)

Dutton, David, 'Anticipating Maastricht: The Conservative Party and Britain's First Application to Join the European Community', *Contemporary Record*, 7:3 (winter 1993)

Dwan, Renata, 'An Uncommon Community: France and the European Defence Community, 1950–4' (D.Phil. thesis, Oxford, 1996)

Elkan, Peter, 'Britain and the Common Market: The Test Case of New Zealand', *World Today*, 18:5 (May 1962)

Ellison, James, 'Harold Macmillan's Fear of "Little Europe" Britain, the Six and the European Free Trade Area' (University of Leicester, Centre for Federal Studies, Discussion Papers on Britain and Europe, BE95/5, October 1995)

Evans, Harold, *Downing St. Diaries. The Macmillan Years 1957–1963* (London: Hodder & Stoughton, 1981)

Evans, John W., *The Kennedy Round in American Trade Policy* (Harvard University Press, 1971)

Fisher, M. H., 'What Chance of Lower Tariffs? GATT and the Kennedy Round', *World Today*, 19:1 (May 1963)

Foreign Relations of the United States, 1961–1963, West Europe and Canada (Washington: United States Government Printing Office, 1994) vol. XIII

Franks, Oliver, 'Cooperation is not Enough', *Foreign Affairs*, 41:2 (January 1963)

Bibliography

Fulbright, J. W., 'A Concert of Free Nations', *International Organisation*, 17:3 (summer 1963)

Furniss, Edgar, 'De Gaulle's France and NATO: An Interpretation', *International Organisation*, 15:3 (summer 1961)

de Gaulle, Charles, *Discours et messages* (Paris: Plon, 1970) vols. III and IV
Mémoires d'espoir (Paris: Plon, 1970 and 1971) vols. I and II
Lettres, notes et carnets 1961–3 (Paris: Plon, 1986)

Gerbet, Pierre, *La construction de l'Europe* (Paris: Imprimerie Nationale, 1983)

Gillingham, John, *Coal, Steel and the Rebirth of Europe, 1945–55* (Cambridge University Press, 1991)

Ginsborg, Paul, *A History of Contemporary Italy 1943–88* (London: Penguin, 1990)

Girault, René and Bossuat, Gérard (eds.), *Les Europe des Européens* (Paris: Publications de la Sorbonne, 1993)

Gorell Barnes, William: *Europe and the Developing World: Association under Part IV of the Treaty of Rome* (London: Chatham House/PEP, 1967)

Griffiths, Richard (ed.), *The Netherlands and the Integration of Europe 1945–1957* (Amsterdam: NEHA, 1990)

Griffiths, Richard and Ward, Stuart (eds.), *Courting the Common Market: The First Attempt to Enlarge the European Community 1961–1963* (London: Lothian Foundation Press, 1996)

Grilli, Enzo R., *The European Community and the Developing Countries* (Cambridge University Press, 1993)

von der Groeben, Hans, *Combat pour l'Europe. La construction de la Communauté européenne de 1958 à 1966* (Brussels: CECA–CEE–CEEA, 1985)

Grosser, Alfred, 'General de Gaulle and the Foreign Policy of the Fifth Republic', *International Affairs*, 39:2 (April 1963)
'France and Germany in the Atlantic Community', *International Organisation*, 17:3 (summer 1963)

Hallstein, Walter, 'The European Community and the Atlantic Partnership', *International Organisation*, 17:3 (summer 1963)
Europe in the Making (New York: Norton, 1973)

Hampshire-Monk, Iain and Stanyer, Jeffrey (eds.), *Contemporary Political Studies 1996*, (Belfast: The Political Studies Association, 1996) vol. I

Hargreaves, J. D., *Decolonisation in Africa* (London: Longman, 1988)

van der Harst, Jan, 'The Netherlands and the EDC' (European University Institute, Working Paper 86/252)

Heater, Derek, *The Idea of European Unity* (Leicester University Press, 1992)

Herbst, Ludolf, *Option für den Westen: Vom Marshallplan bis zum deutsch–französischen Vertrag* (Munich: Deutsche Taschenbuch Verlag, 1989)

Herbst, Ludolf and Bührer, Werner (eds.), *Vom Marshall-Plan zur EWG, Die Eingliederung der Bundesrepublik in die westliche Welt* (Munich: R. Oldenbourg Verlag, 1990)

Herter, Christian, 'Atlantica', *Foreign Affairs*, 41:2 (January 1963)

Hoag, Malcolm, 'Nuclear Policy and French Intransigence', *Foreign Affairs*, 41:2 (January 1963)

Hoffman, Stanley, 'Discord in the Community: The North Atlantic Area as a Partial International System', *International Organisation*, 17:3 (summer 1963)

Horne, Alistair, *Macmillan 1891–1956* and *1957–1986* (London: Macmillan, 1988 and 1989)

Huth, Sabine, 'British–German Relations between 1955 and 1961' (PhD thesis, Cambridge, 1992)

Institut Charles de Gaulle, *De Gaulle en son siècle* (Paris: Plon, 1992) vols. IV and V

Istituto Affari Internazionali, *La politica estera della Repubblica italiana* (Milan: Edizioni di Communità, 1967) vols. I–III

Jacquemyns, Eliane, *L'Europe des Six et la demande d'admission de la Grande-Bretagne au Marché commun* (Brussels: Institut Universitaire d'Information Sociale et Economique, 1963)

Jouve, Edmond, *Le Général de Gaulle et la construction de l'Europe (1945–1966)* (Paris: Librairie Générale de Droit et de Jurisprudence, R. Pichon and R. Durand-Auzias, 1967)

Jowell, Roger and Hoinville, Gerald (eds.), *Britain into Europe: Public Opinion and the EEC, 1961–1975* (London: Croom Helm, 1976)

Kaiser, Wolfram, 'Wie nach Austerlitz? London–Bonn–Paris und die britische EWG-Politik bis 1961', *Integration*, 1 (1993)

'The Bomb and Europe. Britain, France and the EEC Entry Negotiations (1961–1963)', *Journal of European Integration History*, 1:1 (1995)

Using Europe, Abusing the Europeans. Britain and European Integration 1945–63 (London: Macmillan, 1996)

Kane, Elizabeth, 'Tilting To Europe? British Responses to Developments in European Integration (1955–1958)' (D.Phil. thesis, Oxford, 1996)

Kaplan, Lawrence, 'NATO and Adenauer's Germany: Uneasy Partnership', *International Organisation*, 15:4 (autumn 1961)

Kissinger, Henry, 'Strains on the Alliance', *Foreign Affairs*, 41:2 (January 1963)

Kitzinger, Uwe, 'The New France in the New Europe', *World Today*, 16:10 (October 1960)

The Challenge of the Common Market (Oxford: Blackwell, 1961)

'French Thoughts on Britain and the Common Market', *World Today*, 17:9 (September 1961)

Kleiman, Robert, *Atlantic Crisis: American Diplomacy Confronts a Resurgent Europe* (London: Sidgwick & Jackson, 1965)

Kolodziej, Edward, *French International Policy under de Gaulle and Pompidou* (New York: Cornell, 1974)

Küsters, Hanns Jürgen, *Fondements de la Communauté Economique Européenne* (Brussels: Editions Labor, 1990)

Lacouture, Jean, *De Gaulle* (Paris: Editions du Seuil, 1985 and 1986) vols. II and III

Lamb, Richard, *The Macmillan Years, 1957–1963. The Emerging Truth* (London: John Murray, 1995)

Lichtheim, George, *Europe and America: The Future of the Atlantic Community* (London: Thames & Hudson, 1963)

Lieber, Robert J., *British Politics and European Unity: Parties, Elites and Pressure Groups* (Berkeley: University of California Press, 1970)

Liggett, E., 'Organisation for Negotiation: Britain's First Attempt to Join the EEC 1961–3' (M.Litt. thesis, Glasgow University, 1971)

Lindberg, Leon, *The Political Dynamics of European Economic Integration* (Stanford University Press, 1963)

Lipgens, Walter, *A History of European Integration* (Oxford University Press, 1982)

Lippman, Walter, *Western Unity and the Common Market* (London: Hamish Hamilton, 1962)

Loth, Wilfried (ed.), *Die Anfänge der europaïschen Integration 1945–50* (Bonn: Europa Union Verlag, 1990)

Loth, Wilfried, Wallace, William and Wessels, Wolfgang (eds.), *Walter Hallstein. Der vergessene Europäer?* (Bonn: Europa Union Verlag, 1995)

Ludlow, N. Piers, 'Le paradoxe anglais: Great Britain and Political Union', *Revue d'Allemagne*, 2 (1997)

Macmillan, Harold, *Riding the Storm*, (London: Macmillan 1971)
Pointing the Way (London: Macmillan, 1972)
At the End of the Day (London: Macmillan, 1973)

Maillard, Pierre, *De Gaulle et l'Allemagne. Le rêve inachevé* (Paris: Plon, 1990)

Malterre, Pierre, 'L'Angleterre et le Marché commun' (PhD thesis, University of Lyon, 1964)

Marjolin, Robert, *Le travail d'une vie. Mémoires 1911–1986* (Paris: Robert Laffond, 1986)

Marrui, Ali, 'African Attitudes to the EEC', *International Affairs*, 39:1 (January 1963)

Marsh, John and Ritson, Christopher, *Agricultural Policy and the Common Market* (London: Chatham House/PEP, 1971)

Massigli, René, *Une comédie des erreurs 1943–1956. Souvenirs et réflexions sur une étape de la construction européenne* (Paris: Plon, 1978)

Massip, Roger, *De Gaulle et l'Europe* (Paris: Flammarion, 1963)

Matthews, Roy, 'Canada, Britain and the Common Market: A Canadian View', *World Today*, 18:2 (February 1962)

McMillan, James F., *Dreyfus to de Gaulle: Politics and Society in France 1898–1969* (London: Edward Arnold, 1985)

Melandri, Pierre, *Les Etats-Unis face à l'unification de l'Europe 1945–54* (Paris: Editions A. Pedone, 1980)

Merchant, L. T., 'Evolving US Relations with the Atlantic Community', *International Organisation*, 17:3 (summer 1963)

Milward, Alan, *The Reconstruction of Western Europe 1945–51* (London: Methuen, 1984)

The European Rescue of the Nation-State (London: Routledge, 1992)

Milward, Alan, Lynch, Frances, Romero, Federico, Ranieri, Ruggero, and Sørensen, Vibeke, *The Frontier of National Sovereignty. History and Theory 1945–1992* (London: Routledge, 1993)

Monnet, Jean, *Mémoires* (Paris: Fayard, 1976)

Moon, Jeremy, *European Integration in British Politics, 1950–1963: A Study of Issue Change* (Aldershot: Gower, 1985)

Moravcsik, Andrew, 'Why the European Community Strengthens the State: Domestic Politics and International Cooperation' (unpublished paper, Conference of Europeanists, Chicago, April 1994)

Müller-Armack, Alfred, *Auf dem Weg nach Europa. Erinnerungen und Ausblicke* (Tübingen and Stuttgart: Rainer Wunderlich Verlag and C. E. Poeschel, 1971)

Newhouse, John, *De Gaulle and the Anglo-Saxons* (London: André Deutsch, 1970)

Nicholson, Frances and East, Roger, *From the Six to the Twelve, the Enlargement of the European Communities* (Harlow: Longman, 1987)

Noël, Gilbert, *Du pool vert à la politique agricole commune: les tentatives de communauté agricole européenne entre 1945 et 1955* (Paris: Economica, 1988)

di Nolfo, Ennio (ed.), *Power in Europe?* vol II: *Great Britain, France, Germany and Italy and the Origins of the EEC, 1952–1957* (Berlin: Walter de Gruyter, 1992)

Nonis, Francesco E., *L'europa occidentale alla ricerca della sua unità, la cooperazione economica del dopoguerra, le trattative per l'adesione del Regno Unito alla CEE e l'interruzzione del negoziato di Bruxelles* (Rome: Banco di Santo Spirito, 1963)

Nuti, Leopoldo, 'Missiles or Socialists? The Italian Policy of the Kennedy Administration' (unpublished conference paper)

Nutting, Anthony, *Europe Will Not Wait. A Warning and a Way Out* (London: Hollis & Carter, 1960)

Osterheld, Horst, *"Ich gehe nicht leichten Herzens . . . "* *Adenauers letzte Kanzlerjahre – eine dokumentarischer Bericht* (Mainz, 1986)

Pagedas, Constantine, 'Troubled Partners: Anglo-American Diplomacy and the French Problem, 1960–1963' (PhD thesis, King's College, London, 1996)

Parfitt, Trevor, 'Agriculture and the Brussels Negotiations', *World Today*, 19:1 (February 1963)

Paulus, Daniel, *Les milieux dirigeants belges et les demandes d'adhésion du Royaume-Uni à la communauté économique européenne* (Brussels: Université Libre de Bruxelles, 1971)

Paxton, Robert and Wahl, Nicholas (eds.), *De Gaulle and the United States. A Centennial Reappraisal* (Oxford: Berg, 1994)

Peyrefitte, Alain, *C'était de Gaulle* (Paris: Fayard, 1995)

Pfaltzgraff, Robert L., *Britain Faces Europe* (University of Pennsylvania Press, 1969)

Picot, Bernard, 'La France et l'entrée de la Grande-Bretagne dans le Marché commun' (PhD thesis, Lyon, 1965)

Pineau, Christian and Rimbaud, Christiane, *Le grand pari: l'aventure du traité de Rome* (Paris: Fayard, 1991)

Pisani, Edgard, *Le Général indivis* (Paris: Albin Michel, 1974)

Poidevin, Raymond, *Robert Schuman: homme d'état, 1886–1963* (Paris: Imprimerie Nationale, 1986)

Poidevin, Raymond (ed.), *Histoire des débuts de la construction européenne, mars 1948–mai 1950* (Brussels: Bruylant, 1986)

Prittie, Terrence, *Adenauer* (London: Tom Stacey, 1971)

Pryce, Roy (ed.), *The Dynamics of European Union* (London: Routledge, 1989)

Ranieri, Ruggero, 'Italy and the Schuman Plan Negotiations' (European University Institute, Working Paper 86/215)

du Réau, Elisabeth, *L'idée d'Europe au XXème siècle* (Paris: Editions Complexe, 1996)

Reynolds, David, *Britannia Overruled. British Policy and World Power in the 20th Century* (London: Longman, 1991)

Robinson, H. Basil, *Diefenbaker's World: A Populist in Foreign Affairs* (University of Toronto Press, 1989)

Roll, Eric, *Crowded Hours* (London: Faber & Faber, 1985)

Romano, Sergio, *Guida alla politica estera italiana* (Milan: Rizzoli, 1993)

Roth, Andrew, *Heath and the Heathmen* (London: Routledge, 1972)

Roussel, Eric, *Jean Monnet* (Paris: Fayard, 1996)

Schaad, Martin, 'Anglo-German Relations During the Formative Years of the European Community, 1955–1961' (D.Phil. thesis, Oxford, 1995)

Schlesinger, Arthur, *A Thousand Days: J. F. Kennedy in the White House* (London: André Deutsch, 1965)

Schmidt, Gustav (ed.), *Zwischen Bündnissicherung und privilegierter Partnerschaft: Die deutsch–britischen Beziehungen und die Vereinigten Staaten von Amerika, 1955–1963* (Bochum: Universitätsverlag Dr N. Brockmeyer, 1995)

Schröder, Gerhard, *Decision for Europe* (London: Thames & Hudson, 1964)

Schumann, Maurice, 'France and Germany in the New Europe', *Foreign Affairs*, 41:1 (October 1962)

Schwabe, Klaus (ed.), *Die Anfänge des Schuman-Plans 1950/1* (Baden-Baden: Nomos Verlag, 1988)

Schwarz, Hans-Peter, *Die Ära Adenauer: Epochenwechsel 1957–63* (Stuttgart-Wiesbaden: Deutsche Verlags-Anstalt, 1981)

    Adenauer: Der Staatsmann, 1952–1967 (Stuttgart: Deutsche Verlags-Anstalt, 1991)

Schwarz, Hans-Peter (ed.), *Akten zur Auswärtigen Politik der Bundesrepublik Deutschland, 1963* (Munich: R. Oldenbourg Verlag, 1994) vols. I–II

Serra, Enrico (ed.), *Il rilancio dell'Europa e i trattati di Roma* (Brussels: Bruylant, 1989)

Seydoux, François, *Mémoires d'Outre Rhin* (Paris: Grasset, 1975)

Shonfield, Andrew, 'The Commonwealth and the Common Market', *World Today*, 17:12 (December 1961)

Silj, Alessandro, *Europe's Political Puzzle: A Study of the Fouchet Negotiations and the 1963 Veto* (Harvard University Press, 1967)

Snoy et d'Oppuers, Jean-Charles, *Rebâtir l'Europe* (Paris: Duculot, 1989)

Soutou, Georges-Henri, 'Le général de Gaulle, le plan Fouchet et l'Europe', *Commentaire*, 13:52, (winter 1990–1)

Spaak, Paul-Henri, *Combats inachevés, de l'espoir aux déceptions* (Paris: Fayard, 1969)

Spierenburg, Dirk and Poidevin, Raymond, *Histoire de la Haute Autorité de la Communauté Européenne du Charbon et de l'Acier: Une Expérience Supranationale* (Brussels: Bruylant, 1993)

Spinelli, Altiero, *The Eurocrats: Conflict and Crisis in the European Commission* (Baltimore: Johns Hopkins Press, 1966)

Diario europeo (Bologna: Mulino, 1989)

Steineger, Rolf, 'Great Britain's First EEC Failure in January 1963', *Diplomacy and Statecraft*, 7:2 (1996)

Stikker, Dirk, *Men of Responsibility* (London: John Murray, 1966)

van Tichelen, Joseph, 'Souvenirs de la négociation du Traité de Rome', *Studia Diplomatica*, 34 (1981)

Toschi, Simona, 'Washington–London–Paris, an Untenable Triangle (1960–1963)', *Journal of European Integration History*, 1:2 (1995)

Tracy, Michael, *Government and Agriculture in Western Europe, 1880–1988*, 3rd edn (London: Harvester Wheatsheaf, 1989)

Food and Agriculture in a Market Economy. An Introduction to Theory, Practice and Policy (La Hutte (Belgium): Agricultural Policy Studies, 1993)

Trausch, Gilbert (ed.), *Die Europäische Integration vom Schuman-Plan bis zu den Verträgen von Rom* (Brussels: Nomos/Giuffrè/LGDJ/Bruylant, 1993)

Turner, John, *Macmillan* (London: Longman, 1994)

Urwin, Derek W., *The Community of Europe: A History of European Integration since 1945* (London: Longman, 1991)

Varsori, Antonio (ed.), *La politica estera italiana nel secondo dopoguerra (1943–1957)* (Milan: LED, 1993)

Europe 1945–1990s: The End of an Era? (London: Macmillan, 1995)

Vaughan, Richard, *Twentieth Century Europe, Paths to Unity* (London: Croom Helm, 1979)

Warley, T. K., *Agriculture: The Cost of Joining the Common Market* (London: Chatham House/PEP, 1967)

Warner, Geoffrey, 'President de Gaulle's Foreign Policy', *World Today*, 18:8 (August 1962)

'The Nassau Agreement and NATO', *World Today*, 19:1 (January 1963)

Weigall, David and Stirk, Peter (eds.), *The Origins and Development of the European Community* (Leicester University Press, 1992)

Wilkes, George (ed.), *Britain's First Failure to Enter the European Community*,

Bibliography

1961–63: Crises in European, Atlantic and Commonwealth Relations (London: Frank Cass, 1997)

Williams, Shirley, 'When Britain Joins: The Consequences for Internal Politics', *The Political Quarterly*, 34 (January 1963)

Winand, Pascaline, *Eisenhower, Kennedy and the United States of Europe* (London: Macmillan, 1993)

Wurm, Clemens (ed.), *Western Europe and Germany. The Beginnings of European Integration 1945–1960* (Oxford: Berg, 1995)

Young, John W., *Britain, France and the Unity of Europe* (London: Leicester University Press, 1984)

'Churchill's "No" to Europe: the "Rejection" of European Union by Churchill's Post-War Government, 1951–1952', *Historical Journal*, 28:4 (1985)

Britain and European Unity, 1945–1992 (New York: St Martin's Press, 1993)

Younger, Kenneth, 'When Britain Joins: The Consequences for External Policy', *The Political Quarterly*, 34 (January 1963)

'La zone de libre échange devant l'opinion française', *Revue du Marché Commun*, 1 (March 1958)

Index

Index

CAMBRIDGE STUDIES IN INTERNATIONAL RELATIONS